Indra
and
Other Vedic Deities

Contemporary Researches in Hindu Philosophy & Religion (ISSN 0971-9628)

1. Idealistic Thought in Indian Philosophy; by Shuchita C. Divatia (ISBN 81-246-0021-X)
2. Karma and Reincarnation: The Vedāntic Perspective; by Muni Narayana Prasad (ISBN 81-246-0022-8)
3. Stonemill and Bhakti: From the Devotion of Peasant Women to the Philosophy of Swamies; by Guy Poitevin and Hema Rairkar (ISBN 81-246-0059-7)
4. Śaivism: Some Glimpses; by G.V. Tagare (ISBN 81-246-0076-7)
5. Advaita: A Conceptual Analysis; by A. Ramamurty (ISBN 81-246-0067-8)
6. Mind-Body Dualism: A Philosophic Investigation; by Alpana Chakraborty (ISBN 81-246-0071-6)
7. Hinduism and Scientific Quest; by T.R.R. Iyengar (ISBN 81-246-0077-5)
8. Indra and Other Vedic Deities — A Euhemeristic Study; by Uma Chakravarty (ISBN 81-246-0080-5)
9. Brahma-Vāda: Doctrine of Śrī Vallabhācārya; by G.V. Tagare (ISBN 81-246-0112-7)
10. The Science of Enlightenment: Enlightenment, Liberation and God — A Scientific Explanation; by Nitin Trasi (ISBN 81-246-0130-5)
11. Retrieval of Sāṁkhya History: An Ascent from Dawn to Meridian; by Lallanji Gopal (ISBN 81-246-0143-7)
12. The Philosophical Foundations of Hinduism; by A. Ramamurty (ISBN 81-246-0163-1)
13. The Eternal Hinduism; by Baidyanath Saraswati (ISBN 81-246-0249-2)
14. Vedānta and its Philosophical Development; by A. Ramamurty (ISBN 81-246-0000-0)

Contemporary Researches in Hindu Philosophy & Religion, no. 8

Indra and Other Vedic Deities

— A Euhemeristic Study —

Uma Chakravarty

with a foreword by
R.N. Dandekar

D.K.Printworld (P) Ltd.
New Delhi

Cataloging in Publication Data — DK
[Courtesy: D.K. Agencies (P) Ltd. <docinfo@dkagencies.com>]

Chakravarty, Uma, 1933 -
Indra and other Vedic deities.
(Contemporary researches in Hindu philosophy & religion ; no. 8).
Includes bibliographical references (pp.)
Includes Index.
ISBN 8124600805

1. Indra (Hindu deity). 2. Gods, Vedic. 3. Vedas — Criticism, interpretation, etc. I. Title. II. Series: Contemporary researches in Hindu philosophy & religion ; no. 8.

ISBN 81-246-0080-5
First Published in India 1997
Second impression in 2006

Published and printed by:
D.K. Printworld (P) Ltd.
Regd. office : *'Sri Kunj'*, F-52, Bali Nagar
New Delhi - 110 015
Phones : (011) 2545-3975; 2546-6019; *Fax* : (011) 2546-5926
E-mail: dkprintworld@vsnl.net
Web: www.dkprintworld.com

To
the memory of
my father

Foreword

THE Ṛgvedic mythology is essentially an 'evolutionary' mythology. It has been, throughout, reacting and responding to the various vicissitudes in the cultural history of the Ṛgvedic age. Even after a Ṛgvedic god had been first conceived, his character did not remain constant. His personality, as it were, 'grew' — it often assumed a heterogeneous character on account of the different elements which came to be assimilated into it in conformity with the mythological ideology which had been continuously undergoing modification. It is possible to detect three main and presumably consecutive phases of the evolutionary mythology of the *Ṛgveda* — the first phase of the definite realization of the cosmic (moral) order established by Asura Varuṇa, the second phase of the mythologization of history as represented by Vṛtrahā Indra, and the third phase of the hierarchisation of popular religious sects as symbolized by Śipiviṣṭa Viṣṇu. It is the second phase which Dr. Uma Chakravarty has dealt with in the present monograph.

I have met but few scholars who showed such commendable keenness for Sanskrit studies and research as Uma Chakravarty. Ever since the time when she joined the Lady Keane College, Shillong, as the Head of the Department of Sanskrit, Chakravarty seems to have fully realised that teaching and research must always go hand in hand, for, teaching incites and motivates research and research saves teaching from becoming stale. She, therefore, did not miss any opportunity to augment her academic qualifications and expand her research potentiality. For instance, she attended intensive courses of German language and made it a point to participate actively in as many sessions of the All-India Oriental Conference as possible. Her recent sojourn in Germany as a DAAD guest, though short, has evidently proved of no little avail.

Uma chakravarty's doctoral work (1966) related to Kṣemendra, the Kāśmīrian Poet of the eleventh century AD, but, in recent years, she has been delving into Vedic mythology — and that too, fairly fruitfully. To repeat what I have said elsewhere: Various claims have been traditionally made on behalf of the Veda — claims such as that the Veda is *apauruṣeya*, that it is invested with absolute validity, that it is the fountainhead of the entire Indian culture. I would like to add to this list one more claim, namely, that the Veda is an inexhaustible and ever-absorbing subject of study and research.

taraṇirijjayati kṣeti puṣyati (*ṚV* VII.32.9).

Bhandarkar Oriental
Research Institute
July 12, 1996

R. N. Dandekar

Acknowledgement

DURING my intensive German Language Courses at the Max Müller Bhavan, Pune in the late seventies, I used to often visit the Bhandarkar Oriental Research Institute Library. In one of my visits to BORI I met Prof. R.N. Dandekar and expressed to him my desire to work in the field of Vedic studies. But I also explained to him of my difficulties, viz., I taught in a college in Shillong where there were no library facilities for Vedic studies; also being a student of Classical Sanskrit Literature, I did not have a strong enough background for Vedic studies. Prof. Dandekar then suggested to me that I could work on that group of Vedic gods who were euhemeristic, especially the Ṛbhus, Aśvins, Maruts and Indra, i.e., on the mythologization of human heroes.

It was rather too long a time before I entered the world of the Vedas. I used the libraries of Calcutta and Pune during my vacations since those were the only months available to me for my actual work.

I am grateful beyond measure to Prof. Sukumari Bhattacharji whose constant help and guidance have made this work possible.

I am indebted to the authorities of the National Library, Asiatic Society Library, Calcutta, Bhandarkar Oriental Research Institute Library, Deccan College Library and CASS Library, Pune as I collected most of my work material from these libraries.

Discussions with Prof. T.N. Dharmadhikari, the then Director, Vaidik Saṃśodhana Maṇḍala, Pune, Dr. G.U. Thite, Poona University cleared many of my doubts. I feel deeply grateful to them. I am also greatly indebted to Prof. S.D. Laddu, Bhandarkar Oriental Research Institute, Pune, who offered me many useful suggestions during the final preparation of the book. Thanks are due to my friend Dr. Sindhu Phadke also for her generous help in many directions.

I thank the German Academic Exchange Service for granting me a fellowship for three months which I spent at the Freie Universität, Berlin for consulting its library and meeting German scholars of Indology. My thanks are due to those Indologists of Germany and Switzerland whom I met during my study tour. They generously extended to me much of their valuable time for discussions regarding my work.

I am also grateful to Dr. Apurba Kr. Bhattachayya, Mrs. Majushree Sharma and Dr. Keshab Sharma who provided me with copies of some very important books from the libraries of Sorbonne and Harvard Universities.

I am solely responsible for any errors and omissions that may be in the book due to my ignorance and incompetence.

Pune
30th July 1996

Uma Chakravarty

Contents

Abbreviations

ABORI	*Annals of the Bhandarkar Oriental Research Institute, Pune*
AitBrā	*Aitareya Brāhmaṇa*
AO	*Acta Orientalia*, Leiden
ĀpDS	*Āpastamba Dharma Sūtra*
ĀpGS	*Āpastamba Gṛhya Sūtra*
ĀpŚS	*Āpastamba Śrauta Sūtra*
AV	*Atharvaveda*
BṛUp	*Bṛhadāraṇyaka Upaniṣad*
HOS	Harvard Oriental Series
IHQ	*Indian Historical Quarterly*, Calcutta
JAHRS	*Journal of the Andhra Historical Research Society*, Rajahmundry
JaiBrā	*Jaiminīya Brāhmaṇa*
JAOS	*Journal of the American Oriental Society*, New Haven
JAS Ben	*Journal of the Asiatic Society Bengal*, Calcutta
JAS Bom	*Journal of the Asiatic Society*, Bombay

JBBRAS	*Journal of the Bombay Branch of the Royal Asiatic Society*, Bombay
JBHU	*Journal of the Banaras Hindu University, Banaras*
J Bom U	*Journal of the University of Bombay, Bombay*
JGIS	*Journal of the Greater Indian Society*, Calcutta
JGJRI	*Journal of the Ganganath Jha Research Institute, Allahabad*
JRAS	*Journal of the Royal Asiatic Society of Great Britain*, Ireland
KS	*Kāṭhaka Saṃhitā*
KZ	*Zeitschrift fur vergleichende Sprachforschung begründet von*, A. Kuhn, Göttingen
Mbh	*Mahābhārata*
MS	*Maitrāyaṇī Saṃhitā*
Nir	*Nirukta*
PGS	*Pāraskara Gṛhya Sūtra*
ṚV	*Ṛgveda*
ŚatBrā	*Śatapatha Brāhmaṇa*
SBE	*Sacred Books of the East*
SV	*Sāmaveda*
TaitĀ	*Taittirīya Āraṇyaka*
TaitBrā	*Taittirīya Brāhmaṇa*
TS	*Taittirīya Saṃhitā*
VS	*Vājasaneyisaṃhitā*
YV	*Yajurveda*
ZDMG	*Zeitschrift der deutschen morgenlandischen Gesellschaft,* Wiesbaden

Introduction

CATEGORIZING the euhemeristic Vedic gods in one work has not been done as yet though much scholarly work has been published on the Vedic mythology in the last two centuries. This mythological phenomenon may be termed as the 'mythologization of human heroes'. A realistic approach has been taken by a group of scholars — history and myth being complementary to each other. The present work is in line with such a trend and also hopefully fills the gap caused by the absence of a work which treats of such Vedic gods only who had originally been human heroes so different in nature from other gods whose existences are based on nature or on abstract ideas. We include in this group the Ṛbhus, the Aśvins, the Maruts and Indra.

Names have a real significance in the case of euhemerism. Of the forty-five epithets of Indra collected by us many signify his euhemeristic base. We quote below a few: *vajrín, vajrabhṛ́t, vájrahasta, vṛtrakhādá, vṛtrahán, pūrbhít, pūrbhíttama, púraṅdara, yudhmá, satrāsā́ha, śū́ra* (occurring about 150 times in the *ṚV*), *somapā́, somapā́tama, śíprin, hárīśipra, et al.* Such epithets indicating the human origin of a god are hardly met with in connection with abstract deities like Bṛhaspati, Brahmaṇaspati, Prajāpati, etc. Even if they occur they are very meagre compared to the frequency of their use in connection with Indra.

Concrete feats are attributed to the gods who form the subject-matter of this work. The Ṛbhus had earned divinity by dint of their four-fold achievements; the Aśvins had been deprived of their right to the Soma libation temporarily for mixing too frequently among men their devotees, by curing them of their maladies and serving them when they were in difficulty. These feats of these gods form often the subject-matter of many of the *Ṛgveda* verses. The repetition simply indicates the historicity of these events. These concrete feats may be referred to in contrast with vague generalisation as creators, cosmokrators, spiritual hierophanies — Brahman, Puruṣa, etc.

The hymns were intended both for the gods addressed to and the human community who listened to them within the context of the sacrifice or even outside as merely heard litanies.

A god whose concrete feats are recorded whose human adversaries are named and whose conquests over actual enemies and whose real assistance to historical personalities are mentioned was to the extent more tangible, real and convincing to the community. Praise and prayer to such a god generated faith among the supplicants that this god would behave in a similar fashion to his present worshippers. To the first few generations place-names and person-names would be familiar at first hand and repeated recitations and chantings would keep the memory fresh down the generations. Such details point to real human antecedents of the gods who began as human beings and were later deities.

If we divide the Vedic gods in three categories such as:

(a) *Natural phenomena*: Vāyu, Uṣas, Sūrya, Agni and others.

(b) *Historical figures transformed into gods*: The Ṛbhus, the Aśvins, Indra, *et al.*

(c) *Partial or complete abstractions*: Bṛhaspati, Brahman, Brahmaṇaspati, Puruṣa, Ātman, Parjāpati and others, then the second category of gods belong to the stage when the actual memory of living heroes, being deified was still fresh in the community's memory; the records of the

> details are a pointer to this. It is in this context that the second category of gods has a special and unique significance, all ancient mythologies provide parallel instances.

Hence this work with its specific purpose of classifying the historical figures transformed into gods will fill the gap neglected so far.

Many great personalities of the past like Buddha, Mahāvīra, Jesus and Chaitanya were mythologised. In our life-time we have seen outstanding and not so outstanding figures like Rāmākrishna and many religious preceptors being raised to divinity and worshipped with cultic rites. So the phenomenon is not unique or unfamiliar.

A short summary of the work is presented now:

The Ṛbhus

The Ṛbhus have been described as human beings elevated to the status of divinity (*mártyāsaḥ sánto 'mṛtatvám ānaśuḥ, ṚV,* I.110.4). They attained divinity by dint of their four epoch-making achievements: (i) they transformed a dying cow into a milch-cow; this cow, Viśvarūpā by name belonged to Bṛhaspati; (ii) they by their medical skill rejuvenated their dying parents; (iii) they made a three-wheeled chariot for the Aśvins; and (iv) they made the two horses, Haris, for Indra. Their achievements elevated them to the status of divinity, viz. a solar god, a god of fecundity. They earned the right to the third Soma-pressing which they enjoyed along with Indra by making the fourth *camasa*.

The Aśvins

There are three aspects of the mythology of the Aśvins; (i) their being the divine physicians and saviours, (ii) their relation with a maiden, which is an Indo-European archetype and (iii) the divine twinship motif which is a universal motif. — (i) These twin divine physicians cured their numerous devotees suffering from different types of maladies. Bhujyu who was stranded in mid-ocean was rescued by them. This feat of the Aśvins is a parallel to Greek Castor and Polydeukes (Dioskuri). As a result of mixing too much among men, they lost their right to the Soma, which of course they regained by dint of their dexterity. — (ii) The Aśvins' association with a female deity is an archetype. Sometimes she is their beloved, sometimes a sister and at others their mother. A few similar myths belonging to other traditions are: Greek and Roman Castor, Pollux and Helen — a sister, Lithuanian Dieva Sunelei and Saules Dukterys, Latvian Dieva Deli and Saules Meita — a sister in both mythologies, Greek Heraklels, Iphikles and Alcmene — mother, Amphion, Zethos and Antiope — mother. — The third section deals with the worship of the twin gods which is a universal motif. This motif exists in pre-historic, Semitic, Indo-European and American mythologies also.

The Maruts

"Martial storm gods"[1] is the best description of the Ṛgvedic Maruts, Indra's associates. The *ṚV* depicts this group of gods as bright, of howling nature, angry, fearful and similar in appearance — a description equally applicable to the storm gods as well as to the martial gods. The Maruts are the regular enjoyers of the midday Soma libation along with Indra and with other gods as well. Their relation with Indra is very close. In the *TS* and the *AV* the storm god Maruts have been transformed to the rain gods. They play a major role in the Kārīriṣṭi which is performed for rains. This indicates that the society had then become an agricultural one. In the later Vedic literature, however, the Maruts' position was demoted to the status of *devaviśaḥ*, the subjects of gods.[2]

Indra

The last chapter has been divided into ten sections.

Section I discusses the etymology of the word *indra*. Starting from Yāska and ending with Volker Moller (1984) opinions of scholars from the East and West in this regard have been discussed; and our opinion on the same has also been stated. Section II deals with the basic and principal aspect of Indra's character which is that of war god. The majority of the 250 hymns dedicated to Indra depict him as a martial god, and as a devastator of cities/ramparts/forts of the non-Āryan enemies. The invincible weapon *vájra*, the soma drink and chariot drawn by the Haris were instrumental in bringing forth his great victories. Section III concentrates on Indra's protégés on whose behalf he fought against the enemies. Here is a discussion on the protégés and, *vice-versa*, the enemies also. Innumerable were Indra's protégés and only the most prominent of them have been brought under this discussion. Section IV deals with the most important feature of the Indra mythology, i.e., his Vṛtra-killing and releasing the enclosed river waters. Although it is very difficult to decipher who Vṛtra was, what is very clearly stated in the *ṚV* is that, for some reasons still unknown to us, the river waters were obstructed. Indra released the waters and thereby brought great relief to his followers. This is the turning point in the mythology of Indra. A very small Section V is entitiled "Epithets". Epithets of gods throw light on the different aspects of their character and achievements. A survey of these epithets reveals that the major aspects of Indra's character is that of a warrior and that he is anthropomorphised to an extent to which few other gods are. Section VI deals with Indra's relation with other gods. Indra's relation with Sūrya is rather complicated. It has four angles: (a) Indra generated Sūrya and Uṣas; (b) a rivalry between Indra and Sūrya is also observed; (c) they come close to each other; and finally (d) they become identical. Indra being the most important god it became an issue of dignity for the other gods to be related to him. This phenomenon is observed in Varuṇa, Viṣṇu, Tvaṣṭṛ, Sarasvatī and Pūṣan. Section VII deals with those *ṚV* verses which depict Indra as the highest god who settles heaven and earth, whose capabilities are beyond the reach of any other god and whose glory is observed in every object and in every living being.

The theme of section VIII is Indra as has been presented in the *YV*. In spite of the fact that Indra holds quite an important position in the pantheon in this Veda, yet it becomes evident that Indra is now shorn of all the Ṛgvedic glamour. Trickery now becomes his main tool in place of *vájra*. Human elements are observed in greater degree in him. He behaves like an earthly being who has flaws, physical weakness sense of insecurity and not as one possessed of Olympian attitude.

Indra of the *AV* who belongs to both the traditions — the Great and the Little forms the subject-matter of Section IX. The *AV* belonged originally mainly to the so-called lower level of the society. Accordingly, Ṛgvedic Indra's character also changes in their religious book. Now the possessor of the Atharvanic qualities, he suppresses the Sadānvas, the evil spirits which possess the base of the house, with his *vájra*, wears herbs in amulets and consumes the pāṭā plant for strength. He makes somebody important, and gives his worshipper the desired wife. In connection with the setting of a society the necessities of life are determined and they are believed to be fulfilled through the favour of the gods worshipped. In accord with the social backdrop of the upholders of the *AV*, Indra also changes his character.

In Section X the opinions of scholars on Indra's identity have been discussed and analysed, and finally our opinion on the same has been expressed.

References

1. ***See*** *Encyclopaedia of Religion*, Vol. 7, Macmillan, p. 214.
2. The Maruts to us, unlike the Ṛbhus and the Aśvins, are basically nature gods. They have been included in this work because of their close association with Indra. A discussion on Indra remains incomplete without bringing the Maruts into the picture. It is, however, not yet been possible to determine the process which turned the Maruts into Indra's associates.

1

The Ṛbhus

mártāsaḥ sánto' mṛtatvám ānaśuḥ
(*ṚV*,[1] I.110.4)

'being mortals they earned immortality'[2]

saudhanvanā́so 'mṛtatvám érire
(*ṚV*, III.60.3)

'the children of Sudhanvan achieved immortality'

sáudhanavanā ábhavata amṛ́tāsaḥ
(*ṚV*, IV.35.8)

'the children of Sudhanvan became immortal'

IN connection with no other Vedic gods has it been so explicitly stated, as with the Ṛbhus, that they were human beings and later earned immortality. We shall attempt to explore the story of the three brothers, Ṛbhu, Vibhavan and Vāja, mainly based on the Saṃhitā literature.

The *Ṛgveda* is the earliest available source for our knowledge of the Ṛbhus. They are lauded in eleven Ṛgvedic hymns[3] and some stray verses which are mostly dedicated to the Viśvedevāḥ).[4] The Ṛbhu-hymns praise highly and repeatedly their five-fold achievements, which are: reviving of a dying cow, the transformation of their frail and old parents into persons full of youthful strength and vigour, making two horses (Harī) for

Indra, a highly complex and attractive chariot for the Aśvins and making four *camasa*s out of one. And, because of their unbeatable achievements, especially the last one, they had to be awarded immortality and consequently the right of the soma libation.

The *Atharvaveda* in a few places refers to the Ṛbhus but does not give us any new information about them. The *AitBrā* (III.30) tells us the story of including the Ṛbhus amongst gods enjoying in the third libation of Soma. The *Mahābhārata* also mentions the Ṛbhus once and gives them the highest place among the gods.[5]

Etymology of the Word 'ṛbhú'

Before going into the Vedic texts we would like to make a review of the opinions expressed by scholars right from Yāska on the etymology of the word *ṛbhú* with reference to the three brothers, Ṛbhu, Vibhavan and Vāja. We read in the *Nirukta* (I.15) *ṛbhava uru bhānti iti vā । ṛtena bhānti iti vā । ṛtena bhavanti iti vā.*[6] 'Rbhavaḥ are (so-called because) they shine widely (*uru* + *bhā)*, or they shine with sacred rite (*ṛta* + *bhā*), or they live with the sacred rite (*ṛta* + *bhū*).'[7] Then Yāska says, *ṛbhuḥ vibhvā vāja iti sudhanvanaḥ aṅgirasasya trayaḥ putrā babhūvuḥ* (*Nir,* I.16).[8] Yāska's first interpretation represents the Ṛbhus as sunshine and the second one as human beings. Two contradictory aspects of the Ṛbhus' character were revealed to Yāska. *Śabdakalpadruma* simply quotes *Amarakośa* in order to define the Ṛbhus.[9] *Vācaspatyabhidhāna* interprets the Ṛbhus as gods shining widely, *ṛ + bhū + da / deve / tena ṛ — śabdasya svargavāditvaṃ tāñśca pramādāt pūrvam anuktam iti tasya ca svarge puṃstvaṃ bodhyam . . . ṛ + bhā + du uru bhāśamāne.*[10]

The *St. Petersburg Dictionary* states that *ṛbhú* has been formed from the root *rabh* and holds that the Ṛbhus could not be deified human beings.[11] A.A. Macdonell also thinks, '*ṛbhu* is apparently derived from *rabh* to grasp. . . thus meaning 'handy', 'dexterous'.[12] A.W. Ryder takes *ṛbhú* as a proper noun.[13] Alfred Hillebrandt thinks that the root *arb* in the German word *arbeit* is connected in the formation of the Vedic word *ṛbhu.*[14] Sir M. Monier-Williams holds that *ṛbhu* has been formed from the root *rabh* and these three brothers were semi-divine beings.[15] V.S. Apte[16] also describes them as semi-divine beings, sons of Sudhanvan, a descendant of Aṅgiras. Apte, however, does not give any etymology of the word *ṛbhú*. To us it appears that *ṛbhú* has been formed from the root *rabh*.

Genealogy

Ṛbhu, Vibhavan and Vāja, the three brothers, were the children of Sudhanvan who belonged to the family of Aṅgiras. No detailed information about Sudhanvan can be had from the Vedic texts. That the Ṛbhus belonged to the Āṅgirasa family is confirmed by Kutsa, a descendant of Aṅgiras, when he says that some of his relatives, the descendants of Sudhanvan, desiring soma libation went to the residence of Savitṛ.[17] Very often these three brothers are addressed or referred to in plural number of Ṛbhu, which is the name of the eldest brother, and also in the plural number of Vāja, the name of the youngest brother. Only once Vibhavan has been used in the plural number to indicate all the three brothers.[18]

Fourfold Achievements of the Ṛbhus

They were skilled architects. Their dexterity raised them from mortality to immortality (*ábhajanta sukṛtyáyā bhāgáṃ devéṣu yajñiyám* — *RV*, I.20.8).

These three brothers, who will henceforward be referred to as the Ṛbhus, started their benevolent career by reviving a dying cow which was living simply in its hide. Through the Ṛbhus' nourishment it became one full of milk and was united with its calf.[19] The name of the cow was Viśvarūpā[20] and she was given as a gift to Bṛhaspati.[21] The verbs used in connection with the description of the rejuvenation of the cow are: *takṣan* (I.111.1), *tatakṣuḥ* (IV.34.9), *nirapiṃśata* (I.20.3; 110.1), *apiṃśan* (IV.33.4), *upājata* (I.161.6), *ariṇīta* (I.161.7; III.60.2), *abharan* (IV.33.4) and *arakṣan* (IV.33.4).

Vāmadeva who of all the Ṛgvedic poets sang the largest number of hymns (IV.33-37) to the Ṛbhus says, they made a cart for the Aśvins, rejuvenated their parents and the cow, made two horses for Indra, made shoulder-bands (for the gods), separated heaven and earth: the all-pervasive leaders (*naraḥ*) thus performed all such benevolent deeds (*ṚV*, IV.33.8).

Sitanath Pradhan, who believes that the Ṛbhus were euhemeristic, opines on the rejuvenation of the cow: "A *Ṛṣi* whose cow had died leaving a calf asked the Ṛbhus for assistance whereupon the Ṛbhus secured a living cow and covered it with the skin of a dead one from which the calf imagined it to be its own mother."[22] Pradhan's opinion appears rather unreal. N.G. Chapekar, according to whom the Ṛbhus are the names given to sunshine, says about the cow-episode: "For a rational interpretation . . . we should understand the sun by the term 'go'. The other term 'carman', I suggest should be taken to mean a cloud. The term is derived from the root 'car' "to move"; and the cloud moves. The fable thus means that the Ṛbhus extricated the Sun from the cloud."[23] If the Ṛbhus are interpreted as sunshine then Chapekar's opinion is in conformity with the text. But we must explore further to find out if it can be accepted logically.

The sincere, straightforward and dexterous Ṛbhus earned self-confidence after they revived the dying cow. The next attempt was to rejuvenate their moribund, suffering parents who had been long since lying like two posts. Their attempt was successful.

In no time they made them young, full of strength and vigour.[24] The *Ṛgveda*, as usual, does not give any detailed information as to how they performed this apparently impossible task. The verbs, *akrata* (I.20.4), *akṛṇotana* (I.110.8), *cakruḥ* (IV.33.3) *akarta* (IV.35.5), *takṣan* (I.111.1), *tatakṣuḥ* (IV.34.9), *takṣatha* (IV.36.3), have been used by the Vedic poets while describing this function of the Ṛbhus. Stella Kramrisch, who visualises a creation myth in the story of the Ṛgvedic Ṛbhus, holds the cow as the year and the old parents heaven and earth enlivened by them.[25] On its own plane, it is valid, but in our nature of study, i.e., socio-anthropological, it is hardly relevant.

The Ṛbhus, who know their work very well (*vidmanā́pasaḥ* — *ṚV,* I.111.1), made a unique chariot. This three-wheeled vehicle needed no horse, no reins for its movement and could travel in the atmospheric region as well.[26]

The vehicle was such an excellent one that it was, as it were,[27] mentally fashioned. The *Ṛgveda* mentions about eight times[28] this unique achievement of the Ṛbhus and of these eight times it is said three times that they made this for the Aśvins.[29]

The verbs used in this connection are: *takṣan* (I.20.3; 111.1), *tatakṣuḥ* (IV.34.9), *yuyujé* (I.161.6), *yuktvā* (I.161.7), *cakṛuḥ* (IV. 33.8; 36.2); *jātaḥ* (IV.36.1).

The Ṛbhus also created two horses, the Haris, for Indra.[30] From the repeated statement that they mentally fashioned the horses[31] we may infer that the craftsmanship of the Ṛbhus had been developing more and more. The verbs used in this connection are: *tatakṣuḥ* (I.20.2; IV.34.9), *takṣan* (I.111.1); *atakṣata* (I.161.7); *niratakṣata* (III.60.2); *ataṣṭa* (IV.35.5); *yuyujé* (I.161.6); *cakruḥ* (IV.33.10).

'Camasa' — The Fifth Achievement and the Right to the Soma-libation

The Ṛbhus rejuvenated a dying cow, transformed their frail, decrepit parents into youthful persons full of strength and vigour, i.e., they contributed immensely in the world of medicine; they were also fine technicians who could dexterously make a unique chariot the first of its kind, i.e., they brought a revolutionary change in the technology of chariot-making. They must have performed quite naturally, many more such miracles, but somehow, these have not been recorded in the Saṃhitās. The situations demanded some applaud for these three brothers.

Their merit was to be given recognition. Society was then sacrifice oriented. They were planned to be given a place amongst the soma drinking gods. But some practical problems arose. How could human beings be offered soma in the same vessel with the gods? The Ṛbhus now faced the final and the most crucial ordeal in the process of attaining immortality. They were approached with the proposal of making four *camasas* of equal standard out of an original one made by the divine architect Tvaṣṭṛ.[32] The invincible Ṛbhus gloriously passed the ordeal.[33] Looking at the four *camasas* of equal standard. Tvaṣṭṛ[34] at the first instance had a feeling of inferiority complex. He felt ashamed and hid himself among the divine women.[35] Tvaṣṭṛ than became highly indignant; he planned to kill them. Out of fear of Tvaṣṭṛ's rage they changed their original names given by their mother.[36] But this was all a futile egotism on the part of Tvaṣṭṛ. Soon he recognised their merit and praised their achievement.[37] The Ṛbhus thus proved themselves fully competent for sharing the soma libation along with the gods. But unfortunately some more attempts were made to betray them by the god-worshipping society. In place of soma libation they were offered water the Ṛbhus refused to accept that. Then, they were offered water purified by the *muñjā* grass; that was also rejected. So, finally they had to be offered with their hard earned soma libation. So, the three mortals were first offered a mortal's drink, i.e., plain water, then water somewhat sanctified by the *muñjā* grass — but to no avail. And, finally the gods, or the votaries of gods, were obliged to offer them the already promised drink for immortality, soma libation. But, unfortunately they were offered this immortals' drink in the third pressing,[38] which was not considered so sacred. In this connection we may refer to *ṚV,* V.77.2, a hymn dedicated to the Aśvins. Here the priests are urged upon to offer sacrifice to the Aśvins in the morning, while the evening libation is not for the gods, it is just not worthy of the gods.[39] Thus the Ṛbhus underwent a long struggle before earning divinity and finally got the right to the soma libation.

The story of the Ṛbhus' elevation to god-hood through Agni's negotiations, as narrated under *ṚV,* I.161 was definitely a later addition when the Ṛbhus had been finally recognised as immortals and awarded the right to soma libation. This hymn simply glorifies these three unconquerable brothers.

Scholars' Opinions on the Fourth 'camasa'

A review of the opinions on the making of the *camasas* expressed by scholars is very much needed at this juncture. Three different types of opinions are expressed in this respect: the first identifies the *camasa* with the moon and the four into which it was transformed are the four phases of the moon. Macdonell was the first to put forward such an opinion.[40] Keith in support of Macdonell's view says, "the cup of Tvaṣṭṛ may possibly be the moon, and the four cups into which it is expanded may symbolize the four phases of the moon."[41] After about four decades Stella Kramrisch also speaks in the same vein, ". . . as out of the unique cup they made one cup after another until there were four cups, the four phases of the moon which mortals see. . ."[42] The method of interpreting mythological phenomena with cosmic equivalence was current in the entire nineteenth century and continued up to the mid-twentieth century. Methodology has changed considerably since then. Scholars now are interested more in finding as far as possible socio-anthropological data in the mythology.

The second opinion on the *camasa* identifies it with the celestial sphere divided into four parts of three months each. R. Shamashastry in his article based on *ṚV,* I.161 says, "In this hymn we are told that the three men called Ṛbhu, Vibhvā and Vāja, all sons of a king called Sudhanvan, divided celestial sphere into four parts of three months each."[43] We presume that this division of celestial sphere by the human Ṛbhus cannot be a real division but they might so interpret the movement of the sun round the year in the celestial sphere. B.R. Sharma, a believer in the arctic theory, supports Shamashastry's view and adds, "This again may be interpreted as regarding the four directions of the celestial hemisphere when solar rays emanate from the undifferentiated darkness."[44]

The third view is based on the euhemeristic origin of the Ṛbhus. Sitanath Pradhan, an upholder of the euhemeristic theory, says, "The Ṛbhus at that remote age when few knew artisanship amongst Indo-Aryans took a big ladle for sacrificial viands and out of that one piece, made four smaller ladles."[45] The necessity in the fulfilment of which the Ṛbhus made four smaller ladles out of the big ladle has not been pointed out by Pradhan. Moreover, it has been repeatedly mentioned in the Ṛgvedic verses that the Ṛbhus made four *camasas* totally resembling the original one made by Tvaṣṭṛ. Unfortunately, Pradhan has overlooked this very important point on which depended the Ṛbhus' attainment of the divine soma drink.

K.R. Potdar, another propagator of the euhemeristic identity of the Ṛbhus, thinks that the original *camasa* made by Tvaṣṭṛ became insufficient along with further development of sacrifice; so the Ṛbhus who "seem to have attained fame by their clever work in other fields and for that reason they seem to be entrusted with the task of making a small alternative arrangement."[46] N.G. Chapekar considers, "Originally Indra alone was offered 'soma' drink (IV.35.7). The Ṛbhus on their deification took the seats with Indra and were offered the 'soma' juice. Naturally four cups of 'soma' drink had to be kept ready, one for Indra and three for the Ṛbhus. This is how the mircale may be explained".[47] Chapekar urges upon us to question, why Indra alone, when there were other gods who were also offered soma drink.

Our thought on the necessity of the four *camasas* has been already given expression to.

The Ṛgvedic poets repeatedly sing that the Ṛbhus were human beings and earned immortality by hard penance. They, who were born, earned divinity.[48] As soon as they nourished their parents they earned friendship of the gods.[49] They are invoked to come to the sacrifice along with Varuṇa, the Maruts, the Ādityas, Savitṛ, the Parvatas, Sindhu and many others.[50] They are friends of Indra. In the third pressing Indra accepts soma drink with the Ṛbhus.[51] Goddess Dhiṣaṇā had assigned this place for them among the gods.[52] Only through hard labour the Ṛbhus have earned such a rare friendship with the gods.[53] All through, it has been said that they were given the right to the soma in the third libation. But on three occasions they are invoked only to the soma libation and not to the third soma libation.[54] It might be just a manner of expression or could it also indicate that, their right to the third libation was so well established that it needed no separate mention? We have seen how adversely Tvaṣṭṛ reacted to the Ṛbhus' unique success in making four *camasa*s out of one, — Tvaṣṭṛ, whom we may take as the representative of gods or rather of god-worshippers. But, in course of time Tvaṣṭṛ admitted their skill, he highly praised their achievement unimaginable so long. The gods started praising generously the highly skilful workmanship of chariot made by them.[55] Their unique success in making their old bed-ridden parents young became a myth among the gods.[56] The Ṛbhus proved that their merit demanded recognition and ultimately received it.

The Ṛbhus — Solar Deities

Kutsa tells us that some of his relatives desirous of the taste of soma drink went to Savitṛ, And, Savitṛ granted them immortality.[57] Dīrghatamas adds, during their stay with Savitṛ, the *agohya*, who cannot be concealed, the high lands were covered with green grass, the low lands were filled with water.[58] Dīrghatamas poetically put forth the question to the Ṛbhus, "when you had been rambling throughout the worlds, where had your parents been?"[59] They had been wakened from deep-sleep which they had been enjoying in Savitṛ's house. On enquiry they were told that a dog had awakened them. Vāmadeva also repeats that during their stay with Agohya, the lands became fertile and the rivers filled with water.[60] Nowhere does the *Ṛgveda* explicitly tells us that the Ṛbhus are sunshine. Once they were described as *sūracakṣasaḥ* (I.110.4, Sāyaṇa: *sūryasamānaprakāśāḥ*). They ascended the celestial region (I.110.6). As swift as wind, riding horses they traversed heaven (IV.33.1).

Several scholars since the mid-nineteenth century have expressed their opinions on this solar residence for twelve days of the Ṛbhus. Félix Nève who thinks that the Ṛbhus were initially human beings says: "The religious faith which placed the Ṛbhus among the gods had to attribute to them, in order to remain constant, an external and physical action which manifests itself with that of the divinities. It is with this aim it has made the three children of Sudhanvan, the rays of the sun, *sūracakṣasaḥ*".[61] Alfred Hillebrandt identifies the twelve days during which the Ṛbhus stayed with Savitṛ with the period of twelve days' rest at the winter solstice known in the German folk-lore and mythology.[62] Keith with reference to Hillebrandt's opinion says, "But all this is mere conjecture." In addition, he quotes his own opinion (Cf. *JRAS,* 1915, 131-33) ". . . the belief that the Indians and the Germans preserve a common tradition of twelve days' rest of nature at the winter solstice is a most improbable idea."[63] Macdonell sees them as fertility gods in their twelve days' stay with Savitṛ, "the notion that they produce fertility is connected with their sojourn of twelve days in the house of Savitṛ or Agohya, the sun, who cannot be concealed."[64] A.W. Ryder doubts the consistency of identifying the Ṛbhus with sunshine.[65] Stella Kramrisch identifies these twelve days with, "twelve units of their working time during which the year, the old cow and the parents — Heaven and Earth — are made young by the Ṛbhus".[66] B.R. Sharma opines that the twelve days solar residence of the Ṛbhus supports their identification with the solar rays.[67]

The three brothers Ṛbhu, Vibhavan and Vāja went to a retreat — a part of their penance. Nobody knew, where they went.[68] It so happened that it heavily rained during this period, most probably, for twelve days. The sun was totally invisible. After the rains stopped, the earth became naturally very green, full of fertility; the low lands and rivers were filled with water. The three borthers also returned from their sojourn as the rains were over. So the story was born that these altruistic brothers, Ṛbhu, Vibhavan and Vāja, went to the abode of Savitṛ, the *agohya*, became his honoured guests and were granted immortality. During their stay with Savitṛ, they showered rains and consequently made the earth fertile. The Ṛbhus had already been deified because of their meritorious deeds. They were deified as doctors and as carftsmen. But their deification will only be complete when they are raised to the status of fertility gods — solar deities. The process of deification ended gloriously by raising the Ṛbhus to the status of solar deities[69] for the accomplishment of which this story of their residence with Savitṛ was very much necessary. Before solarization they were benevolent gods as doctors and as architects. Now the field of their activities was broadened after passing through the stage of fertiligy gods. They were now given the opportunity to render the best service to humanity. The story narrated in the *Aitareya Brāhmaṇa* (III.30) also speaks about their solarization.

But for a few Viśvedevāḥ hymns the Ṛbhus are hardly ever invoked in others than those dedicated to them. In these hymns also, as is usual for such hymns, they are very mechanically invoked along with many other deities.[70]

In many places of the *ṚV* the word *ṛbhu*[71] has been used as an adjective. As for example in *ṚV,* II.1.10 and III.5.6, *ṛbhu* has been used as an adjective to Agni. In IV.37.5, *ṛbhu* has been used an adjective to the word *rayi* following it.

The word *ṛbhukṣan*[72] represents Ṛbhu, the eldest brother,[73] and all the three brothers when used in the plural number.[74] When Ṛbhukṣan is used in the singular number and personifies the eldest brother, then, mostly, except in two cases,[75] Vāja is also mentioned side-by-side.

Ṛbhukṣan symbolises Indra also in several places.[76] Twice we come across the word *ṛbhvan* used as an adjective to Indra.[77] Ṛbhukṣan has been used as an adjective to Savitṛ in: *tritá ṛbhukṣā́ḥ savitā́ çáno dadhe* (*ṚV,* II.31.6.). *ṚV,* I.51.2 narrates that story that all the gods except the Maruts abandoned Indra. If the word *ṛbhavaḥ* occurring in the verse is interpreted as the Maruts, as was done by Sāyaṇa, only then do we get this story.

Epithets

About a dozen times the Ṛbhus are addressed or referred to as *Saudhanvanāsaḥ,*[78] i.e., the children of Sudhavan. The Vedic texts do not give us any information about Sudhanvan whose children the Ṛbhus are. *ṚV,* V.42.11 uses the word *sudhánvā* while describing Rudra as a good archer. Here it is clearly an epithet of Rudra who is *sviṣuḥ sudhanvā*. Then again *ṚV,* V.57.2 uses Sudhanvānaḥ, i.e., good archers while describing the Maruts as good fighters: *sudhánvāna íṣumanto niṣangíṇaḥ.* Here also it is clearly a descriptive term and cannot by any means be taken as a name for the Maruts. G.V. Devasthali, however, suggests, "it may . . . be perhaps better if we could take *saudhanvana* to mean belonging to or connected with or devoted to Sudhanvan where the epithet Sudhanvan may be taken to stand for the deity (viz. Rudra or the Maruts) itself".[79] To us *Saudhanvanāḥ* (or *Saudhanvaṇāsaḥ*) appears nothing but a proper name. Ryder also holds that Sudhanvan is a name.[80] The Ṛbhus are once described as *mánor nápātaḥ* (*ṚV,* VIII.60.3) who was a human being; Sāyaṇa explains, *manuṣyasya āṅgirasaḥ putrāḥ.* The epithet *śavaso napātaḥ,*[81] children of strength, also hints at thier human identity. Gonda says regarding this epithet "an epithet almost peculiar to them."[82] The Ṛbhus are described as *vājaratnāḥ* (*ṚV,* IV.35.5), *vājāsaḥ* (IV.37.5). *Vāja* means *anna,* i.e., prosperity. In connection with many other deities this term has been used. Gonda, however, wants to connect *vājaratna* with the youngest brother Vāja, "An interesting epithet *vājaratna* — 'whose treasure consists in *vāja*' (IV.34.3, 5) . . . It is hardly a matter of chance that Vāja is identical with the name of one of the Ṛbhus."[83] It is very difficult to say whether Vāmadeva used the word *vāja* connotatively or denotatively. The epithets *sukṛtaḥ, suhastāḥ* also indicate their human character.[84]

We can gather very little personal information about the Ṛbhus. Kutsa tells us that some of his relatives who were Sudhanvan's sons, desiring immortality went to the residence of Savitṛ. So we infer that these three brothers belonged to the family of Aṅgiras. One can infer that they were Sudhanvan's sons as they had been repeatedly referred to as *saudhanvanaḥ*. Sūnu, the seer of *ṚV*, X.176, proclaims himself as the son of the Ṛbhus. About their personal appearance also very little is said. They surpass all in beauty; *śrēṣṭhaṃ vaḥ péśaḥ* (*ṚV*, IV.36.7). Children of Indra, they were strong-jawed (*ayaḥśiprāḥ*, IV.37.4); this speaks probably about their strong determination; they were prosperous (*suniṣkāḥ*) and they had a bright chariot which was drawn by strong horses (IV.37.4).

The Ṛbhus and the Other Gods

Of all the gods Indra is the closest of the Ṛbhus. They are his children.[85] Indra made them his friends because of their deeds of merit[86] Sage Vasiṣṭha feels that, they can defeat all enemies had they been supported by Indra and the Ṛbhus.[87] The three brothers are described as *indravantaḥ*[88] and *Ṛbhu* is described as *indrasvat*.[89] Indra, on the other hand, is *ṛbhumat* and *vājavat*.[90] When the *Ṛbhus*' acceptance on the Vedic pantheon had been finally confirmed, then *Ṛbhu* belonged to Indra, Vibhvat to Varuṇa and Vāja to all the gods (*ṚV*, IV.33.9). But unfortunately the same Indra had objected to their admission into the midday libation which was his alone. So, Prajāpati had to assign them a place in the third soma libation along with Savitṛ.[91] The other deities along which the Ṛbhus are invoked to the sacrificial offerings are Mitrāvaṛuṇau, the Maruts, the Aśvins, the kings, the Ādityas, Parvatas, Savitṛ, Sindhu and the Ṛtus.[92] Once they are addressed as *pūṣaṇvantaḥ* (*ṚV*, III.54.12). Sage Vāmadeva tells us that goddess Dhiṣaṇā assigned this place to the Ṛbhus among the gods.[93] The same sage again marvels to think in which ancient dawn the Ṛbhus had performed their miraculous deeds.[94] Vāmadeva here hints at a very archaic origin of the Ṛbhus.

Scholars on the Identity of the Ṛbhus

A review of the opinions of scholars on the identity of the Ṛbhus might help us in arriving at a ogical conclusion in this respect. As we have already seen, Sāyaṇa also accepts them originally as human beings and later worshipped as sunshine. Félix Nève, the seniormost of the Western scholars on the Ṛbhu-studies, sees in the Ṛbhu-myth, "one of the first attempts of human deifications".[95] He also observes in them a resemblance of German Elves, "Now it is true that the Elves of Germany would be none else than the spirits of ancient generations — souls deprived of a terrestrial body and redressed in a new envelope, the same can be true even of the Ṛbhus whom Indra as has been seen, according to the letters of texts, has glorified as equal of gods of light by assimilating them to the rays of the sun".[96] Weber sees in them the genii of creative past, present and future.[97] According to Bergaigne they are "three ancient skilful sacrificers who acquired immortality and whose number is connected with the triad of sacrificial fires."[98] To Ryder two contradictory aspects — human and solar, of the Ṛbhus are very much evident. He also sees in the number three a resemblance of three steps of Viṣṇu. But on the ground of insufficient evidence Ryder does not dare draw any conclusion.[99] A.A. Macdonell sees the aerial elves in the Ṛbhus and says, "On the whole it seems probable that the Ṛbhus were aerial elves, whose dexterity attached to them various myths illustrative of marvellous skill. But the evidence furnished by the *Ṛgveda* is hardly sufficient to warrant any certain conclusion.[100] Bloomfield[101] and Keith[102] also see the elves in the Ṛbhus. Alfred Hillebrandt refers to the earth becoming fertile after twelve days' stay of the Ṛbhus with Agohya and proposes that the Ṛbhus must be the seasons: "Aus das führt zu der Vermutung, dass Ṛbhu ein alter Name des Jahreszeiten war".[103] He is also sure of their divinity and says ". . . nun ist nicht zu verkennen, dass die Ṛbhus vornehmlich Götter sind nur von Göttern konnte es heissen, dass sie 12 Tage in Agohyas Hause schliefen und nachher Fruchtbarkeit gaben . . ."[104] Oldenberg, however, thinks that such conjectures are the most uncertain and together with many other scholars thinks, insufficient evidences do not permit one to come to any decisive conclusion: ". . . die kurzen Andeutungen in welchen die Lieder von den Erlebnissen der Ṛbhus sprechen geben zu einem einigermassen sicheren Urtheil keine hinreichende Unterlage."[105] Sitanath Pradhan holds the view that the Ṛbhus were chieftains of a remote age.[106] Potdar, a believer in the euhemeristic origin of the Ṛbhus, thinks, "The Ṛbhus making three *camasas* fulfilled that necessity. As society had been still in an evolving state so they were accepted among the gods, though with some protest . . ."[107] According to Chapekar, "Ṛbhus are the names given to the rays of the sun."[108] B.R. Sharma thinks: "The Ṛbhus represent solar deities presiding over the rays of the sun. . . Their threefold division . . . is also applicable to the polar triple phenomenon connected with the sun, namely, the sun and his rays at the decline of winter, the sun in summer and the sun and light gradually disappearing on the eve of winter."[109] Gonda suggests that the Ṛbhus might be originally mortals.[110]

Conclusion

Ṛbhu, Vibhavan and Vāja — the three sons of Sudhanvan — were mortal beings. They were intelligent, dexterous, and benevolent. Their altruistic instinct led them to cure the dying cow which was given as a gift to Bṛhaspati and unite it with its calf, transform their own old frail parents into youthful strong and vigorous persons. They thus proved their therapeutic skill in such remedial activities.

They also showed their skilled carftsmanship by making a unique chariot, of which they made a gift to the Aśvins. We believe, they must have performed many other such wonders but unfortunately these are not recorded in the Saṃhitās. Society marvelled at their generosity and skill. The feeling was common among their followmen that they had to be given some kind of recognition and applaud. Society was sacrifice-oriented; so recognition had to be given in the broader context of the sacrifice. These three brothers were considered no ordinary mortals. Only those endowed with divine power can accomplish such wonders. So, they must be given a share of soma drink in the sacrifice along with other gods. But how could the originally human

Ṛbhus be given that drink which was held so far as exclusive to the gods — the soma drink, in the same cup, the *camasa*, with the gods. Hence three more *camasa*s were badly needed. The skilled artificers, the Ṛbhus, themselves were entrusted with the difficult task of making four *camasa*s out of the original one by the divine architect Tvaṣṭṛ. And, the *camasa*s must totally resemble the original one. Thus they faced the very difficult and final ordeal for attaining divinity. They gloriously passed through the ordeal. They proved themselves as accomplished as Tvaṣṭṛ, the divine architect. Consequently they were given a place among the soma enjoying gods — but with a difference, i.e., they were given this right only in the third pressing (*tṛtīya savana*).

This was the first phase in the process of deification of the hman Ṛbhus. They were recognised as possessors of divine power in the fields of craftsmanship and therapeutic knowledge and skill. Gods possessed of such abilities were not given the highest status in the Vedic pantheon. We may remember in this connection that the divine doctors Aśvins also had to face a number of obstacles in attaining the right to the soma drink in sacrifice.

The highly ambitious, Ṛbhus, now deified, did not stop in their strivings. We have already discussed that during their retreat for a more vigorous penance, which might occupy them for a period of twelve days, it rained heavily without any break. Consequently, the earth became green and fertile. The devotees of the Ṛbhus painfully felt the absence of their beloved deities. As soon as the rains stopped they reappeared. Immediately the story was spun that these three benevolent brothers went to Savitṛ, the *agohya* who cannot be hidden, and because of their residence and intercession with Savitṛ, who had granted them immortality, the earth became fertile. The Ṛbhus, who had so long been expert craftsmen and therapists, were now raised to the status of gods of fecundity. In this way the solarization of the Ṛbhus was accomplished. And, the Ṛgvedic singers describe them as sunshine or as the eyes of the gods (*sūracakṣasaḥ*).

In the beginning the Ṛbhus could heal the earthly maladies, and perform works of craftsmanship of the highest order. Now being solarized they were entrusted with the function of fertility gods and were established in the status of solar gods. The Vedic poets sing to thier glorification that they created the horses (*harī*) for Indra, made shoulder-bands (*aṃsatra*) for the gods and separated heaven and earth.[111] The repeated statement that they made a gift of cart to the Aśvins and that of the cow Viśvarūpā to Bṛhaspati is just to show that they had good connection with other gods. The *Mahābhārata*, however, elevated the Ṛbhus to the status of the highest gods.[112]

Ṛbhu, Vibhavan and Vāja[113] the three human brothers, the sons of Sudhanvan, by dint of their merit (*sukṛtyayā*) earned the same status with Tvaṣṭṛ, the divine architect, achieved immortality and the right to the soma drink and finally achieved the rank of solar deities: gods of very high order.

Notes and References

[First Published: *ABORI*, LXXI (1989).]

1. *ṚV,* = *Ṛgveda*, ed. by Tilak, Maharashtra University, Vaidika Saṁśodhana Maṇḍala, Poona, 1936.
2. All the translations from Sanskrit and German into English in this book are by us. If it is otherwise then translator's name with reference has been mentioned.
3. *ṚV,* I.20; 110; 111; 161; III.60; IV.33-37; VII.48.
4. ***See*** the following verses for stray references to the Ṛbhus: III.54.12; V.42.5; 46.4; VI.50.12; VII.35.12; 37.1; 2; 48.1; 51.3; X.64.10; 65.10; 66.10; 92.11; 93.7: all these verses belong to the hymns dedicated to the Viśvedevāḥ.
5. *Mbh*, III.247, 19a, Critical edn. Poona.
6. *The Nighaṇṭu and Nirukta*, ed. by Lakshman Sarup, Motilal Banarsidass, 1967, p. 194 (text).
7. *Ibid.*, p. 173.
8. *Ibid.*, p. 194 (text).
9. *Śabdakalpadruma*, Vol. I. Calcutta, 1961, p. 287 (*ṛ+bhū+ḍu*) *devatā ity amaraḥ*.

10. *Vācaspatyābhidhāna*, Vol. II, Chowkhamba Sanskrit Series, Varanasi, 1962, p. 1448.
11. Cf. *Sanskrit Wörterbuch*, ed. by Rudolf Roth and Otto Bohtlingk St. Petersburg, Vol. I., p. 1059.
12. *The Vedic Mythology* (reprint), Indological Book House, 1971, p. 133., 1st edn., 1897.
13. "Die Ṛbhus im Ṛg Veda", *KZ*, 1901, p. 18.
14. *Vedishe Mythologie*, Vol. II, Breslau, 1929, p. 135.
15. *A Sanskrit-English Dictionary*, ed. by Sir Monier-Williams (reprint), Motilal Banarsidass, p. 226, Ist edn., Oxford University Press, 1899.
16. *The Practical Sanskrit English Dictionary*, Poona, 1890, p. 310.
17. Cf. *ṚV*, I.110.2, *ābhogáyāṃ prá yád icchánta áitanápākāḥ prā́ñco máma ke cid, āpáyaḥ* I *sáudhanvanāsas caritásya bhūmánā́gacchata savitúr dāśúṣo gṛhám* II
18. **See** *ṚV*, IV.36.3.18.
19. **See** *ṚV*, I.110.8, *niścármaṇa ṛbhavo gā́m apiṃśata sáṃ vatsénā 'sṛjata mātáraṃ púnaḥ* I ***also see*** *ṚV*, I.20.3; III.1; 161.7; III.60.2; IV.33.4; 36.4.
20. Cf. *ṚV*, IV.33.8, *yé dhenúṃ viśvajúvam viśvárūpām* I
21. Cf. *ṚV*, I.161.6, *Bṛhaspátir viśvárūpām úpājata* I
22. "Apotheosis in the *Ṛgveda*", *ABORI*, Vol. XII, 1930-31, p. 58.
23. "The Ṛbhus", *JBBRAS*, Vol. 29, Part I, 1954, p. 81.
24. Cf. *ṚV*, I.20, 4, *yúvānā pitárā púnaḥ satyámantrā ṛjūyávaḥ* I *ṛbhávo viṣṭý akrata* II also Cf. *ṚV*, I.110.8; 111.1; 161.7; IV.33.3; 35.4, 36.3.
25. Stella Kramrisch, "The Ṛgvedic myths of the craftsmen (the Ṛbhus)", in *Artibus Asiae*, Acona 22 (1-22), 1960 (?) p. 120.
26. Cf. *ṚV*, IV.36.I, *anaśvó jātó anabhīśur ukthyo ráthas trickráḥ pári vartate rájaḥ* I
27. Cf. *ṚV*, IV.36.2, *rátham yé cakruḥ suvṛ́taṃ sucétasó. 'vihvarantaṃ mánasas pári dhyáyā* I
28. **See** *ṚV*, I.20.3; 111.1; 161.3; IV.33.8; 34.9; 36.1; 2.
29. **See** *ṚV*, I.20.3; 161.6; IV.34.9.
30. **See** *ṚV*, I.20.2; 111.1; 161.6; 7; III.60.2; IV.33.10; 34.9; 35.5.
31. **See** *ṚV*, I.20.2; III.60.2.
32. Cf. *ṚV*, I.161.2, *ékam camasáṃ catúraḥ kṛṇotana tád vo devā́ abrūvan tád va ā́gamam* I *saúdhanvanā yády evā́ kariṣyátha sākám devaír yajñíyāso bhaviṣyatha* II
33. **See** *ṚV*, I. 110.3;5; 161.2; 5; IV.33.5; 6; 35.2; 4.

34. *Bṛhaddevatā*, however, narrates that the Ṛbhus, the sons of Sudhanvan, were Tvaṣṭṛ's disciples (*sikṣayāmāsa tān tvaṣṭā tvāṣtraṃ yat karma kañcana*). Tvaṣṭṛ, Savitṛ, Prajāpati invited all the gods in an assembly and awarded them immortality in recognition of their merit, etc., etc. Cf. *Bṛhaddevatā*, Part I, III 83-90 (ed. by A.B. Keith, Harvard Oriental Series V (reprint), Motilal Banarsidass 1965, pp. 31-32).

35. **See** *ṚV*, I.161.4, *chakravāṃsa ṛbhavas tád apṛcchata kvéd abhūd yáḥ syá dūtó na ā́jagan yadā́vā́khyac camasā́n catúraḥ kṛtā́n ā́d ít tváṣṭā gnā́sv antár nyānaje* ।

36. **See** *ṚV,* I.161.5, *háṇāma enān íti tváṣṭā yád, ábravic camasám yé devapā́nam ánindiṣuḥ* । *anyā nā́māni´ kṛnvate sutéˊ sácā́ anyaír enān kanyā nā́mabhiḥ sparat* ।।

37. **See** *ṚV,* IV.33.5, *tváṣṭā ṛbhavas tát panayad váco vaḥ* । We presume that Tvaṣṭṛ here represents the whole society.

38. **See** *Ṛv*, I.161.8.

39. *prātár yajadhvam aśvínā hinota*
ná sāyám asti devayā́ ájuṣṭam ।
— Sāyaṇa interprets the second line, *sāyaṃ kāle haviḥ devagāmi na vidyate devā na svīkurvantīty arthaḥ.*

40. *Op. cit.*, p. 134.

41. *The Mythology of all Races* (Vol. VI. Boston Marshall, 1917, Jones Company), p. 48.

42. *Op. cit.*, p. 177.

43. "The Ṛbhus and the four Soma cups", in *Poona Orientatlist*, Vol. VII, 3 & 4, pp. 177-80, 1942-43.

44. "The Vedic Ṛbhus: whom do they represent", in *Sri Venkateshwar University Oriental Journal*, Triupati, Vol. V, Nos. 1-2, p. 56, 1962.

45. *Op. cit.*, pp. 58-59.

46. "The Ṛbhus in the Ṛgveda", in *J. Bom. U.* 21 (2), Sept. 1952, p. 29. A small question arises here, why Tvaṣṭṛ, the original architect of the *camasa*, and definitely a better architect than the human Ṛbhus who were Tvaṣṭṛ's contemporaries, was not entursted with this task, and why the Ṛbhus?

47. *Op. cit.*, p. 84.

48. **See** *ṚV,* I.20.1.

49. *ṚV*, IV.33.2

50. *ṚV*, IV.34.7; 8; 11.

51. **See** *ṚV*, IV.35.7.

52. *ṚV*, IV.34.1.

53. **See** *ṚV*, IV.33.11b; *ná ṛté śrāntásya sakhyā́ya devā́ḥ* ।

54. ***See*** *Ṛ̣V*, IV.35.1; 2; 36.2.
55. ***See*** *ṚV*, IV.36.1.
56. ***See*** *ṚV*, IV.36.3.
57. ***See*** *ṚV*, I.110.2, 3.
58. ***See*** *ṚV*, I.161.11.
59. ***See*** *ṚV*, I.161.12.
60. ***See*** *ṚV*, IV.33.7.
61. *An Essay on the Myth of the Ṛbhus,* Paris, 1847: tr. by G.V. Davane, Ajanta Publications, Delhi, 1985, p. 246.
62. *Op. cit.*, p. 145.
63. *Op. cit.*, Part I, pp. 177-78.
64. *Op. cit.*, p. 133.
65. "Die Ṛbhus in Ṛgveda," in *KZ,* 1901, p. 48.
66. *Op. cit.*, p. 120.
67. *Op. cit.*, p. 55.
68. Cf. *ṚV*, I.161.12 ab, *saṃmī́lya yád bhúvanā paryásarpata kva svit tātyā́ pitárā va āsatuḥ* ।
69. Sāyaṇa in the introduction of his interpretation of *ṚV*, I.161.11 says *purāṇaprasiddhān sudhanvanaḥ putrān karmaṇā devatvaṃ prāptavataḥ ṛbhūn stutyā vedaprasiddhyā sūryarasmirūpān ṛbhūn idānīṃ stauti.*
70. ***See*** *ṚV*, III.54.12; V.46.4; VII.35.12; VII.51.3 (a hymn consisting of three verses, dedicated to the Ādityas but has the character of a Viśvedevāḥ hymn); X.66.10.
71. Sāyaṇa interprets as *mahān, uru bhāsamānaḥ.*
72. Sāyaṇa interprets as *mahat* occurring in I.111.4.
73. Cf. *ṚV*, IV.33.9 cd, *vā́jo devā́nām abhavat sukármā* । *índrasya ṛbhukṣā́ váruṇasya víbhvā* ।। ***also see*** *ṚV.*, IV.34.5; V.42.5; X.64.10.
74. ***See*** *ṚV*, 37.5; VII.37.1; 2; 48.1; X.92.11; 93.7.
75. ***See*** *ṚV*, VII.37.2; X.92.11.
76. ***See*** *ṚV*, I.111.4; 162.1; 186.10; X.74.5; 93.8 — in this verse in the first two lines we read a play with the word *ṛbhu*; *ṛbhúr ṛbhukṣā́ ṛbhúr vidhatá máda ā́te hárī jūyuvānásya vājínā́* ।
77. ***See*** *ṚV*, VI.34.2; X.99.5.
78. Cf. *ṚV*, I.110.2; 4; 8; 161.2; 7; 8; III.60.1; 3; 4; 5; IV.35.1; 8.
79. "Epithets of the Ṛbhus in the Ṛgveda", in *Indian Antiquary* (Third Series), Vol. 2, No. 2 (April 67), p. 13.
80. *Op. cit.*, p. 18; "doch ist Sudhanvan vorläufig kaum mehr als ein Name."

81. **See** *ṚV,* I.161.14; IV.34.6; 35.1; 35.8; 37.4.
82. *The Epithets of the Ṛgveda* (Mouton & Co., 1959), p. 121.
83. *Op. cit.*, p. 121.
84. *ṚV,* VII.35.12.
85. Cf. *ṚV*, IV. 37.4; *índrasya sūno śavaso napātaḥ* ।
86. Cf. *ṚV*, IV.35.7: *sákhīn yā́n indra cakṛṣé sukṛtyā́* ।
87. **See** *ṚV*, VII.48.2; 3.
88. **See** *ṚV*, IV.33.3; 34.6.
89. **See** *ṚV,* IV.37.5.
90. **See** *ṚV,* III.52.6.
91. Cf. *AitBrā,* III.30.
92. **See** *ṚV,* I.111.4; IV.34.2; IV.34.8; IV.34.11.
93. Cf. *ṚV*, IV.34.1 cd — *idā́ hí vo dhiśáṇā devyá hṇām* । *ádhāt pītím sám mádā agmatā vaḥ* ।।
94. Cf. *ṚV,* IV.51.6 ab —

    kva svíd āsām katamā́ purāṇī́
    yáyā vidhā́nā vidadhúr ṛbhūṇā́m ।
    — this verse belongs to an Uṣas-hymn.
95. *Op. cit.*, p. 192.
96. *Op. cit.*, p. 313.
97. *Vedische Beiträge*, Vol. III, p. 37.
98. Quoted from A.A. Macdonell's *Vedic Mythology*, p. 134.
99. *Op. cit.*, pp. 47-49 — . . . "die erste Auslegung nimmt Bezug auf ihre menschliche die zweite auf ihre kosmologische Tätigkeit . . . doch wage ich nicht den Versuch, ein auch einigermassen definitives Urteil abgeben zu wollen . . . doch die Evidenz der Lieder Schwerlich entscheidend, und vorvedisches Material haben wir nicht."
100. *Op. cit.*, p. 134.
101. *Religion of the Veda* (G.P. Putnam's sons, New York & London, 1908), p. 78.
102. *Op. cit.*, Part I, p. 178.
103. *Op. cit.*, p. 131.
104. *Ibid.*
105. *Die Religion des Veda* (Berlin, 1894), p. 236.
106. *Op. cit.*, p. 57.
107. *Op. cit.*, p. 30.
108. *Op. cit.*, p. 81.

109. *Op. cit.*, p. 58.

110. *Die Religionen Indiens* I (Kohlhammer 2nd edn., 1978, 1st edn. 1960), p. 62. "So ist est kein Wunder, dass sie die anfänglich Sterbliche waren, die, Unsterblich erlangten and Indras, Freunde wurden."

111. ***See*** *ṚV*, 34.9.

112. ***See*** *Mbh,* III.247.19a — *ṛbhavo nāma tatrānye devānāmapi devatāḥ* ǀ

113. In the names of the three brothers, Ṛbhu, Vibhavan and Vāja, also the process of their gradual rise can be visualised. Ṛbhu, i.e., dexterity brings forth glory, pervasiveness, i.e., Vibhavan which lead to prosperity, i.e., Vāja.

2

The Aśvins

The Divine Doctors Aśvins and the Soma Drink

THE twin divine physicians, the Aśvins, hold an important position in the Vedic pantheon. About fiftyone hymns have been dedicated to these twin deities. In the *ṚV* the Aśvins hold the fourth position following Indra, Agni and Soma, from the point of view of the total number hymns dedicated to them. In spite of their important position the identity of these twin deities is still a puzzle to indologists as it was even before the time of Yāska. Yāska[1] has recorded four different views of his predecessors on the origin of the Aśvins. The first three of them identify the Aśvins with different natural phenomena like heaven and earth, day and night, and the sun and the moon. The upholders of the fourth opinion, the then historical school, propagated the euhemeristic theory by identifying the Aśvins with two pious earthly kings. Yāska's opinion on the identity of these two deities is: "their time is after midnight, which in consequence is an impediment to the appearance of light. The part in the dark is the atmosphere, and the part in light is the sun".[2] So far around twenty-five opinions have been given on the identity of the Aśvins by the scholars of the East and West. The majority of these have identified the twin deities with different phenomena of earth, atmosphere and sky. K.F. Geldner,[3] however, has opined that they have been succouring Indian saints. G.L.

Chandravarkar[4] holds that they were historical figures of Indo-European origin. He establishes his view by saying that "When the conception of a deity originates from the appearance of a happening in nature its identification with the happening and possibly with no other, remains permanent and is handed down from generation to generation in much the same form. But when the identification is based on imagination, it is probable that more conception than one may arise". Few other Vedic deities have perplexed the scholars of all time as these twin deities.

Another point of controversy in connection with the Aśvins is their right to the soma libation. That the Aśvins had been deprived of the right to the soma libation and that later they regained that right has been recorded for the first time in the *TS*[5] and then in later literature.

A review of the opinions expressed by the scholars on the Aśvins' right to the soma libation appears not to be out of context in this connection.

Alfred Hillebrandt thinks that the Āryan Indians offered libations of soma or *gharma* according to their respective family tradition.[6] A.B. Keith observes, "The Aśvins are particularly connected with honey; they bestrew the sacrifice and worshipper with a honey whip, their car is honey-hued and honey-bearing. They are honey-handed and give the bee its honey. In comparison they are less vitally connected with Soma, though they are said to drink it at each pressing and in some circles they were probably not at first reckoned among the Soma-drinking gods, though for this proofs are rather inadequate".[7] Keith does not speak decisively anything on this point. Václav Machek opines, "With the character of the Aśvins as the youth not yet grown up is no doubt connected that their drink is the *madhu* and not the Soma. It is impossible to look for another reason than analogy of real life: strong drink for heroes and not for boys and young men. Of this simple thing the Indian ritualists made complicated fancies".[8] The multifarious activities of the Aśvins like curing their protégés of different maladies, rescuing Bhujyu from mid-ocean and such others do not speak in support of Machek's view that the Aśvins were boys and young men. Reinhold F.G. Müller sees no confusion in the offering of soma libation of the Aśvins, 'According to the Vedic conception the Aśvins have a place in the Vedic pantheon and rather because of the reason that they are invited specially to the Soma offerings (all through, not less infrequently than the other gods)'. Our conjecture goes in conformity with Müller's except for the fact that the Aśvins were deprived temporarily of this right.[9] K.P. Jog observes, "*KatS,* 13.6; *MS,* 4.6.2. and *TS,* 2.1.10.1 derecognises them among the gods when they refer to the Aśvins not having a claim to Soma offering as the definitive (*nirdhāraṇārthe*) genitive *devānāṃ asomapā* or *asomapau* shows. Such a lesser position of the Aśvins amongst the gods is further indicated from their mention as *devānām-anujāvarau* 'Posthumous' (?) among the gods at *KapS,* 46.6; *KātS,* 13.7; 30.3; and *MS,* 2, 5, 6. This is probably to show that in certain parts of ancient India — or rather, in some of the Vedic schools — the Aśvins were not acceptable to the priestly hierarchy as excellent gods".[10] Textual material, does not, however, support Jog's conjecture. The texts say that the Aśvins lost temporarily their right to Soma.

The Ṛgvedic singers generously offer soma libation to the Aśvins. For about fifty times they have been offered soma in fifty-one hymns dedicated to them. Along with other words of invocation in which they had been offered soma libation five times they had been invoked with the prayer, *píbataṃ somyáṃ mádhu,*[11] thrice with, *sómaṃ pibatam aśvinā,*[12] twice with *pātáṃ sómam ṛtāvṛdhā,*[13] once with, *píbataṃ sómaṃ mádhumantam aśvinā*[14] and once with, *píbātha ín mádhunaḥ somyásya.*[15]

A deliberation on the Aśvins without referring to their close relation with *madhu* is simply impossible. Of the many epithets of the Aśvins that are found in the *ṚV* a few are, *madhuvarṇā* (VIII.26.6) 'honey-coloured', *madhupau* (I.180.2) 'drinkers of honey', *madhupātamā* (VIII.22.17) 'the best drinkers of honey', *mādhvi* (VII.67.4) 'honeyed'. The Aśvins obtained the *madhu-*

lore from the sage Dadhyañc, the son of Atharvan (Cf. *Ṛ̣V*, I.117.12). He imparted this knowledge to the Aśvins by means of a horse's head. The story goes thus; Indra, pleased with Dadhyañc, bestowed on him the '*madhu*-lore' with the warning that he would chop Dadhyañc's head if this lore was divulged to anyone else. The Aśvins put a horse's head on Dadhyañc's neck and induced him to relate the '*madhu*-lore' to them. Indra becoming aware of the fact took off Dadhyañc's head (i.e., the horse's head). Then the Aśvins replaced on his neck his real head.[16] The Aśvins had been the sole possessors of the '*madhu*-lore' all through the Vedic age. What actually the term '*madhu*-lore' (*madhu vidyā*) signified is not known. It is identical with *Pravargya vidyā*, useful at the head of the sacrifice. The *madhu* narrated in the *BṛUp.*[17] describes the all-pervading nature of the 'Soul'. In the *Ṛ̣V* the Aśvins are invoked with *áśvinā píbataṃ mádhu,*[18] *mádhvaḥ pibataṃ madhupébhih āsábhih,*[19] *mádhvā yajñáṃ mimikṣatam,*[20] *pṛnktáṃ havíṃṣi mádhuṇā,*[21] *imé vāṃ nidháyo mádhūnām.*[22] The chariot of the Aśvins is full of honey.[23] It carries a leather bag full of honey from which they have been asked to drink.[24] They are so full of honey that the black bees collect honey from them.[25] The Aśvins pour a hundred jars of *surā* (wine) from the hoofs of their horses (*Ṛ̣V*, I.116.7). *Ṛ̣V*, I.117.6 narrates the same story with the difference that in place of *surā* it uses the word *madhu*.

A scrutiny of the Ṛgvedic hymns leads to the conclusion that the Ṛgvedic singers did not make any discrimination while offering soma and *madhu* libation to the Aśvins. Equal was the passion of the Aśvins for soma and *madhu*. Whether *madhu* and soma were two different drinks or were identical is yet to be established. Mircea Eliade[26] says, "madhu the sweet pressed juice is known as Soma. Cognates to Madhu (GK. *me'thy/ME θU*; old Slavonic *medu*; Icelandic *mjōd / majoār/*; Anglo-Saxon *moedu*) suggest a kind of honey made of celestial origin to which religious value of intoxication and generative power were attributed". In the *Ṛ̣V* the words *soma* and *madhu* are used in such a manner (Cf. *píbataṃ somyáṃ mádhu,* VII.74.2, etc.) that very often it becomes difficult to distinguish one from the other. In many places they are used synonymously.

In the *TS* we learn for the first time that the Aśvins had been denied the right to the soma drink on the ground that they were doctors and that they had mixed much among men and have become impious; the Aśvins, however, established themselves to that much coveted right by dint of their own merit.[27]

A few instances illustrating the Aśvins as divine doctors and friends of their devotees in distress are quoted below from the *ṚV*, in support of the allegations brought against them. The first and the tenth books, i.e., chronologically the later books of the *RV*, depict the succouring nature of the Aśvins in more concrete manner than the other books. Names of about a hundred protégés of the Aśvins are found in the *ṚV*, Some of them had been favoured with gifts, others with protection in distress and still others with medical aid.

Pedu[28] probably tops the list of those who were favoured with the unique gifts. The Aśvins gave him an excellent white horse, the first of its type. Dīrghaśravas[29] and Manu[30] were assisted in the cultivation of land — the first was favoured with showers of rain and for the latter they ploughed the land. Kakṣīvat[31] who was blinded by the darkness of ignorance was enlightened with knowledge. Atri[32] who was thrown into fire by the demons was rescued by the twin deities. Bhujyu[33] who went to fight with his enemies was stranded in mid-ocean; the Aśvins came to his rescue. The twin succouring deities saved Vandana[34] and Rebhā[35] who had been thrown into ditches by demons. Vimada's wife[36] was carried off by some other kings, the Aśvins brought her back to her husband. The divine doctors helped a good number of devotees by granting them medical aid. They restored eye-sight to the blind Kaṇva,[37] Ṛjrāśva[38] and Kavi.[39] The blind and lame Śroṇa[40] was cured of infirmities. Nārṣada's[41] hearing was restored. Śayu's old cow[42] which had stopped breeding regained the power to breed by the skill of the Aśvins. The old Cyavana[43] was rejuvenated and Śyāva[44] was cured of leprosy.

The Aśvins were good surgeons. They operated on the leg of Viśpalā,[45] the queen of king Khela, reset her bones and fitted her with an iron leg. Ghoṣā[46] a spinster had been suffering from leprosy and getting old in her parents' home. The Aśvins softened by her prayer saved her. She recovered perfect health, regained youth and charm and obtained the much cherished husband and home. The Aśvins were expert gynaecologists. They helped at the childbirth of Kamadyū[47] — Vimada's wife and also Saptavadhri's wife.[48] Of about a hundred protégés of the Aśvins, only the more prominent are mentioned here. The *ṚV* does not give any detailed description of these useful and beneficial services rendered by the Aśvins to their worshippers. They are just mentioned one after the other, especially, in the first book. The twin succouring deities granted their wards concrete help by personally coming to them in their distress and not by blessing them from their heavenly home which, however, would have been more god-like.

Gradually there arose in society a taboo against doctors, and the distance between men and gods became wider. The succouring deities Aśvins who were doctors and who did not maintain that distance from mortals were accordingly denied the right to the soma libation. In the *MS*[49] we read that the sacrifice became headless; the gods approached the Aśvins, — the divine doctors and surgeons, for joining the head of the sacrifice. They complied with their request on condition that their right to the soma libation be restored. The Aśvins were given back their right, only after they had been purified by the Bahiṣpavamāna rite, for, doctors were considered impure. The *TS*[50] narrates the same story and says: *apūtā va imau manuṣyacarau bhiṣajāv iti tasmād brāhmaṇena bheṣajam na kāryam.* 'Unclean are these doctors moving among men, therefore, a brāhmaṇa should not practise medicine'.

The *ŚatBrā*[51] in course of narrating the story of Sukanyā and Cyavana states that the gods had excluded the Aśvins from the sacrifice because, as doctors, they were wont to mix much among men. The Aśvins, however, reinstated themselves in their status of Adhvaryu-priests among the gods and acquired their right to soma libation.

Later, the *Mbh* narrates that the Aśvins rejuvenated the old and infirm Cyavana. Śaryāti who gave his daughter Sukanyā in marriage to the old Cyavana hearing the happy news came to congratulate his son-in-law on his rejuvenation. At Cyavana's suggestion Śaryāti performed a sacrifice in which Cyavana officiated as the priest. Cyavana, who in his gratefulness already promised the divine doctors to establish them in their right to soma libation, offered the same to them. Indra protested, and was about to hurl his thunderbolt at Cyavana, who in his turn paralysed Indra's hand; the soma libation was offered to the Aśvins. Moreover, Cyavana created the demon Mada in order to kill Indra. Indra whose hand was already paralysed, became nervous, gave way and acknowledged the Aśvins' right to soma libation. Indra's grounds for protests against the Aśvins receiving soma libation were — first, they had been doctors; secondly, as doctors they wandered much among men assuming different forms.[52] Sukumari Bhattacharji interprets this episode: "Decoding the language of mythology we may say that the cult of the Aśvins won and fought against the opposition of the prevalent Indra cult".[53]

The succouring nature of the Aśvins and their service as doctors are more prominently depicted in the first and the tenth books, i.e., the later books of the *ṚV*. The hymns of the earlier books, on the other hand, depict them essentially as early morning deities, the associates of Uṣas and Agni; their succouring functions are, of course, mentioned from time-to-time. A few hymns of the later books (Cf. 112th, 116th, 117th, 118th and 119th of the first book and the 39th of the tenth book) repeatedly mention the manifold aids rendered by the divine twins to their protégés. Their identity as doctors, as helpers of their devotees in distress became very evident. Apprehensions may arise that around this period the human Aśvins had been deified because of their outstanding services to their devotees.

The Vedic twins gods, the Aśvins, fall in the Indo-European Dioscouri group; their deification must have taken place in their Indo-European home. The Greek counterpart of the Aśvins are Dioscouri who are also popular for their benevolent deeds. Their association with their sister Helen resembles the Aśvins' association with Sūryā. In Roman Cástor and Pollux the saviours of sailors at sea, one sees the image of the Aśvins. The Indo-Iranian branch apparently missed these divine twins. Stig Wikander[54] has, however, found them in the demon Naonhaithya and Atar the son of Ahura Mazdah. Donald Ward[55] observes at the conclusion of his book on the Divine Twins: "Thus the Divine Twins, the sons of the Sky-God, brothers of Sun-maiden, were the well-defined deities of the Proto-Indo-European pantheon and were carried by the various people to their new homelands where the religious complex changed remarkably well through the centuries in the new environment".

Regarding the Aśvins being deprived of soma libation and excluded from circle of gods, we observe the reflections of cult-conflict, viz., between the cults of Indra and the Aśvins. The hymns of the *ṚV*, specially, those of later books, were sung in eulogy of these twin deities. The devotees sang in multifarious ways the benevolent activities of these succouring deities — as men's very present helps in trouble, as doctors, surgeons, gynaecologists, so on and, so forth. But the result of this eulogy was rather adverse, as in society there arose a taboo against the doctors and the gods assumed an Olympian attitude. The Aśvins who did not care to abide by these prohibitions were consequently excluded from the Vedic pantheon and were deprived of the soma libation as recorded in the *TS* and also in later literature. But, as we have seen, this was only a passing phase. Soon the Aśvins had to be recognised as Adhvaryu-priests among the gods and given back their right to the soma libation, as their services as doctors became indispensable because they joined the head of the sacrifice, which had been severed (Cf. *TS,* VI.4.9). So, the loss of right to the soma libation of the divine doctors Aśvins of the

Indian mythology is only a temporary occurrence caused by the conflicts between two cults.

[First published: *JASB* Calcutta, XXXI, 1989, Nos. 1-2.]

The Heavenly Twins and a Maiden

A discussion on the relation of the Aśvins towards Sūryā, the sun's daughter an Indo-European pattern, i.e., a trio of the twin gods and a maiden, as preserved in the Vedic tradition has been intended in this section. An ambiguous relation between Sūryā and the Aśvins is perceived in the Vedas all through.

The story of Sūryā's marriage celebration as narrated in the *ṚV* (X.85) is laid down in a nutshell. All the divine beings, the Vedəs, participated in Sūryā's marriage. The *ṛc* Raibhyā was the bridesmaid, the hymn Nāpāśaṃasa accompanied her as her attendant and the auspicious bridal dress of Sūryā was sanctified by the Gāthā (6). The deity Citti became her pillow; the heaven and the earth were the wells of the wheels of the chariot in which Sūryā travelled towards her husband's place (7). The *stoma*s and the metre Kurīra formed different parts of the chariot. The Aśvins were Sūryā's bridegrooms. The fire-god went forward (as the negotiator of the marriage) (8). Soma desired her as his bride (*vadhūyu*). The Aśvins were her bridegrooms (9). The mind was the chariot in which she moved towards her husband's place; the heaven was the hood of the chariot and the bright (Sun and Moon) were yoked as the bulls that drew her chariot (10). And, all the gods approved of the Aśvins as they proceeded for their marriage with Sūryā, and their son Pūṣan greeted them (14).

The eighth *mantra* of the hymn tells us that the Aśvins were her bridegrooms. In the next *mantra* we read that Soma desired Sūryā, as his bride and the Aśvins became her bridegrooms. The point as to who married Sūryā, Soma or the Aśvins, remains vague. *ṚV,* X.85.7(d) states: *yád áyāt sūryā́ pátim*; X.85.10(d) states: *yád áyāt sūryā gṛhám*; then in X.85.12(d) we read: *sūryā́ rohat prayatī́ pátim* and in X.85.20(cd) *ā́ roha sūrye amṛ́tsaya lokám̐ syonám̐ pátye vahatúm̐ kṛṇuṣva.* In none of the above quoted instances is mentioned the name of Sūryā's husband. The word *pati* being used in singular number one may presume that the *pati* was Soma. Twice in the *ṚV* is stated clearly that Sūryā greeted the Aśvins as her husbands and the Aśvins became her husbands.[56] A polyandrous marriage can be traced. That, Sūryā's association with the Aśvins was very close, that, she liked them is evident from the fact that several times the *ṚV* mentions that Sūryā ascended the chariot of the Aśvins.[57] In this connection we are reminded of the story of the Aśvins and Sūryā as narrated in the *AitBrā* (XVII.1.2), the gist of which is as follows: Pajāpati desired his daughter Sūryā to give in marriage to Soma. But, each and every god wanted to be her bridegroom. Then the gods came to an agreement that he who would win the race would get her. The Aśvins, somehow, managed to be the winners of the race. Shall we go too far, if we infer that this is the occasion on which Sūryā mounted the chariot of the Aśvins? We may perhaps also be permitted to infer that Sūryā's father intended to have Soma as his son-in-law, but Sūryā cherished the association of the Aśvins more.

The relation of Uṣas and the Aśvins is also very close. Uṣas is the most celebrated female deity in the *ṚV*. Both the deities Uṣas and the Aśvins belong to the early morning. They are very often invoked together. Uṣas is their sister (VII.71.1) friend and beloved (IV.52.2; 3). Donald Ward says, "The hymns of the *Rig veda* mention another female divinity who is also associated with the Aśvins. She is Uṣas 'the dawn' who corresponds both mythologically and etymologically to the Gk. *Eos* (Latin *Aurora*) and possibly to the Latvian Austra, Auseklis and to the Lithuanian *Ausra, Ausrine*".[58]

Twin gods are found in many mythologies of the world other than Indo-European, but their association with a female divinity is an Indo-European characteristic. She is sometimes their mother, sometimes sister, sometimes both mother and sister. Since the beginning of this century scholars have been working on this Indo-European pattern of two gods and a goddess. J.

Rendel Harris makes thoughtful comment on the relation between one goddess and two gods. "The simplest form then which we have yet detected of the cult of Dioscuri shows us a woman with two children and suggests to us a double paternity. Here we observe that a woman of the tale appears as the mother of the twins and not as the sister, as in the case of Castor and Polydeuces and the sister Helena, as in the case of the twins of the *Ṛgveda* who take with them on their chariot the virgin Sūryā who is daughter of the Sun. We can hardly hesitate to conclude that the cult of the Dioscuri and Helen is based upon an earlier cult of twin plus their mother."[59]

Discussion on the point of double paternity as mentioned by Harris is avoided here on the consideration that it is not directly connected with our subject of discussion.

Alfred Hillebrandt refers to many twin brothers like Keri and Kema (Brasil), the hostile brothers Jaskeha and Tawiskara (Iroquosi), Hunhuhn-ahpu and Vucub Hunahpu (Popol Vuh) existing in different non-Indo-European folks but, he says that their association with a young lady is the characteristic of the Indo-European people, "Aber das Hinzutreten einer jugendlichen Frau, einer Lichtgöttin, an deren Grund-charakter für Indien niemand zweifein kann, und ihre Verbindung mit den Bruderpaar zu einem mythologischen Dreigestirn bildet einen Unterschied und hebt die arischen Beispiele weit hinaus."[60] According to Hillebrandt the association of a female solar deity with the twin gods is basically an Indian characteristic, which probably becomes difficult to accept as the same pattern occurs in other Indo-Europen mythologies like Greek, Latin, Baltic, etc.

In the Roman mythology we obseve the same trio of two gods and a goddess in Kastor, Polydeukes and Helen and in the Greek in Castor, Pollax and Helen. Helen is their sister. Donald Ward has, however, inferred a polyandrous incestuous theme in the relation of Dioskouri and Helen. "The two daughters of Leukippos whose name is associated with the horse, has been considered to be identical with Helios the Sun. Therefore it is possible that the Leukippides represent manifestation of the single figure of the Sun Maiden. The duality of the Leukippides is probably a secondary development, which occurred when the original polyandrous relationship had become distasteful or was no longer understood."[61]

Dieva Deli (Latvian) and Dieva Sunelei (Lithuanian) are the Baltic counterparts of the Indian Aśvins, so far their relation towards their sister Saules Meita (Latvian) and Saules Dukterys (Lithuanian) is concerned. Their bride and sister Saules Meita (Latvian), Saules Dukterys (Lithuanian), the daughter of the Sun represent Sūryā, the Sun's daughter very much. Dieva Deli rescued her from Menes, the moon, her abductor. This part of the Baltic story reminds us of the story of Sūryā, Soma and the Aśvins. In Herakles, Iphikles and Alcmene their mother, in Amphion, Zethos and Antiope their mother also is repeated the same Indo-European pattern of two gods and a goddess. The trio of two gods and a goddess has found its way in Zoroastrian tradition of Haurvatat, Ameretat and Aramaiti, in the Indian heroic tradition of Kṛṣṇa, Balarāma and Subhadrā; and Rāma, Lakṣmaṇa and Sītā. Much later the same pattern of trio is observed in the story of Buddha, Bhutum and Kalāvatī as narrated in the *Thakurmar Jhuli*, a collection of Bengali folk tales.[62]

The above discussion leads us towards the conclusion that we cannot establish an established relation between the Aśvins and Sūryā. The Vedas do not tell us conclusively, who married Sūryā, the Aśvins or Soma? The same ambiguity is observed in the Baltic myth of the two gods and a goddess. Saules Meita is both sister and bride of Dieva Deli. And, there is also scope to infer such double relation between Castor, Pollux and Helen in the Dioscuric tradition. Does the myth lose its beauty, its charm, when it makes very plain and simple statement? Ambiguity seems to intensify the potency of the myth. Myth and mystery seem to be interlinked.

[First published: Proceedings Fifth World Sanksrit Conference]

The Aśvins: An Incarnation of the Universal Twinship Motif

Worship of twin gods is a unviesal phenomenon in mythology. In the Semitic, pre-historic, Indo-European, African and American mythologies twin gods have been worhshipped. J. Rendel Harris says: "But this belief is not limited to Aryan civilization; it occurs in Semitic also, and can be traced in the earlier chapters of Genesis, and down to the building of Solomon's temple, as well as in Phenicia and Mesopotamia".[63] Gilgamesh and Enkidu (Eaboni), the two brothers-in-arms of the Assyrian mythology, represent this twinship motif. The Assyrian mythology belongs to an epoch much earlier to that of the Indo-European mythology. We read in the *Encyclopaedia of Religion and Ethics*: "In Asia Minor and Palestine the cult of the Twins appears from a very ancient date. Esau and Jacob and other twins found in the Hebrew Scriptures are personages whose pristine form and attributes it is no longer possible to recover from the attrition of time and the erasive energies successfully wielded by the generations of pious editors".[64] Herman Güntert displays prints of three stone slabs found in Germany and Sweden. One of them, belonging to the pre-historic age from Tarun in Bohuslan, demonstrates in stone-carving the twin gods (*Dioskurendarstellung*), while the other stone plate in the shape of a razor, beloning to the early bronze-age from Kivik near Cimbrushnum on the east coast of Schonen, repesents the solar twins sitting on a boat.[65] He also observes 'What the Vedic poets describe, the pre-historic works of art produce that vividly anew'.[66] According to Donald Ward, "Divine Twins are by no means limited to the Indo-European tradition; they are found through the world".[67] He also gives the names of a few dual deities from different traditons. Here we mention a few of them from traditions other than the Indo-European: Alcis, Halfdan the black and Halfdan the white, Ferrutius and Ferrutio, Sintran and Baltram, Huz and Buz.[68] Harris also speaks about the "Children of Tilo" belonging to the African tradition.[69] Ugo Bianchi speaks about the dual divinities from the ideologies of non-literate culture along with twin gods from different traditions. Among them are Tanus and Yolokantamulu, the twin gods among the non-literate Karibean population of American Indians.[70] Much later the twin Christian saints mentioned in the calendars of saints took the place of divine twins. Harris suggests the names of a few pairs of such saints from the French and Italian calendars.

A few names from the French calendar:[71]

Acius & Acclous
Cantius & Cantianus & Cantianella[72]
Donatianus & Crispinian
Ferreolus & Ferretius
Protasius & Gervasius
Vitalis & Agricola

A few names from the calendar of Italian saints:

Picummus & Pilumnus
Mutunus & Tutunus
Sisinnius & Martyrius
Sisinnius & Sisinnidorus[73]

A similar pair of Spanish twin saints are: St. Damian and St. Cosmos.

It is true that the divine twinship motif is a universal phenomenon of mythology; yet the characteristics of the Indo-European tradition are more specifically defined. It is observed by Donald Ward: ". . . there was an exclusive Indo-European tradition of Divine Twins."[74] The Greek Dioscuri (Castor and Pollux) rerepsents very closely this archetype. "Children who are deliverers of men on earth and swift-going ships when stormy gales rage over the ruthless sea".[75] This description of Hesiod readily brings to the mind the succouring Vedic twins, the Aśvins, and their rescuing Bhujyu from the mid-ocean. Of similar type is also the story of Roman Castor and Pollux.

The pattern, two gods and a maiden,[76] is observed probably only in the Indo-European tradition. The association of Dioscuri with Helen, their sister who was abducted by Theseus and later rescued by her brothers, bears close resemblance with the Baltic myth of Dieva Deli and Dieva Sunelei and their sisters and beloved Saules Meita and Saules Dukterys who were abducted by Menes, the moon, but later rescued. Similar is the story of the Aśvins and the Sun Maiden Sūryā. The Iranian twins Haurvatat and Ameretat[77] along with the goddess Aramaiti also forms a similar triad.

The Vedic Aśvins inherit most of the characteristics of the twinship motif. The Ṛgvedic seers eulogise them as succourers, doctors and the deities of the early morning in the main. One comes across more than hundred names of their protégés.[78]

Whether the Aśvins rode any horses cannot be, for sure, known from the Vedic text. But, right from their very names we can see that they are variously connected with horses. Aurṇavābha says, 'They are called Aśvins on account of their having horses.'[79] Śaraṇyu and Vivasvat assuming the forms of horses gave birth to the Aśvins.[80] The Aśvins learnt the honey-lore (*madhuvidyā*), the sole possessors of this knowledge from Dadhyañc after fixing a horse's head on him.[81] The *ṚV* does not tell us whether they rode horses, though their epithets are found to be *svaśvau* (VII.68.1; 69.3), 'possessors of skilled horses' and *aśvāmaghā* (VII.71.1) 'whose treasure is horse'. Many a time the Aśvins are invoked to come to the sacrificial ground on their chariot drawn by horses.[82] In some verses, however, they are invoked to come on their strong horses as fleet as the wind and mind,[83] and swift like falcon (VIII.5.7). No mention of chariot has been made in these verses. Of course three times donkey has been described as drawing the Aśvins' chariot[84] but there is no denying the fact that the Aśvins' horses are more prominent and are more frequently mentioned than donkeys. The association of horses with the dual divinity is an Indo-European phenomenon. Donanld Ward says: "In the *ṚV* the very name of the divine pair expressed their relationship: Aśvinā 'owners of horses'. Similarly the GK Dioskouri were called Leukópōloi 'having white horses' (Pindar, Pyth 1.66)".[85]

Incidentally, the Aśvins gave Pedu their most favourite protégé, a white horse.[86] The Roman Castar and Pollux also had white horses.[87] The horses of the Baltic twins were also seen outside the Sun Maiden's door or on the hill-side feeding on oats. The twin brothers and legendary leaders of the first Anglo-Saxon settlers in Britain in AD 450 were Hengest (hengist) and Horsa.[88] The meaning of both these words being horse.

The Aśvins' association with horses speaks of their solar character. Yāska the theoretician of the sixth century BC says: *aśvinau yad vyaśnuvāte sarvam* (*Nir,* XII.1), "The Aśvins are so called because they two pervade everything".[89] That some scholars derive the word *aśva* from *aś* 'to spread' has relevance in this context.[90] The epithets *sūryāvasū* (*ṚV,* VII.68.3) 'living with Sūryā, 'according to Sāyaṇa, and *divó napātā* (*ṚV,* I.184.1; IV.44.2) 'children of heaven' also indicate the solar identity of the Aśvins.

The Aśvins' association with the boat also hints at their solar identity. They are invoked to come to the prayer in a boat (I.46.7). They protected Bhujyu from mid-ocean in a hundered-oared boat (*ṚV,* I.116.5). In one of the stone plates displayed by H. Güntert, as already referred to, the twin gods are depicted as sitting on a boat and are described by the author as *Dioskuren im Sonnen-boot.*[91] And, he comments on the Aśvins, *Ihre Lichtnatur ist besonders deutlich.*[92] Félix Nève comments on the solar identity of the Aśvins: "The Aśvins would have been glorified rightly in the primitive hierarchy of the gods of light".[93] Regarding the solar identity of the twin deities of South America and southwestern regions of North America, Ugo Bianchi says, "Another important feature of American Indian mythologies of twins is that in South America and in southwestern regions of North America twins are conceived as solar deities."[94] The solar identity of twin gods is not a characteristic of the Indo-European tradition only it occurs in other traditions also.

Apparently two different aspects of the Aśvins are revealed in the Vedic verses. On the one hand they are succuourers, an aspect in which we may categorize them as doctors, fertility gods etc., and on the other hand they are the deities of early morning, the associates of Uṣas, the dawn. The Ṛgvedic singer states that Uṣas follows the all-pervading Aśvins who desire the oblations prepared at night.[95] *ṚV*, VII.71.1 narrates that the dark night is passing away from her sister 'Dawn', making path for the bright sun, and at this hour the singers pray to the twin gods: may they scare away the enemies of day and night.[96] *ṚV*, III.58.1 tells us that the time of the Aśvins is prior to the time of Uṣas:

> *uṣśásaḥ stómo aśvínāv ajīgaḥ* ।
> 'the praise of Uṣas has awakened the Aśvins.'

Probably such descriptions inspired Yāska to fix the time of the Aśvins as follows: "Their time is after midnight which, in consequence, is an impediment to the appearance of light. The part in the dark is atmosphere, and the part in the light is sun."[97] The Aśvins are addressed as *prātaryāvānā* (II.39.2) 'going early in the morning', *śubhrayāvānā* (VIII.26.19) 'having a white path', *rudravartanī* (I.3.3; VIII.22.1; X.39.11), *hiraṇyavartanī* (I.92.18; V.75.2-3; VIII.8.1) 'golden-pathed'. Such epithets clearly show their time. Next to *nāsatyā* the most frequently used epithet of the Aśvins is *dasrā*. Sāyaṇa has interpreted this word sometimes as *śatrūṇām upakṣayitārau*, and at others as *darśanīyau*. Both the interpretations reveal the Aśvins as the deities of early morning. The epithet *nṛtū* (VI.63.5, Sāyaṇa: *nartantau*) also gives an image of the first spread of morning glow. As the Aśvins are the deities of early morning so most of the hymns dedicated to them are applied in the Prātaranuvāka.

The succouring nature of the Aśvins became the cause for their becoming solar deities and consequently the deities of early morning. The sun, the healer of diseases, takes one across sin and blame.[98] The horses of the sun traverse heaven and earth in one day.[99] So it is quite natural for the Aśvins, being solar deities, to take their devotees beyond the multifarious problems of life. That the Aśvins were worshipped as fertility gods[100] also speaks of their solar character. V.C. Srivastava observes, ". . . the physical basis of Aśvins was simply solar in his dual aspects of fertility and light."[101]

Dual deities have been worshipped by peoples irrespective of their belonging to historic or pre-historic, literature or non-literate cultures. Some scholars believe that they were originally historical persons and later deified. Harris speaks on this point: "The anthropologists have been slowly finding out for us that Heavenly Twins can be taken out of the zodiac altogether, that they belong to a time when Chaldean astronomy was not yet dreamt of, and to a period of human development which can only be called historical at all by a very liberal use of the term, and their varied activities and philanthropies are a mirror in which we can read the evolution of human life of many aeons of progress."[102] Donald Ward Says, "One notices that the divine twins are traditionally very human . . . Such evidence has led Leo Sternberg to the assumption that twin cults, wherever they occur, is the result of deification of a pair of human beings."[103] K.P. Jog is also disinclined to accept that the Aśvins are the representatives of natural phenomena, though he has not given any distinct opinion on their identity. He opines, "The connection of the Aśvins with any distinct natural phenomena that can serve as the basis of the Aśvin-concept is the least obvious."[104] The Aśvins as depicted in most of the Ṛgvedic hymns are very much human. Of all the gods they are the closest to their worshippers. Because of failing to maintain the olympian attitude they had been temporarily deprived of the soma libation by the Vedic Pantheon. But, such a friendly attitute is just true to the form of the dual divinity.

Belief in the divine twins is a universal phenomenon of mythology. Their counterparts in different mythologies have been worshipped by peoples all over the world since very early days of human history. The solar character of them is almost universal. The characteristics of this archetype belonging to the Indo-European tradition is more specifically defined. To mention a few: their association with horse and boat, their magical healing power and solar identity, and their also being warriors, saviours at sea and associated with a solar maiden.

It has been observed in life that when two friendly, benevolent and determined persons exert themselves for the good of their fellowmen they render immense service to the society. The fellow creatures on their part in gratitude eulogise them, and, gradually in course of time, quite imperceptibly they are deified. Gratitude for philanthropy lies at the root of this euphemerization.[105] This apotheosis took place at different times among different peoples according to the social needs. The Aśvins are just one example of this archetype. Later in Hindu myth they returned as Rāma and Lakṣmaṇa, Kṛṣṇa and Arjuna, Nara and Nārāyaṇa, and much later we get a glimpse of this twin motif in the Bengali folklore in the story of Buddha and Bhutum.[106] Sukumari Bhattacharji speaks on this point, "Gods reappear again and again in changed garbs to suit the altered needs of the time."[107] In conclusion we would like to say that the Aśvins are one appearance of the many incarnations of the universal twinship motif.

Notes and References

1. *tat kāv áśvinau* । *dyāvāpṛthivyāv ity eke* ।
   ahorātrāv ity eke । *sūryācandramasāv ity eke* ।
   rājānau puṇyakṛtāv ity aitihāsikāḥ ।
   — *The Nirukta and Nighaṇṭu*, p. 206.
2. *tayoḥ kāla ūrdhvam ardharātrāt prakāśībhāvasy ānuviṣṭambhaṃ* ।
   anutamo bhāgo hi madhyamo jyotirbhāga ādityaḥ ।
   — *Op. cit.*, XII.1, p. 206.
3. ***See*** R. Pischel and K.F. Geldner, *Vedische Studien*, Vol. II, Stuttgart, 1897, p. 31.
4. G.L. Chandravarkar, "Aśvins as historical figures" in *J.Bom.U.*, May 1934, Vol. III, Part VI, pp. 63-87.
5. *TS*, II.1.10.1, Cf. *āśvinaṃ dhūmralalāmam ālabheta yo durbrāhmaṇaḥ somaṃ pipāsed aśvinau vai devānām asompav āstāṃ tau paścā somapīthaṃ prāpnutām.*
6. "*neben dem Soma-trank erhálten sie den Gharma, Vorzugsweise aber*

Honig und Surā . . . Ich habe keinen Zweifel, dass es sich um die Einwirkungen verschiedenen Kulturformen handelt. Op. cit., Vol. III, Breslau, 1902, p. 386.

7. A.B. Keith, *The Religion and Philosophy of the Veda and Upaniṣads, HOS* 31, p. 114.
8. Václav Machek, "Origin of the Aśvins", in *Archiv Orientalni,* Vol. XV, pp. 413-19.
9. Reinhold F.G. Müller, "Die vedische Götterärzte", in *Archiv Orientalni,* Vol. 28, 1960, pp. 399-413: "Damit sind die Aśvins auch hier gültig nach den vedischen Ausschauungen in den Kreis der Götter eingefügt, und zwar auch deswegen, weil sie ihnen Anrufungen besonders zum Somagenuss eingeladen werden (durchaus nicht seltner als andere Götter".
10. K.P. Jog, "The Aśvins of the Ṛgveda and their traces in later literature" in Part II, p. 5, *J.Bom.U.*, Vol. 34, 1965. (One observes the similarity of thought between Alfred Hillebrandt and K.P. Jog).
11. *ṚV,* VII. 74.2d; VIII.5.11c; 8.1; 10.4d; 35.22b.
12. VIII, 35.1d; 2d; 3d.
13. *ṚV,* 1.47.3b
14. *ṚV,* VIII.87.4a.
15. *ṚV,* IV.44.4c.
16. Cf. *Bṛhaddevatā,* III.18, 23, pp. 83-84.
17. Cf. *BṛUp*, II.5.
18. *ṚV*, I.15.11a.
19. *ṚV,* I.34.10b.
20. *ṚV,* I.47.4b.
21. *ṚV,* II.37.5c.
22. *ṚV*, III.58.5d.
23. Cf. *ṚV,* I.34.2a.
24. *ṚV,* VIII.5.19.
25. *ṚV*, X.40.6cd.
26. Mircea Eliade, *From Primitive to Zen,* London, 1967, pp. 247-48. G.C. Jhala also thinks that soma and *madhu* are identical. ***See*** G.C. Jhala: *The Aśvins in the Ṛgveda and other Indological Essays*, Munshiram Manoharlal Publishers, 1978, pp. 47-49.
27. Cf. *TS,* VI.4.9.1 — *yajñasya śiro 'cchidyata te devā aśvināv abruvan bhisajau vai staḥ idam yajñasya siraḥ prati dhattam iti tāv abrūtām varaṃ vṛṇāvahai gráha eva nāv atrāpi gṛhyatām iti tābhyām etam āśvinam agṛhṇan tato vai yajñasya śiraḥ prattyadhattāṃ yad āśvino gṛhyate yajñasya niskṛtyai tau devā abrūvan apūtau vā imau manuṣyacarau*

bhisajāv iti . . . Op. cit., p. 322.

28. Cf. *RV*, I.116.6; 117.9; 118.9; 119.10; X.39.10.
29. Cf. *ṚV*, I.112.11ab.
30. Cf. *ṚV*, VIII.22.6ab.
31. Cf. *ṚV*, I.112.11c, 116.7b.
32. Cf. *ṚV*, I.112.7; 16a; 116.8c; 117.3; 118.7; 119.6; 180.4; V.78.4.
33. Cf. *ṚV*, I.112.6; 20; 116.3; 5; 117.14; 15; 118.6; 119.4; 8; 158.3; 180.5; 182.5; 6; 7; VI.62.6; VII.68.7; VII.69.7; VIII.5.22; X.39.4; 40.7. In this connection one remembers the Greek Kastor and Polydeuces, and Castor and Pollux the saviours of sailors at sea, of the Roman mythology.
34. Cf. *ṚV*, I.116.11a; 117.5; 118.6ab; 119.6c.
35. Cf. *ṚV*, I.112.5a; 116.24cd, 118.6b; 119.6a; X.39.9ab.
36. Cf. *ṚV*, I.112.19a; 116.1cd; 117.20cd; X.39.7ab; 65.12c.
37. Cf. *ṚV*, I.47.5ab; 117.8b; 118.7c.
38. *ṚV*, I.110.17b; 117.17c; 117.18cd.
39. *ṚV*, I.116.14c.
40. *ṚV*, I.112.8b.
41. *ṚV*, I.117.8cd.
42. *ṚV*, I.112.16a; 116.22c; 117.20b; 118.8ab; 119.6b; VI.62.7c; VII.68.8bcd, VIII.8.20c; X.39.13b; 40.8a.
43. *ṚV*, I.116.10ab; 117.13ab; 118.6d; X.39.4ab.
44. *ṚV*, I.116.8a; 124c.
45. *ṚV*, I.112.10ab; 116.15; 117.11d; 118.8ab; 182.1cd; X.39.8d.
46. *ṚV*, I.117.7cd; X.39; X.40.
47. Cf. *ṚV* X.65.12 (***See*** Geldner's introductory note to his translation of this hymn. K.F. Geldner, Der *Rig Veda*, IV, *HOS* 36).
48. Cf. *ṚV*, V.78.7, 8, 9.
49. *MS*, ed. by Damodar Satavalekar, Satara, IV.6.2, pp. 377-78: *aśvinā asomapau, tā upādhāvan, yathā bhiṣajam upadhāvanty evaṃ idaṃ yajñasya śiraḥ pratidhattam iti, tā abrūtāṃ, bhāgo nāv astv iti, vṛṇāthām ity abrūvan stā abrūtāṃ, grahaṃ nau gṛhṇantu, somapītham aśnāvahā iti, tad vā aśvinau prattadhattaṃ tasmād āśvinībhir abhiṣṭuvanty aśvinau hi prattadhattāṃ, tau vai bahiṣpavamānenaiva pāvayitvā tābhyāṃ pūtābhyāṃ yajñiyābhyāṃ bhūtābhyām agṛhṇan . . .*
50.. *TS*, VI.4.9.

G.S. Ghurye observes the traces of Hayagrīva-incarnation of Viṣṇu of later age in this Yajurvedic story of the sacrifice becoming headless. *Vedic Age*, Popular Prakashan, Bombay, 1979, p. 110.

51. *ŚatBrā*, IV.1.5.14-15, Kashi Sanskrit Series, 127, 2nd edition (1st edition 1913), p. 330:
tau ha ūcatuḥ upa nau hvayadhvam iti te ha devā ūcur na vām upahvayiṣyāmahe bahu manuṣyeṣu saṃsrṣṭam ācariṣṭaṃ bhiṣajyantāv iti tau ha ūcatuḥ viśirṣṇā iti upa nu nau hvayadhvam atha vo vakṣyāvaḥ iti tathā iti tāv upahavayanta tābhyām etam āśvinaṃ graham agṛhṇan tāv adhvaryū jajñasya abhavatām.

52. *Op. cit.*, III.123-25.

53. *The Indian Theogony*, Cambridge, 1970, p. 239.

54. *Myth and Law Among the Indo-Europeans*, ed. by Jaan Puhvel. Donald Ward, "Separate Functions of the Indo-European Divine Twins" University of California Press, Berkeley & Los Angeles, 1970, p. 195.

55. Donald Ward, *The Divine Twins,* University of California Press, Berkeley and Los Angeles, 1968, p. 91.

56. I.119.5cd — *ā́ vām patitvám sakhyā́ya jagmū́ṣī yóṣā'vṛṇīta jénvā yuvā́m páti* ||
IV.43.6 (cd) — *tád ū ṣú vām ajirám ceti yā́nam yéna pátī bhávathaḥ sūryā́yāḥ* ||

57. ***See*** I.34.5; I.116.17; I.117.13; I.118.5; I.119.2; IV.43.6; IV.44.1; VI.63.5; VIII.8.10.

58. *Op. cit.*, p. 11.

59. J. Rendel Harris, *Cult of the Divine Twins*, Cambridge, 1906, p. 8.

60. Alfred Hillebrandt, *Vedische Mythologie* (Kleine Ausgabe), 1910, pp. 38-39.

61. *Op. cit.*, p. 11.

62. Daksinaranjan Mitra Majumdar, *Thakurmar Jhuli,* 21st. edn., pp. 29-58.

63. *Op. cit.*, p. 154.

64. *Encyclopaedia of Religion and Ethics*, ed. by James Hastings, Edinburg, T&T Clark, 1960 edn., Vol. XII, p. 498.

65. Hermann Güntert *Der arische Weltkönig und Heiland,* Haale (Saale), Verlag Von Max, Niemeyer, 1923, p. 272 "Was vedische Dichter Schildern, führen aus wiederum prähistorische Kunstwerke anschaulich vor."

66. *Ibid.*, p. 274.

67. *Op. cit.*, p. 2.

68. *Ibid.*, p. 6.

69. *Op. cit.*, p. 28.

70. ***See*** *The Encyclopaedia of Religion,* Vol. 15, Macmillan Publishing Company, 1987, pp. 99-107.

71. *Op. cit.*, pp. 63-66.

72. This triad brings to the mind the Greek triad, Castor, Pollux and Helen, the Indian Aśvins and Sūryā, and the Baltic Deiva Deli, Dieva Sunelei and their female associates, Saules Meita and Saules Dukterys. On this point has been discussed in the previous section.

73. *Op. cit.*, pp. 80-95.

74. *Op. cit.*, p. 1.

75. Hesiod, *Homeric Hymns*, "To the Dioscuri", XVII.

76. We have already discussed on this point in the previous section.

77. Cf. C. Bartholomae, *Altiranisches Wörterbuch*, Strassburg, 1905, p. 1791. *haurvatat, haurvat: Ganzheit, Volkommenheit . . . in Dualverbindung mit am r tat,* v. 51.7; 45.10; 44.18; 47.1; *"Gib mir. . . Unsterblichkeit und Wohlfahrt durch den heilligen Geist . . . Kraft und Bestand".*

78. On this point has been already discussed in this book.

79. *The Nighaṇṭu and the Nirukta*, p. 184. *aśvair aśviānv ity aurṇavābhaḥ* ǀ XII.I, p. 106.

80. ***See*** *Bṛhaddevatā*, III.18-23.

81. ***See*** *JaiBrā*, III.126.

82. ***See*** *ṚV,* I.118.4; 5; VII.68.1; 69.1; 72.1.

83. *ṚV*, I.181.2:

    ā́ vām áśvāsaḥ śúcayaḥ payaspā́ vā́taraṃhaso divyā́so átyāḥ ǀ
    manojúvo vŕ̥ṣaṇo vītápṛṣṭhā ehá svarā́jo aśvínā vahantu ǁ

84. ***See*** *ṚV*, 1.34.9, 116.2; VIII.85.7.

85. *Op. cit.*, p. 12.

86. ***See*** *ṚV*, I.116.6, 117.9, 119.10; X.39.10.

87. Cf. Ovid, *Metamorphoses*, tr. by Mary M. James, Penguin Book, 1975, p. 189. "But now the twin brothers Castor and Pollux not yet raised to be stars in the heavens rode up together, a striking pair on their horses."

88. ***See*** *Encyclopaedia Britannica*, Ready Reference and Index, Vol. IV, 15th edn. 1973, p. 1019.

89. *Op. cit.*, p. 184.

90. N.G. Chapekar, "Nāsatya", in *ABORI*, Vol. 45, 1964, pp. 29-37. "More plausible is *Aśva*, is derived from *aś* to spread. The rays of the luminous bodies spread instantly over the whole universe." Hermann Güntert however, thinks that the Aśvins were originally horses of Sūrya's chariot and later promoted to solar deities. ***See*** *Op. cit.*, p. 269.

91. *Op. cit.*, p. 272.

92. *Op. cit.*, p. 253.

93. *Op. cit.*, p. 250.
94. *Op. cit.*, p. 102.
95. *ṚV*, I.46.14 — *yuvór uṣā́ ánu śríyaṃ párijmanor upā́carat* ।
ṛtā́ vanatho aktúbhiḥ ।।
96. VII.71.1 — *ápa svásur uṣáso nág jihīte ṛṇákti kṛṣṇī́r aruṣā́ya pánthām* ।
áśvāmaghā gómaghā vāṃ huvema dívā náktaṃ śárvm asmád yuyotam ।।
also Cf. *ṚV*, VIII.9.17; 18.
97. *Op. cit.*, p. 184; *Nir*, XII.1; *tayoḥ kāla ūrdhvamardharātrāt prakāśībhāvasya anuviṣṭambham* । *anutamo bhāgo hi madhyamaḥ* । *jyotirbhāga ādityaḥ* ।
98. *ṚV*, I.115.6 —
adyā́ devā úditā sū́ryasya nír áṃhasaḥ pipṛtā nīr avadyā́t ।
tán no mitró váruṇo māmahantām áditiḥ síndhuḥ pṛthiví utá dyáuḥ ।।
99. Cf. *ṚV*, I.115.3.
100. Cf. *ṚV*, I.112.9; 12; 16; 116.22; 117.20; 24; 118.8; 119.6; VI.62, 7; X.39.4; 40.8; 184.3.
101. V.C. Srivastava, "The Aśvins in the Rigveda", in *JAHRS*, XXX (I-IV), 1964-65, p. 62.
102. *Op. cit.*, Introduction, p. 2.
103. *Op. cit.*, p. 7.
104. K.P. Jog, "Aśvins of the Ṛgveda and their traces in the later Indian literature", in *J.Bom.U.*, September 1964, p. 48.
105. In this connection we would like to remember the *karmadevas* who have been defined in the *ŚatBrā* (14.7.1.35) as, *ye karmaṇā devatvaṃ abhisampadyante*. 'who have earned divinity through action.' ***Also see*** *TaitĀ*, 8.8.3 and *TaitUp*, 2.8.3.
106. Already referred to in the previous section.
107. *Op. cit.*, p. 248.

3

The Maruts

THE *Ṛgveda* dedicates thirty-five hymns to the Maruts.[1] Besides these thirty-five hymns they are also invoked along with Agni, Indra, Viṣṇu and Nirṛti in a few stray verses and are also invoked along with many other deities in the hymns to the Viśvedevāḥ. The two major aspects of the Ṛgvedic Maruts' character are, firstly, they are storm gods and then they are Indra's associates and friends, so warriors.

Etymology of the Word 'marut'

Nothing has yet been decisively said on the etymology of the word *marut*.[2] The majority of scholars think that *marut* has been formed from *mṛ* 'to shine', whereas others think it is from *mṛ* 'to die'. According to Yāska[3] *marut* comes either from *mi* + *ruc* 'to shine' or from *mahad* + *dru*, 'to run fast'. To him the Maruts were atmospheric storm-gods. Otto Böhtlingk and Rudolf Roth prefer to interpret *mṛ* in the word *marut* as 'to shine' rather than as 'to die', keeping in mind the brilliant description of this group of gods as portrayed in the *ṚV*.[4] Hopkins also indicates that *marut* has been formed from *mṛ* 'to shine' when he says, "their name means the shining ones".[5] Monier-Williams interprets *marut* from *mṛ* 'to shine' and in that connection refers to the word *marīci*.[6] According to Macdonell[7] and Keith,[8] who identify the Maruts with storm-gods, *mṛ* in *marut* means 'to shine'. According to Hillebrandt, Benfey, A. Kuhn, Von Schroeder, R.N. Dandekar and Sukumari Bhattacharji the Maruts were the "souls of the dead" and *marut* has been formed from *mṛ* 'to die'.[9] In spite of the fact that in places the Ṛgvedic Maruts have been portrayed fearful, destructive, because of their being storm-gods, the overall picture of these gods in the *ṚV* is very bright and brilliant and this prompts us to hold that *mṛ* in *maruts* means 'to shine'.

Storm-Rain-Gods

The Maruts are born of the bright lightning (I.23.12).[10] The Rudriyas shower rains even in windless deserts (I.38.7). As the mother cow making sound nourishes its calf so the lightning nourishes the Maruts while they shower rains (I.38.8). They darken the day with clouds which are laden with water and drench the earth with showers of rains (I.38.9). They, on their onward march, make the stable unstable and the heavy, light (I.39.3). They do harm to harmful, shake and saturate the earth with water which they collect from heaven (I.64.5). Like wild elephants they devastate forests (I.64.7). They roar like lions (I.64.8). The irresistible Maruts shake the mountains, uproot trees and separate the branches from them (I.39.5; 85.4). They yoke Pṛṣatīs (their animals) in their chariot and as soon as the tawny coloured animals draw them in their chariot the whole earth and mankind are frightened (I.39.6). Hearing the howling of the Maruts the earthly houses with their residents shake (I.38.10). The following verse gives a vivid description of the youthful, invincible Maruts:

> *yúvāno rudrā́ ajárā abhoggháno*
> *vavakṣúr ádhrigavaḥ párvatā íva* ।
> *dṛḍhā́ cid víśvā bhúvanāni pā́rthivā*
> *prá cyāvayanti divyā́ni majmánā* ।। I.64.3
>
> The youthful, ferocious, ever-fresh (Maruts), destroyers of their non-worshippers, intent on fulfilling the prayer of their devotees, with the steadiness of a mountain shake with their strength the whole of existence — heavenly and earthly.

They are invoked to come in their bright, all-pervasive chariot, decorated with lightning and armed with weapons. One sees "in the all-pervasive chariot of the Maruts" nothing but the clouds full of water and twinkling with lightning. The showers, as bright as honey, are welcomed by the people (I.87.2 also V.54.2).[11] As the fire is uncontrollable so also is the sound of the Maruts (I.143.5). As they pervade the atmospheric regions, as their horses run as if being self-drawn, then indeed the universe with its buildings, etc. is frightened; wonderful indeed is their march! As they move on resounding the mountains with their howlings and shaking the surface of heaven, the big trees are threatened and the creepers move from one place to the other (I.166.4; 5). The strong Maruts, as bright as fire and as fearful as the beasts of prey, pervade the regions with torrential rains and send the clouds helter-skelter (II.34.1). They make the clean water of river Paruṣṇī unclean and shatter the clouds (*adri*) with the felly of their chariot (V.52.9; ***also see*** V.53.6; 7). The waters showered by the Maruts possess medicinal value, so, quite naturally, the devotees desire their company (V.53.14). All devastations caused by the Maruts are only apparently ominous; actually they are blessings to their worshippers (V.57.3). They wash away the islands that are formed on the river-surface during the dry season (VIII.20.4). During their fearful march the waters flow, the earth shakes but she does not become slim (X.77.4).[12]

Warrior Gods

The verses depicting the Maruts as warrior gods bear a totally different note from the verses portraying them as nature gods. They seem to represent two sides of the same coin. They are invoked to kill Vṛtra along with Indra.[13] The bright Maruts are born along with their weapons, with their Pṛṣatī animals; their shouts signal the death of their enemies. With whips in their hands as they proceed making horrifying sound then they adorn their path as it were (I.37.3). Their steady weapons never fail them in the battle-fields (I.39.2). The leaders whose joy lies in the drink of soma, carry immensely strong weapons in their hands

(I.64.10). All the warriors are frightened as these bright warriors resembling powerful kings, are engaged in frightful battles (I.85.8). They are implored to protect their devotees from deceitful enemies (II.34.9). While fighting against the enemies they at the same time create more powerful weapons as it were (V.52.6).[14] Guarded by shoulder-bands and yoking the spotted antelopes (horses?) as they march forward, they win all battles (V.55.6). The verse under V.57.2 gives a complete picture of the Maruts as fighters — the sons of Pṛśni carrying all kinds of weapons set on their auspicious march in chariots drawn by strong horses.[15] Through the Maruts' help alone powerful warriors defeat their enemies in the battlefield (VII.56.23). No other warrior ever looked so bright as do the Maruts in their armour and weapons (VII.57.3). The worshippers of the Maruts are never harmed in the battle-field (VII.59.4). They are ferocious, showerers (of fulfilment of desires) and strong-armed; they are not scared of their personal security. Their beautiful chariot is furnished with steady weapons like bows, etc. Their victory in the fore-front of the battlefield is always guaranteed (VIII.20.12).

Anthropomorphic Features

The Maruts adorn their body with bright golden ornaments. The golden necklaces dangling on their chests endow them with a very bright look. They put on golden bracelets on their arms and anklets on their ankles. Dazzling golden headdresses embelish their heads. As a woman decorates her limbs with beautiful ornaments so do the Maruts. They wear a very bright look as they proceed on their equally bright chariots. They carry weapons on their beautifully ornamented shoulders and arms. They also carry a whip in their hands. When they make very loud sound with their whips the listener, though actually hearing it from a long distance, feels that it has been made on the selfsame spot. The mother-cow (Pṛśni) dresses up her calves and makes them look very attractive. The blissful sons of Rudra set out on their onward march in their chariot. The source of their energy lies in their weapons which they carry on their shoulders. Like a bridegroom, brightly ornamented, the Maruts proceed on their chariots. They are all of equal age and form. Their young father Rudra and resourceful mother Pṛśni have made their days all blissful.[16]

Though the Maruts have been endowed with anthropomorphic features yet one can perceive that at the base of all such descriptions lies the reality of nature in the form of storm, rains and wind. Geldner observes with reference to this, "Trotz aller anthropomorphischen Umbildung schwebt doch gerade bei den Marut das natürliche Phänomen der urplötzlich aus der hervorbrechenden Gewittersturms den Dichter immerwieder vor".[17] 'In spite of all anthropomorphic modifications the Maruts are, however, always present in the poet's mind as natural phenomenon representing thunder storm that suddenly breaks through cloud'.

The Bright Maruts

The Ṛgvedic Maruts are all through described as dazzling with brightness. "They are as bright as the sunshine".[18] "The greatness of the Maruts who are bright as the sun, is worthy of eulogy".[19] They who are wonderful and sun-coloured, are marching upwards".[20] The following epithets speak of their bright appearance, *tveṣádyumnāya* (I.37.4), *tveṣā́ḥ* (I.38.7; 15), *bhrā́jadṛṣṭayaḥ* (I.64.11; V.55.1; X.78.7), *citrábhānavaḥ* (I.85.11), *rukmávakṣasaḥ* (II.34.2; 8; V.55.1; 57.5; VIII.20; 22; X.78.2); *híraṇyaśiprāḥ* (II.34.3) and *sū́ryatvacaḥ* (VII.59.11).

The Howling Maruts

The howling nature of the Maruts indicates primarily their identity as storm gods and secondarily as war gods. The god Agni who makes sound is comparable to the Maruts only.[21] The mountains, though great and old, and the heavenly regions tremble at the sound made by the Maruts (V.60.3). The wonderful and bright Maruts shake the heavens during their onward march which is always accompanied by sound.[22]

The Maruts' Anger

The Vedic Indians were scared of the Maruts' wrath. Often they were besought by their devotees to shake off their anger against them. They are approached with obeisance and prayer so that they may shake off their anger, release the horses from the chariot, come to the sacrifice and accept the oblations offered to them (I.171.1). They are described as terrific (*bhīmásaṁdṛśaḥ* — V.56.2). "As to err is human so may the maruts withdraw their weapons raised against their devotees, for, they long for their favour and not for their enmity" (VII.57.4).[23] Sometimes they are approached for their favour through other gods. I.94 is an Agni-hymn. In its twelfth verse Mitra and Varuṇa are prayed to by the Maruts' worshippers, so that the great anger of the Maruts against them be pacified and they may be highly pleased with them.

The Fearful Maruts

All regions, the whole universe and the well-built houses (*harmyá*) on earth shake in great fear as the Maruts march on I.116.4. They are earnestly implored to throw far away their weapons and be auspicious to their devotees (I.172.2). The helpless sage Vasiṣṭha tries to convince his own self by saying that the Maruts, in spite of their destructive activities, would not inflict any harm upon him and his people (VII.56.9). Sacrifices are offered to the Maruts whose advent can be known from a long distance. As they march they cause termors in the earth which at that time resembles nothing but a frail boat full to its brim (with passengers).[24] Every creature is afraid of the high-minded Maruts who are born of brightness and are very strong and dreadful (VII.58.2). The fearful Maruts are nothing but storms in origin. The storm brings forth life through devastation. The Maruts also stand for the well-being of their worshippers. The epithets *dhṛṣṇú* (I.37.4), *riśā̆dasaḥ* (I.39.4), *udbhídaḥ* (V.59.6), *ghorávarpasaḥ* (I.64.2), *ugrā́ḥ* (I.166.6) speak of the Maruts' fearful nature.

All the Maruts are Equal

It is repeatedly mentioned that the Maruts are all equal. They are of equal age, equal mind and hail from the same place.[25] They are simultaneously born and simultaneously they send showers (V.55.3). Like the spoke of a wheel, neither of them is inferior while none is superior either (V.58.5ab). Neither of them is the eldest nor the youngest, nor is any the middle one.[26] Such a phenomenon of equality in all aspects indicates their identity as storm gods; the storms are all alike eternally and universally; this also indicates their identity as soldiers, for, the soldiers look alike in their uniforms. The following epithets bear relevance in this connection; *sapsarā́saḥ* (I.168.9), *yamā́ iva* (V.57.4), *sánīḷāḥ* (VII.56.1), *sábandhavaḥ* (VIII.20.21), *samanyavaḥ* (II.34.3; 5; 6; VIII.20.1).[27]

The Maruts as Birds

The Maruts are several times compared with birds. They who are of one mind are invited to the soma libation like a flock of swans (II.34.5). Like flock of birds they fall from heaven (V.59.7). Like falcons the Maruts come to the oblations offered to them (I.165.2; VII.56.3; VIII.20.10).[28] Stormy clouds flying at high speed lie at the base of such poetic imagination.[29] The epithet *nī́lapṛṣṭhāḥ* (VII.59.7) for the Maruts, is very appropriate in this connection.

The Maruts and Soma Libation

In sacrifices the Maruts are offered with the usual soma libation, sometimes independently, sometimes with Agni and other gods and mostly with Indra. "May the Maruts who are of one mind come to the soma-offering like a flock of swans (II.34.5). Soma is pressed between the two stones for the Maruts" (I.88.3).[30]

The Maruts' Animals — the Pṛṣatīs, the Horses

The well-built chariot of the Maruts is drawn by the Pṛṣatīs. The Maruts were born along with the Pṛṣatīs (I.37.2).[31] When the

Maruts yoke the tawny coloured horses to their chariots, the earth with all its inhabitants is frightened (I.39.6).[32] As they, drawn by the Pṛṣatīs, travel, they shower rains.[33] The epithet *Pŕ̥ṣadaśvāsaḥ* is often used for the Maruts.[34] The question arises, who these Pṛṣatīs are. The *Nighaṇṭu* says, *pṛṣatyo marutām* (I.15.6). Sāyaṇa while commenting on the word in I.37.2 says *vidyutyuktā mṛgyaḥ*. Geldner translates the word as *scheke*.[35] Sāyaṇa and Geldner hint at their identity as natural phenomenon. Clouds, being tinged with lightning are the animals of the storm gods Maruts, appears to be a very rational imagery.

Horses also in places are stated as the Maruts' animals.[36]

The Parents of the Maruts

The Maruts' mother is Pṛśni and they are called *pṛśnimātaraḥ*.[37] Pṛśni bore them in her womb (VI.66.3; VII.56.4). She gave birth to the resplendent Maruts (I.168.9). *Go* also is mentioned as their mother (I.85.3; VII.94.1). Rudra is their father. They are called *rudrā́ḥ*,[38] *rudríyāḥ*[39] or *rudríyā́sah*,[40] *rudrásya sūnúḥ* or *sunávaḥ*,[41] also *rudrásya máryāḥ*.[42] Rudra gave birth to the Maruts in Pṛśni's womb.[43] Rudra is called *marútvat*[44] (II.33.6). To us Pṛśni is cloud laden with water and so quite naturally the Maruts, the storm gods, are her children. (Cf. Keith, *op. cit.*, p. 53: "Pṛśni is the mother of the Maruts, perhaps the spotted storm-clouds").

On one occasion the Maruts have been stated to be the sons of Bharata (II.36.2) and on another as the children of Aditi and heaven (X.77.2).

Rodasī, the Female Associate of the Maruts

Like Sūryā the Aśvins' chariot, Rodasī, the symbol of brightness (*tveṣápratīkā*) and the leader of the sky, ascends the chariot of the Maruts for enjoyment and the Maruts place the young lady in their car (***see*** I.167.5; 6). The sacrificer invokes the chariot of the Maruts in which the noble and blissful Rodasī has taken her seat (cf. V.56.8-9).

Griswold holds that Rodasī is "perhaps a personification of the lightning, since she is described as 'self-luminous'."[45] We also maintain that Rodasī represents lightning without which the imagination of storm gods remains incomplete.[46]

The Maruts and Other Gods

INDRA

The Maruts without Indra is unimaginable. They are *índrajyeṣṭhāḥ* (I.23.8), *índravantaḥ* (V.57.1). Indra on his part is *marútstotra* (I.101.11), *marúdvṛdhaḥ* (III.13.6), *marútta* (I.101.8) and *marútvat*.[47] Of all these epithets of Indra, *marútvat* occurs most frequently. Indrāṇī introduces herself as *marútsakhā*.[48] In the *AV*[49] also Indra is *marútvat*. The Maruts earned the right to the soma libation, they got a place in the Soma sacrifice after their association with Indra (I.87.5). Whatever favour the Maruts show to their devotees, Indra never contradicts that. All the gods out of Vṛtra's fear left Indra, only the Maruts were by his side;[50] this story is referred to in the *AitBrā* also. As a result the Maruts enjoyed the midday Soma-pressing along with Indra; the Marutvatīya graha and the Marutvatīya pragātha were introduced in favour of the Maruts (***see*** *AitBrā,* III.20). Their status in the Vedic pantheon was high. A note of serious discord between the Maruts and Indra is recorded in the Ṛgvedic hymns from I.165-171. The Maruts were being charged by Indra of leaving him alone at the time of killing Ahi (*ahihátya,* I.165.6). The Maruts, however, retorted by saying that all the achievements of Indra's life had been possible only because they were by his side and they have the capacity to perform much more. Indra was not subdued and was about to kill his brothers, the Maruts (I.170.2). Through sage Agastya's meditation the dispute was somewhow put down. Happily did Indra say, *áchānta me chandáyāthā ca nūnám*, "you have pleased me before and you please me now" (I.165.12). Agastya, later discloses the truth to the Maruts that he prepared the offering for them but Indra had demanded it. Out of fear of Indra he concealed the same elsewhere (I.171.4).[51] The same charge against the Maruts by Indra has been referred to in VIII.7.31 also.

Based on the hymns to the Maruts the relation between Indra and the Maruts has been discussed so far. We would like to have a glance at the same, as it has been reflected in the relevant Indra-hymns. Indra did not know what point of Vṛtra's body he should strike at, in order to kill him. The Maruts passed to him the important information and Vṛtra was killed (III.32.4). Indra's Vṛtra-killing was felicitated by the songs sung by the Maruts. On that occasion Pūṣan and Viṣṇu cooked a hundred buffaloes for the Vṛtra-killer and three lakes of soma were prepared for him (VI.17.11). The Maruts being requested sang songs in praise of Indra and then alone was it possible for the Vṛtrahā to kill with his hundred-edged *vájra* his invincible enemy (VIII.89.1; 3). The Maruts also sang in praise of Indra when he shattered the ninety-nine castles (of Śambara) (V.29.6).

In spite of the manifold anthropomorphic description of the Maruts, in the Family Books (sp. Book V) they are basically nature gods representing storm, wind and rains. To be precise, they are nature anthropomorphised. How and following what evolutionary process they became Indra's friends and associates is difficult to say. In the onward march of the storm lies a sort of uniformity, a kind of discipline. This characteristic is quite patently present in marching soldiers. These common elements might have been the grounds for the transformation of basically storm gods into warrior gods as has already been thought by Prof. Dandekar. He observes, "the Maruts are like brothers among whom none is the eldest or the youngest (V.59.6; 60.5). They are equal in age (I.165.1) and are of one mind (VIII.20.1; 21) . . . These peculiarities of the Maruts must have presented to the mind of the Vedic poet the picture of the formation of well-disciplined soldiers in their uniforms. When, therefore, the memories of the original character of the Maruts were being gradually dimmed, the Vedic poets naturally thought of associating them newly with their war god, Indra".[52]

THE MARUTS AND AGNI, VIṢṆU, VARUṆA, VĀYU, NIRṚTI, ETC.

But for Indra the Maruts' relation with other gods is rather formal. I.19 is jointly dedicated to Agni and the Maruts. Throughout the whole hymn the refrain is: *marúdbhir agna ā́ gahi*. V.60.8 invokes Agni and the Maruts together to the soma libation (***also see*** I.31.1; VIII.7.32). Viṣṇu and the Maruts, his associates, are mentioned together in V.87.1. Both Varuṇa and the Maruts are paid homage together in VIII.41.1 (a Varuṇa-hymn). Vāyu generated the Maruts from the udders of heaven (I.134.4). The singer prays to the Maruts, 'let not Nirṛti kill them' (I.38.6). VII.58.1 states that the Maruts pervade the heavenly regions from regions of Nirṛti.[53] Does it hint at their identity as mortals, i.e., from mortality they raised themselves to immortality? Apart from these deities the Maruts are also invoked along with Indra-Vāyū, Bṛhaspati, Mitrāgnī, Pūṣan, Bhaga, Ādityas, Ṛta, Brahmaṇaspati, Aśvins and Uṣas.[54] The Maruts had evidently a distinct place along with other divinities in the Vedic pantheon.

The Protégés of the Maruts

The *ṚV* refers to a number of the Maruts' protégés. Trita had been fighting with his enemies; the invincible Maruts stood by his side and consequently Trita's enemies were defeated.[55] The thirsty Gotama besought the Martus for water. Softened by the sage's prayer they shifted near him a well from another place (I.85.10; 11). The Maruts also contributed immensely towards the achievement of the status of a sage on the part Śyāvāśva (V.61). Called by the sage Uśanas as the well-armed Maruts, brightly dressed with golden headdresses, etc. proceeded towards him, even heaven cried out in fear (VIII.7.25; 26). They also gave protection to Turvaśa, Yadu and Kaṇva (VIII.7.18). They gave wealth consisting of horses to Bharata (V.54.14). Now the question arises, who was Bharata — a fore-father of

Śyāvāśva he being the seer of the hymn? The Maruts have been mentioned once (II.36.2) as Bharata's children also.[56]

Maruts — the Maryas

The Maruts are often describe as *máryāḥ*. They are *rudrasya máryāḥ* (I.64.2; VII.56.1) — the sons of Rudra; *divó máryāḥ* (V.59.6) — the children of heaven. Sāyaṇa interprets *maryāḥ* as *mārakā manuṣyarūpā vā* (**see** *bhāṣya* of X.77.2). Geldner translates *maryāḥ* as 'Jüngen'.[57] The nature of the Maruts as storm gods, as soldiers, is strong and vigorous and so quite naturally *maryāḥ* became a very appropriate epithet for them.[58]

According to Stig Wikander, **mario* = Skt, *marya* = *Männerbund*, i.e., a band of young men. He is of the opinion that, among the different ethnic groups of the Āryans there was the custom of initiating groups of young men with observance of special rites. After this initiation which resembles death (cf. Skt. *dvija*) they were considered as reborn. The Maruts are the divine counterparts of such earthly *Männerbund*.[59] To us Wikander's opinion appears too far-fetched.[60] Louis Renou also holds that the Maruts are a band of 'young men' (*marya*).[61]

The Maruts: Gaṇa, Śardhas, Vrāta, Viśaḥ

The Maruts form *gaṇa, śardhas, vrāta*, i.e., they form a group by themselves (cf. *mā́rutāṁ śárdhas* (V.46.5) *mā́rutāṁ gaṇám* (VI.16.24). The following verse is very relevant in this connection:

> *vrā́taṁvrātaṁ gaṇáṁgaṇaṁ suśastíbhir*
> *agnér bhā́maṁ marútām ója īmahe* | (III.26.6ab)

Here *vrāta, gaṇa*, or *śardhas* means a group in general and is quite different from the group of Rudras whose number is fixed at eleven, or the group of Vasus who are eight in all, or that of the Ādityas who are always twelve. V.52.17, of course, mentions them as seven by seven: *saptá me saptá śākínaḥ*, then according to VIII.96.8 they are sixty-three: *tríḥ ṣaṣṭís tvā marúto vāvṛdhānā́ḥ*. But, they are mentioned forty-nine or sixty-three in the *ṚV* once and for all.

In the *TS* (II.2.5.6) their number is fixed at forty-nine through a story which narrates that Indra, jealous of Vāyu who was in the state of a foetus in Aditi's womb, chopped the foetus into seven parts, and then each of these into seven again, thus making the total number forty-nine. In later Vedic literature seven are the different names of wind.[62]

In the *ṚV* the idea of the Maruts as group deities consisting of fixed number does not exist. They are many Maruts (*marutaḥ*), i.e., plural of the stem *marut*.

They are mentioned twice (VIII.12.29; 13.28) as Indra's people (*viśaḥ*). The idea that the Maruts are Indra's people developed more in the *TS* and in the Brāhmaṇas. In the *ṚV* the Maruts, apart from being Indra's people, have a separate independent identity which they almost lost in later Vedic literature.

The Maruts Euhemeristic

Once the Maruts are addressed by the sage Kaṇva, "O you the children of Pṛśni! had you been mortal and had I been immortal!"[63] Geldner interprets, "Had I been in your position and you in mine, I would then have made your worshippers immortal".[64] In I.85 the poet mentions twice (2; 7) that the Martus have made an abode in the heavenly region from the world of Nirṛti (i.e., the goddess of death). These instances speak of their euhemeristic origin. Compared to the massive representation of them in the *ṚV* as nature gods these few references are, however, meagre.

It has been observed by us that, the more the Maruts get closer to Indra the more they behave like human beings. In a few hymns of the first (I.165-71) and eighth (7.12) *maṇḍala*s they are represented in the main as Indra's associates, friends and also as rivals. They are depicted quite euhemeristically in those hymns.

Such euhemeristic representation of the Maruts led some scholars to conclude that the Maruts were originally human beings. According to Satavalekar the Maruts were human heroes, great patrons who having decorated themselves with ornaments served their mother-land and so quite naturally *go*, the mother earth, was their mother. According to him the word *marut* has been formed from *mar* 'to die' — *ye maraṇaparyantam utthāya yudhyante.*[65] Nigam Sharma maintains that, as the Ṛbhus, originally human beings, by their dexterity raised themselves to the status of divinity, so also did the Maruts. They are successful young soldiers of Indra.[66] Uma Gupta refers to the *ṚV,* I.72.2 and says, "the Maruts — 'mortal bands' with their spouses worshipped Agni for three autumns and thus though 'mortal bands' won the holy names for worship and dignified their bodies".[67]

Regarding the opinions of these scholars we would like to comment that, they have given a partial opinion on the identity of the Maruts and have totally neglected the primary aspect of their character which lies in storms, rains and winds, and which has been presented in the majority of hymns to the Maruts. That the Maruts were originally not human beings is also evident from the fact that in the early Vedic age no conflict arose regarding the Maruts' right to the soma libation; they had been very naturally and with dignity enjoying this right whereas the Ṛbhus had to struggle hard in achieving this right. Much contradiction arose regarding the Aśvins' right to the soma libation also.[68]

The Maruts are also medicine-men. They are capable of curing the malady of the diseased.[69]

Geography and History in the Marut-Hymns

The Maruts made unclean the waters of the river Paruṣṇī (V.52.9). The sage Śyāvāśva purified his treasure of cows, etc. in the water of the river Yamunā (V.52.17). The Maruts went to the countries Śaryaṇāvat and Ṛjīka (VIII.7.29).

The Literary Beauty of the Marut-Hymns

As while paying obeisance to the goddess Uṣas the Ṛgvedic singers become highly imaginative and poetic so also they become vibrant with their poetic imagination while paying homage to the Maruts. In places the adjectives are placed one after the other as if in a chain.[70] A few of them describe them as storm-gods, some as soldiers[71] while still others give a mixed description of these divinities.[72] Again in some verses a flavour of fine similes is inferred. The Martus, the destroyers, are compared with wild elephants.[73] The Maruts, the storm-gods, are like swans with dark-coloured backs[74] — the moving dark clouds represent the black-backed swans. VII.56.16 reminds us of the figure of speech Mālopamā in which the Maruts are compared with a fleet of horses, a group of men enjoying a festival, children playing in palaces and with playful calves.[75]

The Maruts in the Atharvaveda

Some changes are observed in the character of the Maruts in the *AV*. The storm gods of the *ṚV* are transformed into rain-gods. IV.15 of the *AV* has been entitled by Satavalekar as *vṛṣṭiḥ*; in the seventh, eighth and ninth verses of this hymn the refrain is *marudbhiḥ pracyutā meghā varṣantu pṛthivīm anu* "let the clouds, started forward by the Maruts, rain along earth".[76] IV.27.4 says, how the Maruts carry water up to heaven from oceans and then again shower them on earth; they are the masters of water.[77] As in the *ṚV* here also the Maruts are as bright as the sun,[78] *indrajyeṣṭhāḥ* (III.19.6), the associates of Indra and warrior gods (III.19.6; V.21.11). Some magical elements are added in their character: "Let Indra confound the army; let the Martus slay with force; let it go back conquered" (III.I.6).[79] The singer asks the Maruts to pierce the enemy with baffling darkness (III.2.6).

Pṛśni is their mother (V.21.11), but their father is Paśupati (V.24.12). They are also the children of height (I.26.3: *pravato napāt*).

The Maruts in the Taittirīya Saṁhitā, Brāhmaṇas and in the Sūtras

Although the principal traits of the Maruts' character are apparently present in the *TS* and in the Brāhmaṇas, yet there is no denying the fact that compared to the Ṛgvedic Maruts, the Maruts of the later Vedic literature have lost their prominence and grandeur. They no more attract us by their adventurous, bright and fearful onward march. They have become stereotyped and limitations are inflicted on their rights and privileges. In the later Vedic literature they have been permanently placed in the position of *devaviśaḥ* — divine subjects.

It has been already observed that in the *AV* the Maruts have been transformed from storm-gods to rain gods and the same trend has been maintained in the *TS* also. The *TS* represents a society which was sacrifice-oriented. So the Maruts have been referred to in connection with sacrifices only.

The Kārīriṣṭi is performed for rains. The Maruts have a major part in rain-bringing. They are invoked in many verses in this sacrifice (***see*** *TS,* II.4.7.10). As has been already referred to they are represented as seven winds in the *TaitĀ*. Our conjecture is, as they are wind gods and rain-gods, so they are *krīḍins* (*TS,* I.8.4), i.e, playful in their manner.

Some war-like elements in their character can also be traced in the *TS*. In the Apratiratha hymn (IV.6.4) they are desired to lead the divine soldiers with Indra as their leader. Their martial nature can be inferred from the expressions like *marutāṁ prasave jeṣam āptaṃ manaḥ*, *marutām ojase svāhā* (*TS*, I.8.14.2; 15.1).

The Maruts are Indra's friends.[80] They are also *indrajyeṣṭhāḥ* 'with Indra as their head' (*TS,* V.5.9). Indra killed Vṛtra but he was not sure whether he had really killed his enemy. The Maruts revealed the truth to Indra on condition that the first offering is to be given to them.[81] Besides these, the Maruts are invited along with Indra in the Kāmyeṣṭi sacrifice. In the Ṣoḍaśin sacrifice they are the participants in the midday sacrifice. Besides being enjoyers of soma, *caru, āmikṣā* (clotted[82] curd), they are also given the seventh limb of the horse in the horse-sacrifice.[83] The Maruts were about to devastate the sacrifice; Prajāpati, somehow, pacified them by offering animal-fat to them (*TaitBrā*, I.3.4.4). According to Ṛgvedic texts, Pṛśni was the Maruts' mother and now she becomes the animal to be offered to them.[84]

That the Maruts are seven multiplied by seven, i.e., forty-nine in number, has been mentioned only once in the *ṚV* (V.52.17). But the *TS* associates them with this number invariably: "The Maruts with seven syllables won the seven-footed *Śakvarī*[85] (I.7.11); the *puroḍāśa* baked in seven potsherds is to be offered to them, they are seven in troops.[86]

The most significant development in the mythology of the Maruts which in the *TS* and the Brāhmaṇas is observed is that, they are now placed in the position of the subjects of the gods, i.e., *devaviśaḥ*. "The Maruts are the subject class among the gods; verily by subjects among the gods he wins for him the subjects among men".[87] (*TS*, II.2.5.6). "Vaiśvānara is kingly power, the Maruts the people; having offered to Vaiśvānara, he offers those to the Maruts; verily he attaches the people to the kingly power . . . He utters aloud (in the direction of the *Agnīdh*) for Vaiśvānara, he offers the offerings of the Maruts muttering; therefore, the kingly power speaks above the people"[88] (*TS*, V.4.7.7). From the above statements it becomes evident that the kingly power always had the threat[89] from the subjects, and there was constant effort on the part of the royalty to subjugate people. Such elements were not present in the Ṛgvedic texts. In the later Saṁhitās and early Brāhmaṇa period monarchy had been gradually taking shape[90] which the Ṛgvedic Aryans, who had been so busy in fighting against the non-Aryans and settling down in the new land, were not previously familiar with.

The Maruts who were resplendent "Martial storm gods"[91] Indra's associates and friends in the *ṚV*, who were strong enough to challenge even Indra's strength, now lose their grandeur, their privileges which they had been enjoying as gods, and are placed in the position of the subjects of the gods. It is true that they had been enjoying soma libation along with Indra, the reason, we presume, is as they were Indra's people so they were royal people, i.e. belonging to the royal entourage, escorting the king to the sacrifice, so they must be shown due honour along with their master. They are now associated with sins also. The *ŚatBrā* (II.5.2.7) states that the sacrificer's wife who has committed the sin of having intercourse with one who is not her husband, invokes the Maruts in the Varuṇapraghāsa rite of the Cāturmāsya sacrifice in order to be absolved of the sin. The Maruts are connected with the *aśvattha* tree — "*Aśvattha* is the might of the Maruts" (*TS*, II.3.1). A review of the *Śrautasūtras* tells us that the Maruts had been enjoying the same status in the *Saṁhitā*- and the *Brāmaṇa*-period. But in the *Gṛhyasūtras*, to be more specific in the *Pāraskara Gṛhyasūtra*, they have fallen very low. While dealing with the Prauṣṭhapada sacrifice this *Gṛhyasūtra* states: "Having cooked milk-rice for Indra and cakes, and having put cakes round (the fire), he sacrifices the two *ājya* portions and *ājya*-oblations to Indra, to Indrāṇī, to Aja Ekapād, to Ahi Budhnya and to the Proṣṭhapadas. After he has eaten (his portion of the sacrificial food), he offers *bali* to the Maruts. For the Śruti says, 'the Maruts eat what is not sacrificed'. (This *bali* he offers) in the *Aśvattha* leaves, because it is said. 'The Maruts stood in the *Aśvattha* tree".[92] Here we wonder at the poor oblations offered to Indra. Gone is his so delicious pools of *soma*-drink! If Indra is offered with the milk rice then keeping in conformity with the general trend in the fall of the standard of offering to the gods, it is quite justified that such a *bali* is offered to the Maruts, the Maruts who are *ahutādas*.[93] The rites prescribed in the *Gṛhyasūtras* are performed by the house-holder without any priestly help in a very informal manner, bereft of the pomp of the *śrauta*-sacrifices, so it is quite natural that the oblations offered to the deities were also of quite an ordinary standard, without the grandeur of a *śrauta*-sacrifice.

Opinions of Scholars on the Identity of the Maruts

So far, scholars have come up with eight different opinions[94] on the identity of the Maruts. Majority of them, right from Yāska, hold that they were basically nature gods representing storm, rains, etc. Heinrich Zimmer was, probably, the first Western scholar to support the view that the Maruts were storm gods. He gives a description of the terrible Indian monsoon, translates *ṚV*, V.83 and in that connection adds "Zweifelsohne hat man manche andere prächtige Schilderung des Gewitters des Zuges der Maruts auf den Südwest Monsun zu beziehen".[95] According to Adolf Kaegi, "Rudra's sons and companions are richly adorned, well-armed Maruts, the gods of thunder-storm, the heavenly singers".[96] A. Barth maintains, "Indra's faithful companions, the Maruts, probably the bright ones, gods of storm, of the lightning . . ."[97] Hopkins says about these deities, "They are red storm-gods, following Rudra, their father, and accompanying the storm-bringer Indra . . . Their mother is the variegated cow Pṛśni, the mother cloud. Their name means shining, gleaming ones . . . an unadulterated type of nature god".[98] Edmund Hardy holds discussion on the Maruts in the chapter entitled "Regen und Wind" which signifies his opinion on the Maruts' identity.[99] H. Oldenberg accepts the Maruts primarily as nature gods connected with storm and wind "Die Beziehung der Maruts auf Sturm und Gewitter, insonderheit auf den Monsun, der alljährlich die grossen Regen bringt drängt sich auf".[100] According to A.A. Macdonell, "They (the Maruts) are storm-gods".[101] To A.B. Keith also the Maruts are, "the deities of wind in their aspect as bearing the storm clouds".[102] We have already referred to the view of K.F. Geldner, an upholder of the view that the Maruts were storm-gods. M. Winternitz also believed that the Maruts were storm-gods.[103] To Jan Gonda, the Maruts were, in the main, storm-gods and were also at the same time benevolent earthly bards and Indra's associates: "Vielleicht sollte man sie für atmosphärishe, besonders gewitterige Sturmmächte halten die nach Analogie irdischer Verhältnisse als Helfer, Barden, Heernschaar Indras interpretiert wurden".[104] We have already discussed the view regarding the Maruts' identity of Stig Wikander, to whom the Maruts were the heavenly counterpart of an earthly band of young men and also Louis Renou, to whom the Maruts were, "a band of young men". The euhemeristic view regarding the Maruts of O.H. de A. Wijesekara, S.D. Satavalekar, Nigam Sharma and Uma Gupta has been already discussed.

According to R.C. Hazra,[105] the Maruts were originally followers of an anti-Indra Iranian god Maruttash — a warrior god, originally a nature divinity associated with peasantry and with wind, rain and growth of food-grains. The Maruts which is the Indian name of the individual Iranian divinity Maruttash were defeated by Indra. They submitted themselves before Indra, became his associates and friends and because of their benevolent nature as nature gods enjoyed all the privileges due to a Vedic deity: "So, there is hardly any doubt that it was the Maruttash of Iranians who later became the Maruts of India".[106]

Hazra is also of the opinion that the Maruts were later associated with Rudra — originally a non-Āryan deity: "for giving him a Vedic stamp, and thus making his entrance into Vedic fold easier, they (the Aryans) thought it advisable to associate him with the Maruts as their father and progenitor".[107] Among the reasons for associating Rudra with the Maruts, as shown by Hazra, one is that, both were outlandish. As pre-Vedic history of the Āryans is still to be explored, so it is very difficult to prove the historicity of such inference. Hazra also thinks that, the group deities, the Rudras, i.e., the host of Rudras, were quite different from the Maruts for whom *rudrāḥ* was just an epithet because of their howling nature.[108]

L.D. Barnett compares the Maruts with the Iranian Fravasis and says: "The Maruts are a host of genii dwelling in heaven and constantly waging battles in the sky against the power of darkness and evil especially revealing themselves in the lightning and thunders of the storm that bring rains to parched land of Northern India and revive the force of nature . . . Owing to peculiar climatic conditions of India, this function of ruling the storm and thereby giving rains has overshadowed the aspects of the Maruts in the Vedic India and misled the modern scholars into regarding them as primarily and originally storm gods".[109] We would like to observe here that, not only to modern scholars, even to Yāska the Maruts were atmospheric gods representing storms and rains. And, it is difficult to infer the Indian counterparts of the Iranian Fravasis from the textual evidences.

Many a scholar supported the view that the Maruts were in origin souls of the dead and later they evolved into Indra's associates and storm gods. A. Kuhn, Benfey, Von Schroeder, Meyer, Hillebrandt, Dandekar, Sukumari Bhattacharji belong to this group of scholars. Historically their opinion might be valid, but the Ṛgvedic texts do not bear any evidence in support of their opinion. Macdonell says in this regard: "A. Kuhn, Benfey held the Maruts to be personification of the souls of the dead and with his view Meyer and Von Schroeder substantially agree. This origin is historically possible but the *ṚV* furnishes no evidence in support of it".[110] A.B. Keith also thinks in the same light: "The only other view of importance is that they are the souls of the dead who go in storm and wind but of this at least *ṚV* has no hint; nor is the etymology from *mṛ* 'to die' enough to serve as a base for the explanation, since their appellation may equally come from a root *mṛ* 'to shine' or 'to crush', either of which would well accord with their figure".[111] Jan Gonda who believes that the Maruts were primarily storm-gods, comments in this regard: "Anderen haven mit geringen Erfolg versucht diese Gottheiten als die im Sturm dehinfahrende Seelsnschaar zu deuten wofür die Texte aber so gut wie keinen Anhalt geben".[112]

Conclusion

The same deity appears in different forms at different times to his worshippers. Sometimes the god is all benign to his devotees, at others he appears in destructive mood. And, this is quite natural. The same nature with advent of spring and rains showers bliss on humanity, and with drought and flood causes massive havoc on it. The Maruts, also in like manner, possess mutually contradictory elements in their character which fact led the scholars of the past and present to see them in different perspectives and draw different conclusions on their identity. The same is the case with many other deities, especially with the Aśvins.

The Ṛgvedic Maruts are basically storm gods accompanied by rain and wind. As they are storm gods so they are bright, noisy, full of anger, fearful, equal in form and age; they are like swans with black backs (*nīlapṛṣṭhāḥ*); their mother is Pṛśni — the mottled cloud, and the fearful Rudra is their father; Rodasī who according to the Vedic texts is lightning, is their female associate; their chariot is drawn by spotted deer (Pṛṣatīs) which represent clouds tinged with lightning. They are highly anthropomorphic. Being brightly dressed and decorated with resplendent golden ornaments, carrying weapons in their hands they march forward shaking heaven and earth, forests, mountains and endangering fears in the minds of the earthly people. But, this is only their outward manifestation. At the base of all such descriptions lies nature. The Maruts, the storm gods, are only apparently anthropomorphic; to us they are nature anthropo-morphised.

The martial elements in the character of the Maruts are also very prominent. Guarded by shoulder-bands, with whips and all kinds of weapons in their hands they proceed in their chariots drawn by the Pṛṣatīs, against their enemies to win battles. Their weapons never fail them in the battlefield. They are ferocious and their victory in the fore-front of battlefield is always guaranteed. That they howl, manifestly full of anger, fearful and are all the same in appearance — all this is not only because they are storm-gods but also because they are soldiers. One sees in their warlike activities the function of the invading Āryans. So, they are described as *maryas-*, a band of young men, and they move in groups (cf. *śardhas, gaṇa, vrāta*, etc.).

Among all the gods the Maruts' relations with Indra is the most intimate. They are his friends and associates. In connection with Indra they become more euhemeristic. They sing Indra's praise; they also quarrel with him. In the episode of slaying Vṛtra, they aided Indra more by inspiring him, by singing laudatory songs and giving war counsels than by actually fighting for him. Along with Indra they enjoy the drink of soma in the sacrifices.

The wonderful experiences the newly arrived Āryans had when they observed the stormy wheather of this new land, and the image of the invading hosts left a deep impression in the minds of the Ṛgveic poets. Such experiences received poetic expressions in the songs to the Maruts who in some hymns represent the stormy weather and in others the actual Āryan warriors. Two more or less similar characters are mingled in one name — the Maruts. It is difficult to say, which of these characters is earlier, as poems belonging to this category are spread all over in the *ṚV*, irrespective of earlier or later books. The majority of the hymns dedicated to the Maruts, however, depict them more as nature gods than as gods of war.

The Maruts, the Ṛgvedic storm gods, have been transformed into rain-gods in the *AV*, *TS* and in later Vedic literature. They have a major part to play in the Kārīrīṣṭi which is performed for rains. This tells us that the Āryans, now settled in India, started depending on rain for agriculture. The society now has become sacrifice-oriented. In the *TS* and the Brāhmaṇas the Maruts are mentioned only when it became necessary to refer to them in connection with the narration of sacrifices.

The most prominent change in the character of the Maruts, as observed in the later Vedic literature, is that, they are now finally confirmed in the status of the *devaviśaḥ*, i.e., the subjects of the gods, whereas in the *ṚV* they are very infrequently mentioned in that manner. Thus, a great fall in their position is noticed. Though they were offered the usual soma libation in the sacrifices, yet it becomes very evident that they have now lost their grandeur, their brightness with which they made their onward march in the Ṛgvedic era. That they were not deprived of the soma libation, we believe, is because of the fact, they were Indra's people, the royal entourage, *indrajyeṣṭhāḥ* 'with Indra as their chief' — the royal people must, by all means, be rendered due honour and hospitality. The constant effort of subjugating the Maruts (cf. *TS,* V.4.7.7) who were divine subjects, are nothing but the reflections of the efforts of subduing the subjects by the newly arisen power of 'kings', local overlords of petty principalities. This power was under constant threat from subjects and from the society which was under the rule of monarchy as monarchical rule now has been fully established (cf. the eighth *pañcikā* of the *AitBrā*). Till the days of the Śrautasūtras the Maruts, though classified as *devaviśaḥ*, i.e., 'the divine subjects', yet were offered due soma libation along with other divinities. While the other Gṛhyasūtras are silent about the Maruts, in the *Pāraskara-gṛhyasūtra* they were ear-marked as *ahutāda*, i.e., the eaters of *bali*-offering. *Bali* is a very ordinary type of offering of rice and grain and that also the sacrificer offers after he has eaten his own share, i.e., the mere left-overs, definitely signifying a considerable humiliation for the Maruts.[113]

Contrary to the Ṛbhus who, born as human beings, raised themselves to the status of solar dieties, the gods of fecundity, by dint of their noble deeds, the Maruts, originally storm gods, warrior gods, Indra's friends and associates, proud receivers of soma libation were demoted to the low status of *bali*-eaters. Later, in Sanskrit literature Marut is used in the singular and is the name of the wind god. Like the majority of Vedic deities, the Maruts also have hardly any function to perform in a Hindu rite.

Notes and References

[First Published: *ABORI:* Amṛtamahotsava Volume.]

1. The Marut-hymns of the *ṚV*: I.37-39; 64; 85-88; 165; 167; 168; 171-172; II.34; V.52-61; VI.66; VII.56-59; VIII.7; 20; 94; X.73 (?); 77; 78.
2. Cf. Manfred Mayrhofer: *Kurzgfasstes Etylogisches Wörterbuch des Altindischen,* Band II, Heidelberg, (1963), p. 589: 'Eine überzeugende Deutung dieses wichtigen Götternamens steht noch aus'.

3. **See** *Nighaṇṭu and Nirukta*, XI.3, p. 193 (text).
4. *Sanskrit Wörterbuch*, Vol. 5 (1868), St. Petersburg, p. 570. "Die Ableitung neuerer von *mar* sterben ist unvereinbar mit dem Bilde welches der Veda den Marut gibt".
5. E.W. Hopkins : (1885) *The Religions of India* (Reprint 1970), Munshiram Manoharlal, New Delhi, p. 97.
6. *Op. cit.*, p. 790.
7. *Op. cit.*, p. 81.
   "The root appears to be *mar* but whether in the sense 'to die' or 'shine' it is hard to decide. The latter meaning, however, seems to accord best with the description given of the Maruts in the *ṚV*".
8. *Op. cit.*, pp. 39-40.
   "There can be little doubt that the Maruts are the storm-gods, — wind in the qualified sense".
9. "A. Kuhn, Benfey held the Maruts to be personifications of the souls of the dead and with this view Meyer and Von Schroeder substantially agree". — quoted from macdonell's book (*op. cit.*, p. 81).

   Sukumari Bhattacharji: (1968) "Rudra, the Rudras and the Maruts", *Anvīkṣā*, Vol. III, Part 1, p. 52.

   "The derivation of the word Marut is not clear but it appears to have been formed from verb *mṛ* = to die (a parallel Greek verb *maraino* = to die) of which Mārtaṇḍa is a cognate".
10. All references are from the *ṚV*.
11. We presume, such descriptions indicate that the Āryans started by depending on rain waters for their agriculture.
12. The following Ṛgvedic verses may also be taken into consideration: I.85.4; V.54.2; VIII.7.4; 28; 20.1.
13. *ṚV*: I.23.9; *hatá vṛtráṁ sudānava índreṇa sáhasā yujā́* ।
14. This indicates intensity of fighting.
15. The text goes as follows:

    vā́śīmanta ṛṣṭimánta manīṣíṇaḥ
    sudhánvāna íṣumanto niṣaṅgíṇaḥ ।
    svā́śvāḥ stha suráthāḥ pṛśnimātaraḥ
    svāyudhā́ maruto yāthanā śúbham ।।
16. The following Ṛgvedic verses depict the anthropomorphic features of the Maruts: I. 37.3; 64.4; 85.1; 3; 88.2; 3; 5; 166.10; 168.3; II.34.3; 13; V.53.4; 54.11; 55.1; 56.1; 57.6; 58.2; VII.56.13; 57.3; VIII.7.25; 32; 20.11.
17. K.F. Geldner : *Der Rig Veda*, 1951; Harvard Oriental Series, Vol. 33, p. 47n.
18. *ṚV*, V.55.3C : *virokíṇaḥ sū́ryasyeva raśmáyaḥ* ।

19. *Ibid.*, V.55.4ab : *ābhūṣéṇyaṃ vo maruto mahitvanáṁ didṛkṣéṇyaṃ sū́ryasyeva cákṣaṇam* ।
20. *Ibid.*, VIII.7.7ab : *údu tyé aruṇápsavas citrā́ yā́mebhir īrate* ।
21. ***See*** *ṚV,* I.127.6.
22. Cf. *ṚV,* VIII.7.3; 7; 17.
23. Such descriptions remind us of Rudra, the Marut's father.
24. *ṚV*. V.59.2:

    ámād eṣāṃ bhiyásā bhū́mir ejati náur ná pūrṇā́ kṣarati vyáthiryati ।
    duredṛ́śo yé citáyanta émabhir antár mahé vidáthe yetire náraḥ ।।
25. *Ibid.*, I.165.1ab:
    káyā śubhā́ sávayasaḥ sánīlāḥ ।
    samānyā́ marū́taḥ sáṃ mimikṣuḥ ।।
26. *Ibid.*, V.59.6ab :
    té ajyeṣṭhā́ ákaniṣṭhāsa udbhídó 'madhyamāso máhasā ví vāvṛdhuḥ ।

    Also see *ṚV,* V.60.5.
27. *samanyavaḥ* appears to be a pet expression with Gṛtsamada in connection with the Maruts. He uses the same thrice in one hymn (II.34.3; 5; 6).
28. Prof. R.N. Dandekar thinks that because the Maruts were souls of the dead so they have been described as birds: "But perhaps the most suggestive point in this context is that the Maruts are often represented as birds. It may be recalled that according to the primitive mythological thought the spirits of the dead often wander about in the forms of birds." *Vedic Mythological Tracts*, 1979, p. 237 (first published in 1953). We would like to observe here that, not only the Maruts but some other gods also have been compared with birds, *ṚV*, III.8.9 deserves mention in this connection:

    haṁsā́ iva śreṇiśó yátānāḥ śukrā́ vásānāḥ sváravo na ā́guḥ ।
    unnīyámānāḥ kavíbhiḥ purástād devā́ devā́nām ápi yanti pā́thaḥ ।।

    In the *ṚV,* VIII.35.7-9, the Aśvins are compared with the *haridrā* birds, swans, and falcons respectively.
29. This brings to the mind the *bordoi silā*, the Assamese legendary bird, which at the first norwester goes back to its own abode from its mother's inflicting great devastation on earth. In this connection we also remember *kālvaiśākhī*, the stormy norwester of Bengal, occurring in the months of April-May.
30. ***Also see*** *ṚV,* I.23.7; 10; 88.3; 101.9; II.34.6; VII.59.6; VIII.94.3; 4; 9-12.

    This point will be discussed in details later, while we shall discuss the Maruts' relation with Indra.
31. ***Also see*** *ṚV*, V.55.6; 58.6.
32. ***Also*** *ṚV*, V.57.3; 58.6; 60.2.
33. ***See*** *ṚV*, VIII.7.28; ***also see*** I.85.4; 5.

34. ***See*** *ṚV,* I.89.7; 186.8; II.34.4; III.26.6; V.42.15; VII.40.3.
35. *Op. cit.*, p. 46.
36. ***See*** *ṚV,* I.38.12; 85.6; 88.2; V.54.10; 55.1.
37. ***See*** *ṚV,* I.23.10; 38.4; 85.2; 89.7; V.52.16; 57.3; 58.5; 59.6; VIII.7.3; 17.

    Sāyaṇa gives different interpretation of Pṛśni in different places: *nānāvarṇayuktāyāḥ bhūmeḥ putrāḥ* (I.23.10); *pṛśnināmakakāmadhenu-putrāḥ* (I.38.4); *pṛśnyāḥ mādhyamikāyāḥ vācaḥ sambandhinam* (II.34.10; VI.48.11; VIII.76.3). Regarding the last of these interpretations we would like to observe that the idea of the *mādhyamikā vāc* did not exist at the time when the Ṛgvedic verses were composed.
38. ***See*** *ṚV,* I.39.4; 7; 64.3; 85.2; 166.2; II.34.9; 13; V.57.1; 60.2; VIII.7.12; 20.2.
39. ***See*** *ṚV,* II.34.10; VIII.20.3.
40. *Ibid.*, I.38.7; V.57.7; 58.7.
41. *Ibid.*, I.64.12; 85.1; VI.50.4; 66.11; VIII.20.17.
42. *Ibid.*, I.64.2; VII.56.1.

    Sāyaṇa exposes *rudrasya maryāh* as *rudrasya mahādevasya putrā́ḥ* and according to Geldner they are "die Jünglinge des Rudra". Geldner is more logical; Mahādeva got his place in the Hindu pantheon much later.
43. II.34.2cd:
    rudró yád vo maruto rukmavakṣasaḥ
    vṛ́ṣā́jani pṛ́śnyāḥ śukrá ū́dhani ||
44. Prof. R.N. Dandekar shows four stages of mythology of the Maruts. According to him, in the first stage the Maruts "have been independent divinities and were regarded as the hosts of spirits of the dead. (2) The Martus were later associated with Rudra after the latter god was included in the Vedic pantheon mainly as the god of death". In the third and the fourth stages the Maruts were associated with Indra (*op. cit.*, p. 238).

    We would like to observe with reference to the first stage of the Marut mythology, as classified by Prof. Dandekar, that, the Ṛgvedic texts do not give any evidence in favour of the fact that the Maruts were souls of the dead. And, regarding the second stage, it is true that they were very much associated with Rudra but that was only in name; they had no common platform of activities with Rudra as they had with Indra. We think that, in those days life, in all aspects, was quite helpless and insecure because of the total absence of any security measures to fight against tumltuous destructive nature. People often became victims of cruel nature. This destructive aspect of nature got a form in the imagination of the fearful god Rudra. The storm gods, were also apparently destructive and so a relation was drawn between them and Rudra. But, as storm gods they had a positive function to perform: as they travelled in their chariot they made earth pregnant as a man his wife. (cf. V.87.7).

45. H.D. Griswold: *The Religion of the Ṛgveda*, (1st Indian print, 1971) Motilal Banarsidass, p. 204, n. 1.

46. According to Sāyaṇa-*bhāṣya* (I.167.5) Rodasī was the wife of the Maruts, Keith also says, "their lovely wife, Rodasī" (*op. cit.*, p. 39). The texts, however, never describe her as their wife. ***Also see*** *Sanskrit Wörterbuch*, Vol. 6, p. 443.

47. *ṚV*, I.20.5; 23.7: 80.11; 100. 1. I.101 is an Indra-hymn consisting of eleven verses; in the first seven verses the last line is a refrain which reads: *marútvantaṃ sakhyā́ya havāmahe*. ***Also see*** I.142.12; III.47.5; VIII.36.1.

48. *ṚV*, X.86.9 : *utā́hám asmi vīríṇī́ndrapatnī marútsakhā.*

49. *AV*, ed. by W.D. Whitney, Pt. I; VI.104.3; (HOS 7&8).

50. *ṚV,* VIII.96.7:
vṛtrásya tvā śvasáthād ī́ṣamāṇā víśve devā́ ajahur yé sákhāyaḥ ।
marúdbhir indra sakhyáṃ te astv áthemā́ víśvāḥ pṛ́tanā jayāsi ।।

Also see *AitBrā*, III.20: *maruto haimaṃ nājahuḥ prahara bhagavo vīrayasva iti evainam etām vācaṃ vadanta upātiṣṭhanta iti* ।

51. A conflict between the Indra-cult and Marut-cult, the upholder of which is sage Agastya, is reflected in this conflict between Indra and the Maruts.

52. *Op. cit.*, p. 193.

Prof. R.N. Dandekar has shown four stages of the mythology of the Maruts. Here we are concerned with the third and the fourth stages. He thinks, because of their disciplined formation the Maruts were associated with Indra. And, in the last stage, when Indra came to be looked upon as a rain-god, the Maruts became storm-gods (*op. cit.*, p. 230).

Our findings tell us that the Maruts were earlier storm-gods and later evolved into warrior gods, Indra's associates. In the Family Hymns the Maruts were basically storm gods but anthropomorphised. Moreover, their relationship with Indra is depicted more in the Indra hymns, belonging to the first *maṇḍala*, than in the hymns dedicated to the Maruts. The history of the Āryans tells us that Indra was originally a warrior god. When the Āryans, after fighting many battles with the non-Āryans, settled in India then they became an agricultural people and started depending on rains for a good harvest. At that time their necessity was more for a rain-god than for a warrior god. So, quite naturally, the most important warrior god Indra evolved into rain-god.

53. Nirṛti in the whole of the *ṚV* has been mentioned in connection with the Maruts twice (I.38.6: VII.58.1) only. Basing on these two instances we find it difficult to draw the conclusion that the Maruts were originally

associated with Nirṛti as has been mentioned by Prof. Dandekar (*op. cit.*, p. 236).

54. ***See*** *ṚV,* I.14.3 (Indra-Vāyū, Bṛhaspati, Mitrāgnī, Pūṣan, Bhaga, Ādityas); 15.2 (Ṛtu); 40.1 (Brahmaṇaspati); 44.14 (Varuṇa, Aśvins and Uṣas).

55. ***See*** *ṚV,* II.34.10; VIII.7.24.

56. O.H. de. Wijesekara ("Ṛgvedic Bharata; A survival from Aryan Pre-history", in *University of Ceylon Review*, Vol. VII.3, 1949, p. 160), observes in this regard, "An analysis of Rudra's character in the *ṚV* shows he is only the primitive hunter deified (Cf. Pali *ludda-ka* for hunter) . . . The Maruts are also such hunters (*mar-ut*, originally killer)." He further thinks that the warriors are an evolution of primitive hunters. He also thinks, that the Bharatas were fighters from *bhṛ* to carry off, hence to rob, plunder, raid; *bhara* = battle. So the Maruts who were originally hunters later became warriors, the associates of Indra.

    According to Wijesekara, the Maruts evolved from the Bharatas which, of course, tallies with the *ṚV*, II.36.2. Since Āryan pre-history is still hypothetical, Wijesekara's opinion cannot be finally accepted. Moreover, the linguistic interpretation of the words *rudra* and *marut*, given by him, yet remains to be proved.

57. *Op. cit.*, p. 84.

58. The Ṛgvedic poets had the tendency to use a particular epithet in connection with a particular deity. For example, *dasra* means 'beautiful', 'charming' in general, but the poets of the *ṚV* are fascinated with this epithet especially for the Aśvins (Cf. I.3.3; 46.2; 117.21; III.58.3; VII.68.1 — and there are many more instances).

59. Stig Wikander: (1938) *Der arishe Männerbund*, Lund, Cf., pp. 75-83.

60. Cf. also Mayrhofer (*op. cit.*) "*mar in maryaḥ*, da die göttliche Entsprechung zu den menschlichen *maryas* sind, Wikander 83, — ganz unglaubhapt, Juret, RHA 6 (1940) 18."

61. Louis Renou : (1947) *Vedic India*. tr. by Spratt Philip, Calcutta, 1957, p. 63.

62. The *TaitĀ*, V.24.1 names the seven winds as follows: *dhuniśca dhvanaśca dhvanayaśca niliptaśca viliptaśca vikṣipa iti* । ***also see*** *VS,* 39.7.

63. *ṚV*, I.38.4:
    yád yūyáṃ pṛśnimātaraḥ mártāsaḥ syā́tana ।
    stotā́ vo 'mṛ́taḥ syāt ।।

64. *Op. cit.*, p. 48, n. 4, Geldner's interpretation is long-drawn but bears relevance.

65. S. Satavalekar : "*Vedamantreṣu vīrapuruṣāṇāṃ varṇanam,*" in *Gurukul Patrikā*, (1965) 18 (1-2); pp. 35-36.

66. Nigam Sharma : (1967) "Marudgaṇaḥ", in *Gurukul Patrikā*, 20 (1-2), pp. 39-43.
67. Uma Gupta : (1987) *Materialism in the Vedas*, New Delhi, p. 55.
68. On the Ṛbhus and the Aśvins' right to the soma drink has been discussed already by us.
69. Cf. *ṚV*, VIII.20.26cd.
kṣamā́ rápo maruta ā́turasya ná íṣkartā víhrutaṃ, púnaḥ ।
70. One such verse is quoted below:

    hiraṇyáyebhiḥ paviḃhiḥ payovŕdhā új jighnanta āpathyò ná párvatān ।
    makhā́ ayā́saḥ svasŕto dhruvacyúto dudhrakŕto marúto bhrā́jadṛṣṭayaḥ ।।
    I.64.11.

    Also see I.87.1.
71. *ṚV*, V.57.2:
vā́śīmanta ṛstimánto manīṣíṇaḥ sudhánvāna íṣumanto niṣaṅgíṇaḥ ।
sváśvāḥ stha suráthāḥ pṛśnimātaraḥ svāyudhā́ maruto yāthanā śúbham ।।

    Also see VII.56.11.
72. *ṚV*, V.58.2.
tveṣáṃ gaṇáṁ tavásaṃ khā́dihastaṃ dhúnivrataṁ māyínaṃ dā́tivāram ।
mayobhúvo yé ámitā mahitvā́ vándasva vipra tuvirā́dhaso nŕn ।।
73. *ṚV*, I.64.7c: *mṛgā́ iva hastínaḥ khādatha vánā.*
74. *ṚV*, VII.59.7 ab: *sasvás cit hí tanvaḥ śúmbhamānā ā́ haṁsā́so nīlapṛṣṭhā apaptan* ।
75. *átyāso ná yé marúto sváñco yakṣadŕśo ná śubháyanta máryāḥ* ।
té harmyeṣṭhā́ḥ śíśavo ná śubhrā́ vatsā́so ná prakrīḷínaḥ payodhā́ḥ ।।
76. Tr. by W.D. Whitney : *Atharva Veda Saṁhitā*, Vol. I, pp. 173-74.
77. *āpaḥ samudrād divam udvahanti divaḥ prthivīm abhi ye sṛjanti* ।
ye adbhir īśānā marutaś caranti te no muñcantu aṁhasaḥ ।।

    "Waters from ocean to the sky carry up, they who pour them from the sky upon the earth — the Maruts who go about lording it with the waters; let them free us from distress." tr. *op. cit.*, Vol. 1, p. 196.
78. ***See*** *AV*, I.26.3, p. 11.
yūyaṃ na pravato napātaḥ marutaḥ sūryatvacasaḥ ।
79. Tr. *op. cit.*, Vol. I, p. 85.
80. *TaitBrā*, I.5.5.3: *indro marudbhiḥ sakhibhiḥ saha.*
81. *TaitBrā*, I.6.7.5: *asmabhyam eva prathamaṁ haviḥ nirupyatām* ।
This story is also referred to in the *AitBrā*, III.9.
82. In the Vaiśvadeva rite an oblation on seven potsherds is offered to them (*TS*, I.8.2). In the Varuṇapraghāsa *rite āmīkṣa* is offered to them (*TS*, I.8.2). In the Śākamedha-rite *caru* is offered in the midday sacrifice to the

Sāntapana Maruts and the same is offered to the Gṛhamedhin Maruts in the evening (*TS,* I.8.4).

83. *TS,* V.7.21: *marutāṁ saptamī.*
84. *TS,* V.6.12: *pṛśnis tiraścīn pṛśnir ūrdhva pṛśnis te mārutaḥ* ।
85. Tr. by A.B. Keith : *Veda of the Black Yajurveda, HOS*, 18, p. 110.
86. *TS*, II.2.11.1: *saptakapālo mruto bhavanti saptagaṇā vai marutaḥ.*
87. Tr. *op. cit.*, p. 152.
88. *Ibid.*, Vol. 19, p. 435.
89. Cf. *TaitBrā*, II.7.11.3: ed. by Mahadev Shastri, p. 424(?). *maruto vai devānāṁ bhūyiṣṭhāḥ* — such statements indicate the strength of the subjects — here the Maruts.
90. Cf. *AitBrā*, eighth *pañcikā*, (37-39) describing the consecration of the king.
91. Cf. the *Encyclopaedia of Religions*, Vol. 7, p. 214.
92. *Pāraskara Gṛhvasūtra*, II.15.2-4; tr. by H. Oldenberg; *SBE* 29, p. 331.
93. *Pāraskara Gṛhyasūtra* has quoted *ahutādo vai marutaḥ* from *ŚatBrā*, IV.3.2.16 in support of the rule that the Maruts should be offered *bali*-offering. In the technical sense the term *ahuta* is applied to the *bali*-offering. *Śāṅkhāyana Gṛhyasūtra* (ed. by Sehgal, S.R.: Delhi, 1960, I.107) defines *ahuta: ahuto balikarmaṇā.* Prof. R.N. Dandekar identifies the Maruts originally with the souls of the dead. Their association with *aśvattha* tree, their being *ahutādas* are some of many grounds for such inference (***see*** *op. cit.*, pp. 236-38). Chronologically the Sūtras belong to the last phase of the Vedic period. Had the Maruts been originally the souls of the dead, then the references to the *aśvattha* etc. were expected in the *ṚV* also, the *ṚV* being the earliest phase of the Vedic literature.
94. The different opinions of scholars on the identity of the Maruts may be roughly summed up as follows:
    - (i) Storm-gods: Heinrich Zimmer, Adolf Kaegi, E.W. Hopkins, H. Oldenberg, K.F. Geldner, A.A. Macdonell, A.B. Keith, M. Winternitz, J. Gonda.
    - (ii) A band of heavenly young men: Stig Wikander.
    - (iii) A Band of Young Men: Louis Renou.
    - (iv) Patriots: S.D. Satvalekar.
    - (v) Hunters: O.H. de A. Wijesekara.
    - (vi) Those who later earned divinity through noble deeds: Nigam Sharma, Uma Gupta.

      The last four opinions (iii, iv, v, vi) are based on the euhemeristic origin of the Maruts.
    - (vii) Host of genii dwelling in heaven: L.D. Barnett.

(viii) Souls of the dead in the Pre-Ṛgvedic age: A. Kuhn, Benfey, von Schroeder, Meyer, A. Hillebrandt, R.N. Dandekar, Sukumari Bhattacharji.

95. Hienrich Zimmer: (1879) *Altindisches Leben*, Berlin, p. 43.

96. *Op. cit.*, p. 39.

97. A. Barth: (1881) *Religions of India*, tr. by J. Wood., London, p. 13.

98. *Op. cit.*, p. 97.

99. Edmund Hardy: (1893) *Vedisch-Brahmanische Periode der Religion des alten Indien,* Münster, pp. 83-85.

100. *Op. cit.*, pp. 225-26.

Oldenberg does not totally rule out the possibility of the Maruts being the souls of the dead and in that connection he refers to the *Mysterium und Mimus* 121ff. by L. Von Schroeder, Hillebrandt's *Vedische Mythologie*, Vol. III, 238ff, but at the same time this remains a puzzle to him and he considers that the Ṛgvedic texts do not give any clear picture on the identity of the Maruts as the souls of the dead: "Irgend klare Spuren die auf Seelenschar der Maruts deuten, liegen meines Erchatens allerdings nicht vor" (*op. cit.*, p. 226).

101. *Op. cit.*, pp. 81.

102. *Op. cit.*, p. 152.

103. Winternitz, M. : (1907, 1st German ed.). *A History of Indian Literature*, Vol. I, (tr.) Mrs. Ketkar, S., Calcutta University, 1962 (3rd edn.), p. 65; p. 81.

104. *Op. cit.*, p. 61.

105. R.C. Hazra: (1981) "The historical background of the Maruts' (or Rudras') Association with Indra and Rudra and of the Puranic Story of their origin", *Purāṇam* 23(2) pp. 110-48, 1981.

106. *Ibid.*, p. 132.

The question arises, how far it is linguistically justified to derive *marut* from Maruttash, while the majority of the scholars hold that the word has been formed from *mṛ* "to shine", or "to die". ***Also see*** Mayrhofer, Band II, pp. 590-91.

107. *Ibid.*, p. 144.

108. *Ibid.*, p. 145.

Prof. Dandekar, however, thinks just in the opposite direction. According to him, the Maruts were first associated with Rudra, the god of death, and then with Indra, the warrior god (*op. cit.*, p. 238n).

In this connection we would like to refer to Ernst Arbman who also maintains that the Maruts and the Rudras, the group deities, were distinct from each other: "Dass die Maruts also Indras Gefolge an den Kämpfen dieses Gottes gegen die Feinde der Götter und Menschen teilnehmen, entspricht nur ihrem leichtem heldenhaften Wesen — wie könnte man sie Rudras finsteren Mordtaten beteiligt denken." *Rudra*, Uppsala, 1932, p. 16.

We have already expressed our view in this regard.

109. L.D. Barnett: (1929) "A Study of the Indo-European Psychology", in *JRAS* Part IV, p. 737.

Barnett refers to *ahi-bhānu* (I.172.1) 'radiant as serpents', *ahi-manyu* (I.64.8; 9) 'having fury of serpents' and connects the Maruts, because of their association with snakes, with the Italian 'genius', who was already figured in art as a young man with a snake (*ibid.*, p. 738). We would like to comment here that, it was quite natural for the Vedic poets to compare the terrible storm with the brightness, fury and violence of a snake without having any connection with the Italian 'genius'. A.B. Keith also thinks in the same same light (***See*** *op. cit.*, p. 39).

110. *Op. cit.,* p. 81.

111. *Op. cit.,* p. 39.

112. *Op. cit.,* p. 61.

113. We have already discussed that in the Gṛhyasūtras the standard of offerings to the gods, in a general way, sank very low.

4

Indra

HERMAN Lommel comments on Indra's identity, "Indra is the most celebrated and the most important god of the Vedas. Of all the ancient Indian gods his character has the largest number of facets and therefore his character is the most difficult to understand. If anybody understood it, he would have understood the major part of the Veda. . ."[1] An attempt to a logical analysis of his character with its manifold facets, might reveal to us the real identity of him in its entirety.

I. On the Etymology of the Word 'indra'

An attempt to get the etymology of the word 'indra' would focus light on the principal and basic aspect of his character. Before coming to our point of view in this regard we would like to make a survey of the opinions of our predecessors — from Yāska to Volker Moller.[2]

A. Of the thirteen derivations of the word *indra* given by Yāska[3] we prefer the following two: *indater vaiśvarya-karmaṇaḥ* । *indañcatrūṇāṃ dāryaitā vā* । *drāvayitā vā*[4] "or, the word is derived from (the verb) *ind,* meaning to be powerful, i.e., being powerful, he tears the enemies asunder, or puts them to flight".[5] Yāska's last derivation of *indra*: *ādarayitā ca yajvanām*.[6] 'Or he honours the sacrificers'[7] — might be pointing to the growing importance of sacrifice in society. The *Bṛhaddevatā* does not say anything directly on the etymology of *indra*. It speaks about the four aspects of his character. They are: (i) he is the god of waters, i.e., the rain god, (ii) killer of Vṛtra, and a performer of acts of strength,[8] (iii) as he lords over all so he is Indra,[9] and (iv) he is one of the twelve Ādityas.[10] — The *Bṛhaddevatā* notes that the feature of super-eminence of Indra's laudation is his accomplishment of every kind of feat of strength.[11] The execution of feats of might in course of time entrusted him with the highest function of ruling over all. The inclusion of Indra among the twelve Ādityas belong to a period when the mythology of the Veda was more developed and was in the process of taking a definite shape.

B. Thirteen different opinions on the etymology of the word *indra* expressed by twenty-five or more scholars are reviewed below in a nutshell.

 (i) Roth and Böhtlingk at the conclusion of their article on *Indra* says, "Man wird zu keiner befridigenden Lösung des Wortes kommen, so lange man das द् als wurzelhaft betrachtet. Geht man dagegen von der Wurzel इन्, इन्व् aus, an welcher sich das suff. द mittelst eines epenthischen द् anfügt so ergibt sich der vollkommen zutreffende Sinn: *Bezwinger, Bewältiger*, der *vermögende*; zu weiterer Bestätigung vgl. इन्द्रिय".[12] "So long as द् is considered a part of the root it is not possible to arrive at a satisfactory solution. Contrarily if one starts with the root इन्, इन्व् and adds the suffix द् to it after the insertion of the epenthetic द्, then one, reaches at the perfectly correct meaning: 'the conquerer', 'the master', 'the powerful'." With reference to the above Charpentier refers to Jacobi, who observes that one cannot speak of a root like *in*; all the formations *i-nā, i-nu* and *inv-a* are derived from the root *i.*[13] We, however, would point out that, root *in*/*inv* exist very much in the Saṃhitās. Many words have been formed from this root. Some of them are *invathaḥ* (*ṚV,* 1.119.7b) *invatu* (*ṚV*, 1.162.6d; 12d; IV.53.7d; *et al.*; *invasi* (*ṚV*, V.28.2c; VIII.13.32c; *et al.*), *invire* (*ṚV*, V.6.6c). Only a few instances have been quoted above. It is, however, to be noted that in the above examples the root *in*(*v*) has not been necessarily used in the sense of 'to conquer' or 'to overpower'. In some verses it means 'to cover', in others 'to go'. Our point of view is that the root *in*(*v*) has been used by the Vedic poets.

(ii) Befney[14] following a very complicated process concludes that *indra* has been formed from **sind* + *ra* which on its part has been originated from *syand* meaning 'drop'. Regarding Benfey's opinion Charpentier comments: "allerdings original — aber ganz unannehmbar"[15] 'by all means original but not acceptable'.

(iii) Max Müller holds, *indra* is exclusively an Indian word and is derived from the same root from which 'indu' 'drop' 'juice' has been formed.[16] Max Müller reminds one of Yāska: *indave dravatīti vā* । *indau ramata iti va* (X.8), "he runs for the sake of *soma* (*indu* + *dra*), or he takes delight in *soma* (*indu* + *ram*)." Muir, Macdonell, Fick, Kirste share Max Müller's opinion.

(iv) Grassmann maintains, "Die Ableitung ist sehr unsicher, des Wahrscheinlichste ist wohl noch, da es (*indra-*) wie *indu*, von der Wurzel *indh* statmmte in dem der Nasal biswilen . . . eine Umwandlung der Aspirate in die Media veranlasst".[17] "The derivation is very uncertain. The highest possibility lies in that it as *indu* originates from the root *inndh* in which the nasal causes an occasional change of aspirate in the middle'. In Grassmann's interpretation, as has been already pointed out by Charpentier, we observe that the two of the thirteen interpretations of Yāska, i.e., *indra* has been formed from *indu* as well as from *indh*, have been combined into one. Bergaigne, Bollensen hold more or less the same opinion as Grassman.

(v) Bezzenberger puts Zend *andra* (*indra*), Pehl. *andar* and Slav. *indra* on the same par. He opines that **ant* = Skt. *nad* (from which *indra* has been derived). But Bezzenberger's view has not been supported by any other scholar.[18]

(vi) Charpentier finds Jacobi's view (*i-nr*)[19] acceptable but at the same time puts forward his own hypothesis:

(vii) "Also wäre *indra* moglicherweise aus älterem **in-ra* zu erklären, was sich denn ist einwandfrei mit ἀνήρ, ανδρ — zusammenstellen liesse. Auch der Bedeutung wegen wäre eine derartige zusammenstellung gut verwandbar, was sich besonders durch das abgeleitete *indriya* —, 'Manneskraft', beweisen lässt"[20] 'Indra also could possibly be interpreted to be formed from "*in-ra*, then it can satisfactorily be grouped with ἀνηρ, ἀνδρ-. For the sake of meaning also such a grouping is well-thought of which particularly lets itself prove through *indriya* — manly virility' — derived from it.' Charpentier thinks more or less in the same light as Roth and Böhtlingk. That Charpentier, unlike many scholars, thinks that the word *indra* is originally not Vedic and may be linked up with parallel Greek words gives it a much broader perspective.

(viii) Hermann Güntert[21] holds that the basis of *indra* lies in **oid* meaning 'to swell' and he also gives plausible explanation of *n* and *r* occurring in the word. R.N. Dandekar finds Güntert's view the most convincing.[22]

(ix) Hillebrandt refers to the opinions of several scholars in this regard but prefers not to give any of his own: "Mythologisch hat all dies weing Wert. Indras Name ist der Inbegriff aller Kraft."[23] 'Mythologically, all these have little value. Indra's name is the embodiment of all strength.'

(x) For Benveniste's view we quote Keith, "Benveniste suggests with Kretschmer that the name of Indra is borrowed from Hittite or Luwi, but asserts that there is no proof that 'Innara' in Hittite was a divine name".[24] Keith refuses to accept Benveniste's view and comments "If the base of Indra is Indo-European, it seems wholly unnessary to find in it a Hittite loan-word.[25]

(xi) L.A. Waddel observes a link between Sumerian King In-Dar, In-Duru or In-Dur with the Vedic Indra. "His (i.e., King's) personal name in Sumerian . . . was Dar, Dur or Tur with the prefix of 'king' or 'Lord' (In or Ash or An), it was In-Dar, In-Dur or In-Tur, i.e., the 'King Dar, King Dur or Tur".[26]

(xii) Mayrhofer thinks that 'Indra' is originally an adjective meaning 'strong', 'powerful' and links it up with the Serbocroat *jedar* 'full, powerful, strong' — "Wegen *indriyam* und *indra* in der Bedeutung "Furst, Erster" scheint *Índraḥ* ein altes Adjektivum für "Stark, mächtig" zu sein, weshalb sich zusammestellung mit serbokroat, *jedar* voll. kräftig, stark (aksl. *jedro* indro-s?) empfielt".[27]

(xiii) Volker Moller says that *indra* originally means 'strong, powerful' and has been derived from *inoti* 'stimulating, overpowering'. He also observes that the basic nature of Indra is that of a war god. "Indra (urspr. wohl, 'stark mächtig', auch von *inoti* 'treibend', 'bewältigend' abgeleitet). Der hervorragendste Gott der vedischen Zeit; in seiner ursprünglichen Naturbedeutung wie auch als Gott der Krieger ist er Gegenstand einer vielfalt von Mythen und wird in über 250 Hymnes des *ṚV* gepriesen".[28]

C. Of the thirteen opinions on the etymology of the word

> *indra* six are in favour of establishing that the root from which *indra* has been derived has the meaning 'to infuse strength, invigorate' and the like. We can mention the names of Roth-Böhtlingk, Charpentier, Mayrhofer, and Moller in this connection. Hermann Güntert and R.N. Dandekar also observe that from the root *id-*oid,* 'to swell' — swelling manly virility, *indra* has been formed.

Our conjecture is, *indra* has been formed from the root *in(v)* with the suffix *ra* and with the epenthetic *d* (*in+d+ra*). Such a linguistic phenomenon is not rare in the Vedic literature[29] and is probably common among the NIA languages also.[30] In this connection we would cite *candra* as a parallel example. It, occurs many a time in the Vedic literature. *Candra* has been formed from the root *can* meaning "to delight in" (Monier-Williams: *Sanskrit-English-Dictionary*), "sich einer Sache freuen" (*St. Petersburg Dictionary),* with the suffix *ra* and the epenthetic *d*; *tandra* ("von तन्" *St. Petersburg Dictionary*) is also an example to quote in this regard (cf. *AitBrā,* VII.15 *Sūryasya paśya śremāṇaṃ yo na tandrayate caran,* **also see** *ŚatBrā,* 8.5.2.6). We would further add that *mantra, tantra, yantra*[31] etc. also have been formed following more or less the same process. We get support in arriving at such a conclusion from Roth-Böhtlingk, Charpentier and Volker Moller.[32]

According to Monier-Williams the root *in(v)*, *inv* or the root *in: inoti* means "to advance upon, press upon, drive; to infuse strength, invigorate; to use force" . . . and the word *ina* means "able, strong, energetic . . . bold, mighty; *ṚV*, a lord, master, a king". The words *ina, inasya, inatama* occur nineteen times[33] in the *ṚV*. And, of these ten times (or eleven I.155.4 Indra or Viṣṇu?) they have been used by the poets of the *ṚV* to denote Indra. In this connection it may be apt to quote *ṚV,* III.49.2 (a hymn to Indra).

(a) *yáṁ nú nákiḥ pṛ́tanāsu svarā́jaṃ*
(b) *dvitā́ tárati nṛ́tamaṃ háriṣṭhā́m* ।

(c) *inátamaḥ sáttvabhir yó ha śūṣáiḥ*
(d) *pṛthujráyā amināď áyur dásyoḥ* ||[34]

Inátamaḥ occurring in (c) in the above verse has been translated by Wilson as "supreme in sway", by Griffith as "the most vigorous" and by Geldner as "der der höchste Gebieter ist", 'he who is the highest master'.

The word *indra* was initially an adjective — a very apt epithet for the leader of the Vedic Āryans, a leader who vanquished enemies and released waters. Precisely, one who fulfilled all the dire necessities of life of his people. Later the epithet, following a very normal course was transformed into his name.[35] Such a phenomenon is not unusual in life. The very etymology of the word *indra* hints at the historical background the Vedic Āryans and their leader passed through.

II. Indra, the War God

The majority of the 250 Indra-hymns speak about his warlike nature. He was the benevolent leader of his Āryan followers. He was fully equipped, with a chariot drawn by the Haris — his two horses, his unique weapon the *vájra* with which he fought against his enemies; the soma drink prepared with great care by the priests and by the gods was always ready at hand in profuse quantity for his exhilaration.

The non-Āryan enemies can be identified from their names; they are also often referred to as the *dā́sa*s and *dásyu*s whereas the Āryan enemies are never described in such specific terms, but the textual matter reveal their identity.[36]

A GOD OF STRENGTH

'The terrible Indra is born since the beginning of time for the performance of mighty deeds'.[37] 'The virile father gave birth to the manly (son), and the woman (*nārī*, i.e., the mother) bore him for the good of men'.[38] 'All deeds of valour are consummated in Indra'.[39] 'Which mighty deed has not been performed by Indra!'[40]

VII.30.1 eulogises Indra in words of might and strength like, *śávas, śuṣmín, śū́ra, kṣatrá, páuṃsya* etc.

> *ā́ no deva śávasā yāhi śuṣmin*
> *bhávā vṛdhá indra rāyó asya* ।
> *mahé nṛmṇā́ya nṛpate suvajra*
> *máhi kṣatrā́ya páuṃsyāya śū́ra* ॥

A few terms used chiefly in connection with Indra, as a killer, are discussed here: *vṛtrahátya, ahihátya, dasyuhátya, śambara-hátya,* and *śuṣṇahátya*. The second member of these compounded words directly speak about killing — killing of the enemies. *Vṛtrahátya*, i.e., killing of Vṛtra in its different declensional forms like *vṛtrahātyena, vṛtrahátyāya, vṛtrahátye, vṛtrahátyeṣu* occur about twenty-three times in the *ṚV*.[41] In the same way *ahihátya* occurs about five terms,[42] *dasyuhátya* six times,[43] *śambarahátya*[44] and *śuṣṇahátya*[45] once each. These words tell us that the killing of Vṛtra. Ahi, *dásyu*, Śambara and Śuṣṇa became such important events in life of Indra worshippers that terms based on these events were coined. The frequency of their use indicates the strength of that enemy mentioned in that particular term. They were Indra's enemies because they occur, with few exceptions, in the Indra hymns. It is difficult to say whether Vṛtra is a proper name, or is used to mean 'enemy' in a general sense, one who resists (from *vár* to resist), but it definitely narrates about Indra's slaughtering his enemies. The same is applicable to *áhi, dásyu*, i.e., that they were not enemies of that particular name but they symbolize the enemy. There were other non-Āryan enemies of Indra like Kuyava, Pipru, Kṛṣṇa *et al*. But, why was no terms denoting the slaughter of these adversaries coined? We would presume that, this indicates comparative insignificance of these enemies in Āryan life. *Vṛtrahátya, dasyuhátya* later meant killing of enemy in a general sense and not a particular enemy of that name. For example, the theme of *ṚV*, X.95 is a dialogue between Purūravas and Urvaśī. In the seventh verse of this hymn it is stated that the gods strengthened Purūravas for *dasyuhátya*, i.e., the killing of enemies, what we wanted to reach at through this discussion is that the principal aspect of Indra's character was fighting, killing of enemies. Ludo Rocher observes in this connection "There are 110 forms derived from *vadh* in the *ṚV* . . . More than half of the forms derived from *vadh* appear in hymns of which Indra is the *devatā*. These are the 59 cases: . . . The first thesis which I shall propose in this article is that the connection between Indra and *vadha* is even closer than has been generally acknowledged."[46]

PÚRAḤ

The martial feats of Indra are reflected in the narration of devastation of cities, killing a host of enemies, sometimes their women and children in their mother's wombs. A survey of a few verses describing Indra's demolishing cities/forts/ramparts (*púraḥ*) belonging to the *dā́sa-/dásyu* — enemies is intended here. The masters of these cities were Śuṣṇa, Śambara, Pipru, Vaṅgṛda, Śarat, etc.

'O Indra, the beloved of your worshippers, you destroyed the cities of Pipru'.[47] 'You destroyed the hundred cities of Vaṅgṛda'.[48] 'You the holder of *vájra* while fighting for Purukutsa (you) devastated the seven cities'.[49] 'O unblamable Indra, you suppressed the people speaking untrue words, demolished Śarat's seven cities, let the waters flow and killed Vṛtra in favour of young Purukutsa'.[50] Armed with weapons, confident of his strength, Indra roamed about devastating the cities of the *dā́sas*.[51] I.53.7 gives a vivid description of mighty and frightful Indra — fighting in the warfield and devastating the cities.[52] 'When they placed the *vájra* in his arms he killed the *dásyus* and rent their fortresses made of *áyas*'.[53] VIII.98.6 represents three aspects of Indra's identity — (i) the destroyer of cities and killer of *dásyus*, (ii) bestower of prosperity on humanity (i.e., his people) and (iii) the lord of heaven:

tvám̐ hí śáśvatīnām índra dartā́ purā́m̐ ási ।
hantā́ dásyor mánor vṛdháḥ pátir diváḥ ।।

Indra's emergence from a war god to the highest god — the lord of heaven through his benevolence towards his people is observed in this verse.

The epithets *pūrbhít* (III.51.2), *pūrbhíttama* (VIII.53.1), *purohā́* (VI.32.3), *purandara* (I.102.7) also represent Indra as a devastator of cities.

The cities devastated by Indra belonged to the non-Āryans, the indigenous settlers in the land. They were rich, well-established in life. This can be easily inferred from the *ṚV* texts which, however, are the only source material because of the absence, so far of any historical or archaeological evidence in this regard. The text always narrate the devastation of the cities belonging to the *dāsa*s. About whether the Āryans possessed cities they are totally silent. The Āryans were the invaders. They entered into the new land in search of prosperity and a new home. They were desperate to the utmost, for they had nothing to lose. The non-Āryans, the previous settlers, on the other hand were well-established in life. They were probably city-dwellers in the main; they arrested rivers, presumably, for agricultural purpose. Militarily, however, they were inferior to thier Āryan enemies. With Indra as their leader and with the benefit of possessing horses and the invincible weapon *vájra* a group of Āryan people headed by Indra attacked them, devasted their cities, broke the enclosures of waters and thus shattered the enemies' whole economy. Later, out of gratitude towards their leader they sang his praise and offered soma libation profusely in the sacrifice.

A *púr* seems to mean a city/rampart/fort rather than cloud as has been interpreted by many scholars.

VÁJRA

The word *vájra* in its different forms, with *taddhita* suffixes and in compounds occurs about two hundred and seventy-five times in the *ṚV*. The *vájra* is the weapon with which Indra fought many battles, killed his enemies — the Āryans, the non-Āryans, the enemies in a general way and above all Vṛtrāhi his strongest enemy.

Tvaṣṭṛ made this *vájra* for Indra, Indra declares: *máhyaṃ tváṣṭā vájram atakṣat āyasám.* 'Tvaṣṭṛ made the *vájra* made of *ayas*[54] for me.' (X.48.3a; ***also see*** I.32.2; 61.6; V.31.4; VI.17.10). The *ṚV* also tells us that Uśanas made the *vájra* for him. 'Uśanas made the exhilarating *vájra* — the killer and suppressor (of enemies), and gave you.'[55] The *vájra* in some verses is described as golden, 'Indra's *vájra* the killer of enemies is golden.'[56] In some other verses it is described as made of copper (iron?).[57] It is thousand-knotted; 'Indra the friend of the Maruts, lacerated Vṛtra's head with his thousand-knotted *vájra*';[58] the *vájra* is also thousand-edged. Vṛtra failed to frighten Indra by the fearful shakings of his body or by the terrific sounds he made. Indra, on the other hand, threw his thousand-edged *vájra* on him: *ná vépasā ná tanyaténdraṃ vṛtró ví bībhayat* ǀ *abhy énaṃ vájra āyasáḥ sahásrabhṛṣṭir āyatā́rcan ánu svarā́jyam* (I.80.12). The *vájra* was lying inside the ocean, covered with water, whoever came near it became its victim (VIII.100.9). Indra was aksed to hold the thunderbolt in his right hand and resist all kinds of evil powers: *dhiṣvá vájraṃ dákṣiṇa indra háste viśvā ajurya dayase ví māyā́ḥ* (VI.22.9cd). Accompanied by Sūrya Indra with the *vájra* in his hand, destroys the *dā́sa*-enemies. '(We who are) strengthening your splendid vigour placing the bright *vájra* in your hands O bright Indra, strengthen yourself and, accompanied by Sūrya suppress the *dā́sa*-people'.[59] The demonic power rose against Indra, Indra also boldly resisted and suppressed them with his *vájra*, his old friend (***see*** III.30.6c; 33.7; VI.21.7; VI.27.7 *et al.*). The Maruts' friend Indra sharpens his *vájra*; he sharpens it in the same manner as does the bull its horns (I.55.1d; ***also see*** I.130.4). With his *vájra* Indra killed his strongest enemy Vṛtra (I.121.11; IV.19.3; VI.20.9 *et al.*). As Indra held the thunderbolt in his arms in order to kill Ahi, the mountains made loud sounds, the cows and priests sang in his praise (VIII.96.5).

The following epithets also show the very important part played by the *vájra* in the Indra myth.

Vájrin 'the possessor of the *vajra*' occurs about eighty times in the *ṚV*, *vajriva* signifying the same idea is come across twenty times in this Saṃhitā. *Vajriva* has been all along used in the vocative case. *Vájravāhu* 'with the *vájra* in his arms and *vájrahasta* 'with the *vájra* in his hands occurs seventeen times each. *Vájradakṣiṇa* who has *vájra* in his right hand (according to Sāyaṇa) occurs twice.[60]

We are not going into the discussion of the technical part of the *vájra*-as, the material the *vájra* was made of, its shape, or its counterparts in other mythologies like Greek 'Harpoon' or Finish *vasara,* etc.

Wilhelm Rau observes 'the word *vájra* was previously translated as 'thunderbolt but nowadays by it is meant club (?) (German *Keule*) a weapon which can be thrown at somebody and with which somebody can be hit at = mace, massue. In our work (i.e., *Metalle und Metallgeräte im vedischen Indien*) *vájra* represents mainly a weapon used in war by a god, above all, by Indra and the like was also used by men. At least one part of the *vájra* was made of copper because its colour is described reddish brown'.[61] Rau further thinks that we must also take into consideration the possibility that the word *várja* along with the change of the material out of which it was produced changed its form.[62]

Tapan Kr. Das Gupta thinks, 'In spite of the fact that in the majority of cases whenever the Vedic poets speak about *vájra* by that they mean the weapon of the god Indra, i.e., though this word, above all, is used in connection with myth, the statements in this regard are so exact, so detailed and in such a high degree free from contradictions that there cannot arise serious doubts about the fact that the Vedic poets had before their eyes a similar concrete object'.[63]

The vivid Ṛgvedic descriptions of the *vájra* signify to us nothing but the fierce and unassailable weapon used in the war of the Āryans against the non-Āryans, specially by Indra. This weapon played a very important part in the conquest of the non-

Āryans. In the Ṛgveda the most prominent aspect of Indra's character is that of a war god. In course of time the pre-Āryan storm myth returned among the Āryans when the nomadic Āryans had become agriculturists in the new land and consequently the necessity for a rain god became more pressing than that of a martial god. At this juncture the war god Indra evolved as a rain god, a god of fecundity and simultaneously the word *vájra* also changed its singnificance from Indra's weapon to his thunderbolt when he had become a rain god.[64]

SOMA

Indra's excessive love for the soma drink is beyond controversy. He is the best drinker of soma; full with soma his belly swells like the ocean.[65] He proceeds towards the soma libation with the same urge as the horse approaches the mare.[66] The more Indra is in the rapture of Soma the more he showers wealth in the form of cows, etc. to his worshippers.[67] Invigorated by Soma, Indra fights his enemies, kills them and devastates their cities. When Indra is entangled in long battles, his wife also offers the soma drink to him in the house.[68] Invigorated by Soma Indra exhibits his martial feats; in the battlefield he enjoys Soma the best. Stimulated by Soma he destroys ninety-nine ramparts of Śambara (***see*** VI.47.2; VIII.33.7).[69] The strongest of Indra's enemies was Vṛtra. He became competent to kill him after being invigorated by Soma. Indra's friend Agni (according to Sāyaṇa) cooked three hundred buffaloes and prepared three pools of Soma for him in order to render him strong enough to kill Vṛtra. After consuming all this he killed Ahi (V.29.8) and released the rivers (II.19.2).[70] The refrain; *sómasya tā́ máde índraś cakāra* (II.15) 'in the exhilaration of Soma Indra did all these', signifies the important part played by Soma in the Indra-myth.

Indra drank soma just after his birth (III.32.9ab; 10ab). Indra drank the ambrosia (*pīyū́ṣa*) which he had desired and which was hidden in the mountain; his mother gave soma the infant as the first thing to drink in her parental home (according to Sāyaṇa even before she gave him breast-milk she gave him soma).[71] Indra defeated Tvaṣṭṛ after his birth and drank soma from the vessel (III.48.4cd).[72]

This soma was brought to him from heaven by the hawk (*śyena*). 'Indra found the soma from heaven kept in a hidden place as the nestling of the birds are kept in vast endless rocks'.[73] 'The bird in mental speed went across the city made of *áyas*[74] reached heaven and brought *soma* for the *vájra*-holder.'[75]

We find the following description noticeably anthropomorphic. 'After he had had his Soma drink which was offered to him in a vessel he stood up and shook his jaws with great force'.[76] 'In one gulp Indra drinks thirty pools (sarāṃsi), of Soma full to the brim'.[77] 'Even a deer (*Goura*) does not know his drinking spot better than Indra knows the whereabouts of Soma'.[78] 'Indra is asked to hasten towards the soma drink which is swarmed with black bees'.[79]

Indra is *sómapāḥ somapā́bnām* (I.30.11b) 'the soma drinker of soma drinkers'. He is enriched by the soma drink — *sómavṛddha* (VI.19.5). He is the best soma drinker — *sómapātama* (VIII.12.1a) and he is the lord of Soma — *sómapati* (I.76.3c; VIII.21.3c).

Here we have touched those aspects of Soma which are related to Indra, the warrior. A warrior needs a stimulating drink initially for the exertion of his martial feats and later it becomes a part of his life-style. Same was the case with Indra. He needed this invigorating drink before he went to fight with his non-Āryan enemies for the good of his Āryan followers. Later, this drink was offered to him as oblation in sacrifice. It is ture, many other deities enjoy this oblation, but Indra is the only deity to enjoy all the three oblations and the midday oblation was solely for him (*mā́dhyandinaṃ sávanaṃ cā́ru yát te,* III.32.1b).[80]

THE HARIS

The Haris are the two horses who draw Indra's chariot. Indra, for whom the offering has been prepared in proper form, is asked to yoke his horses to his chariot (I.177.4; III.32.1d). He is also asked to stand for a while, while the horses are being yoked (III.35.1). The horses after becoming ready for the drive, bring Indra to the sacrifice (III.35.2). Indra who has reached the sacrificial ground is asked to release the horses so that they may have their fodder (III.35.3.7).[81] As Indra holds the thunderbolt in his arms the two horses carry him along with his devotees; he who is eternally famed, who is the lord of prosperity ascends the chariot (X.23.3).

The Haris are tawny (I.6.2 *śoṇau* — Sāyaṇa *raktavarṇau*). They are well-built, strong horses (III.43.4b); possessors of beautiful manes (VIII.14.12; 17.2). Though the Haris are usually described as tawny, once their hair has been said to have the colour of the peacock (*mayūraromabhiḥ*, III.45.1b). In most of the verses related to the Haris, they are simply asked to bring Indra to the sacrificial ground and nothing about Indra's martial feats are referred to. III.30.6b, however, urges Indra to proceed in his chariot drawn by the Haris towards his enemies in order to kill them with the *vájra*. Indra declares, "I yoke to my chariot the strong fleet horses, the performers of many feats." (X.49.2c).

Normally, the horses of Indra are two. In some verses, however, instead of the dual number Hari is used in the plural: *ā́ tvā vahantu hárayaḥ vŕ̥ṣaṇaṃ sómapītaye* 'May the Haris bring the manly Indra to the drink of soma' (I.16.1ab; ***also see*** IV.20.2; VII.29.2; VIII.34.1; X.96.1 *et al.*). This might be just in the form of laudation.

Harivah 'possessor of Haris' is an epithet of Indra:

> *índrā́ yāhi tū́tujāna úpa bráhmāṇi harivaḥ* ।
> *suté dadhiṣva naś cánaḥ* ॥
>
> 'O Indra, the *hariva*! come quickly to our prayer,
> accept our offering; the Soma has been pressed'.
> (I.3.6 ***also see*** III.30.2; IV.16.21 *et al.*).

The other epithets of Indra in this regard are *haryaśva* (III.30.12b; VII.19.4b; VIII.21.10), *hariṣṭhā* (III.49.2b; VI.17.2c *et al.*), *harivat* (VII.20.4c; 32.12c).

The Ṛbhus made the Haris for Indra.[82]

INDRA AND WAR

The verses mentioned below from the *ṚV* deal directly with Indra fighting his enemies.

'He who cherishes fame strengthened by his vigour, devastates the artificial houses (of the enemies) . . .'[83] '(Indra), the destroyer, fights with his warlike vigour and performs feats devastating the cities of the enemies one after another'.[84] 'Escorted by you we shall conquer one who resists; protect our share in every battle, make the path for earning prosperity at ease, O Indra, and ruin the strength of the enemy'.[85] 'You, as such, we place you in the fore-front of strength, you resemble a boat which goes across (i.e., attains the fulfilment of desires)'.[86] 'You have made this earth (death-) bed for the *dā́sa*s'.[87] 'O Bṛhaspati, attack the warriors of the *ásura*s who have guarded themselves well, with your piercing weapons, kill our enemies with your devastating power in the same manner as you ever did'.[88] 'He the possessor of all-surpassing prowess with his strength and magical powers (*māyābhiḥ*) ruined the crooked *dásyu*s'.[89] The Indra-worshipper urged by his sense of intolerance, appeals to his deity: 'O Indra, when will you engage the men with men and the heroes with the heroes of the enemies and win the battles for us! Conquer the cows the best of them (*tridhā́tu*) and win abundant wealth for us'.[90] 'The opponents can resist neither his right arm nor the left (arm)'.[91] X.99.3 narrates to us that the righteous Indra went to fight, he searched the treasures of the enemy, and he the irresistible one found out their hidden treasure after killing them the *śiśnadeva*s.[92] The *Ṛgveda* records only once that Indra killed the *dásyu*s who were *anā́sa*s (V.29.10c). It is, however, difficult to say finally on the *anā́sas*[93] basing on one evidence.

III. Indra's Protégés

The motif of a god giving shelter and succour to his protégés is associated more with the Aśvins, the heavenly physicians, than with Indra. Indra's other feats like killing Vṛtra, releasing waters etc. are comparatively fascinating and marvellous and thus attracted scholars' interest much more than this minor element of his character, viz. giving protection to particular protégés against their enemies, against their physical disabilities, etc.

These protégés of Indra[94] may be divided into four categories:

(i) To the first group belong those whom Indra protected by killing their enemies, and by destroying their ramparts. The enemies of this class of protégés were, presumably the non-Āryans — the *dā́sa*-s or the *dásyu*-s.

(ii) The different groups of Āryan people often clashed with each other. On one side were the Indra-worshippers and on the other, the Indra haters or, in the language of the *ṚV*, the *anindrá*-s (VII.18.16 etc.). Such Indra-worshippers who had been given protection against their Āryan enemies, belong to the second category.

(iii) To the third category belong the usual Indra worshippers. They offered sacrifices to Indra, and Indra returned their favour by fighting against their enemies, by recapturing their lost treasury, i.e., by showering material prosperity on them.

(iv) The Indra worshippers whose physical disabilities had been treated by Indra belong to the fourth category of his protégés — a motif rather more associated with the Aśvins, the divine doctors.

INDRA'S PROTÉGÉS AGAINST THE DĀ́SA-/DÁSYU-ENEMIES

Kutsa

Kutsa is a Ṛgvedic seer. He is also called Ārjuneya.[95] In spite of the fact that following the usual trend of the Ṛgvedic texts, the episodes connected with Kutsa are so complicated with the intermingling of various elements and are narrated in so abridged a form that it is difficult to distinguish one Kutsa-episode from the other, or to make out a complete story out of the texts. Yet four phases of the Kutsa-episode can be observed in the *Ṛgveda-saṃhitā*. They are: (i) his enmity with Śuṣṇa and Kuyava — the *dāsa-/dasyu*-enemies, (ii) introduction of Uśanas, Indra's counsellor, (iii) Indra's stealing one of Sūrya's wheels for the sake of Kutsa, and (iv) Indra's adverse behaviour towards Kutsa. No scholar, right from Sāyaṇa, has ever given an etymology of the word Kutsa, though we find different etymological interpretations of the word *śuṣṇa*. Sāyaṇa says, it is — from *śuṣ* meaning *śoṣaṇārahita-* 'one who never dries up'. Perry interprets *śuṣṇa* as 'greedy'[96] and Gonda as 'voracious'[97] presumably from *vaś* 'to eat'. According to some it is 'a drought demon' (from *śuṣ*, to dry up, cf. Śuṣna: the *Monier-Williams, Dictionary*). The use of *aśuṣa* as Śuṣṇa's adjective may, however, also be a play of words by the Ṛgvedic poets as thought of by Geldner.[98] According to the *St. Petersburg Dictionary, śuṣṇa* is from *śus* meaning *zischer, pfeifer*, 'one who whistles, whizes'. Śuṣṇa was the greatest enemy of Kutsa who was given all round protection by Indra against this enemy. Indra killed Śuṣṇa by his magical power (*māyā*), (I.11.7, ***also see*** I.103.8; 121.9; 175.4). Indra in the exhilaration of Soma imprisoned *Ś*uṣṇa I.56.3). He devastated his ramparts (I.51.11d). Indra who never failed in a battle, killed Dhuni, Cumuri, Śambara and Śuṣṇa and destroyed their ramparts (VI.18.8). Indra attacked Śuṣṇa from all sides, devastated his ramparts and killed him with his *vájra* (V.32.4 ***also see*** VIII.96.17). He destroyed the mobile ramparts of Śuṣṇa (VIII.1.28). Indra declares: *ahám śúṣṇasya śnáthitā* (X.49.3c) 'I am the killer of Śuṣṇa'. All this Indra did for the sake of Kutsa, his favourite, the son of Arjunī (***see*** VI.26.3b; VII.19.2cd). When Indra attacked Śuṣṇa he travelled in the self-same chariot, drawn by fleet horses, with Kutsa (IV.16.11), Uśanas and the gods. They travelled together to the house (of Kutsa-Sāyaṇa) at the time of Indra's attacking Śuṣṇa. Indra gave protection not only to Kutsa but also to his son: *ā́vo yád dasyuhátye Kutsaputrám* । *prā́vo yád dasyuhátye kutsavatsám* (X.105.11cd). According to Perry Śuṣṇa is a demon of drought and bad harvest.[99] Hillebrandt agrees with Oldenberg on the point that the heavenly and earthly elements are so intermingled that it is difficult to recognise the historical and mythological sources of the Vedic myths.[100] This is equally applicable to Kutsa-Śuṣṇa myth. Hillebrandt also adds that Śuṣṇa might either be an earthly enemy, or the eclipse of the sun, or the darkness of the sun (*svarbhānu*). According to him in order to interpret this myth one must side with one of these alternatives and he prefers to accept the last view. But by so doing does he not neglect the other two aspects of this myth? Moreover, if we interpret Śuṣṇa as the darkness of the sun then how do we link it with the story of Kutsa whom the *ṚV* has depicted as an earthly being? According to many scholars, Kutsa was a human being. Keith observes: "Kutsa in the case of his real personality must be a king, and this is not inconsistent with being called a royal seer: royal seers are not unknown".[101] Gonda also hints at the human identity of Kutsa as he observes: "Thus there may possibly have existed a more or less coherent story of Kutsa, the hero who is associated with Indra in the exploits of winning the sun and in defeating demon Śuṣṇa".[102]

Kutsa's other enemy was Kuyava (I.103.8; II.19.6; IV.16.12). he was very prosperous non-Āryan chieftain and was killed by Indra for Kutsa's sake. His abode was concealed in the waters of the rivers and he controlled the waters of the rivers Añjasī, Kuliśī and Vīrapatnī (I.104.4). The word *kuyava* means 'bad harvest'. As Kuyava controlled the river waters so he caused bad harvests for his enemy who consequently gave him such a name.[103] The following *Ṛgveda* story also speaks about Kuyava's prosperity. His two wives had been taking bath in milk. This became intolerable for Kutsa, the seer of the hymn I.104. He prayed to Indra. "May Kuyava's two wives be drowned in the depths (or in the slopes — *pravaṇe*?) of the river Śiphā (I.104.3). Ludwig's comment in this connection is very interesting. "While poor Aryan who can only wish for the wealth which he does not possess has not even ordinary water to wash himself in, the wives of the enemy, in the insolent pride of their riches bathe in milk." (Quoted from Griffith, *The Hymns of the Ṛgveda*): Indra in favour of Kutsa killed Kuyava (II.19.6; VII.19.2). A conflict between

Indra and Sūrya is reflected in the repeated statement that Indra in order to favour Kutsa stole one of Sūrya's wheels (*yátrotá bādhitébhyaś cakrám̩ kútsāya yudhyáte* | *muṣāyá indra sū́ryam* || (IV.30.4, ***also see*** V.29.10; VI.31.3). Oldenberg comments on this Indra-Sūrya conflict — with reference to Kutsa — that Kutsa, the son of Arjunī, was a hero, and that he might be a historical or an ideal figure. The myth of the sun was added to the Kutsa-myth in order to adorn this historical or half-historical myth.[104] We cannot imagine what causes might be lying behind this Indra-Sūrya conflict. If we say that a cult conflict could be inferred in it then we simply attempt to evade the question. The Ṛgvedic texts do not enlighten us much on the identity of Uśanas. He was more of Indra the counsellor than a devotee. As already referred to, he accompanied Indra in the selfsame chariot while Indra drove his chariot against Śuṣṇa in Kutsa's favour.

Surprisingly enough, Kutsa the son of Arjunī, the great favourite of Indra, resembled Indra so much in appearance that his faithful wife[105] could not distinguish which of these two was Indra (cf. *sarūpā* in IV.16.10). Kutsa's other name Ārjuneya and this extreme similarity in appearance of the two lead us to the conclusion that the woman Arjunī got this son Kutsa from Indra. Kutsa, though a great favourite of Indra, was subdued by him along with Atithigva and Āyu in order to favour a greater devotee, Suśravas, — great young Āryan king who in a battle was surrounded by twenty kings and their sixty thousand and ninety-nine soldiers (lit. people I.53.9; 10; ***also see*** VIII.53.2).[106]

We are not going into the historicity of the myths connected with Indra, Kutsa, Śuṣṇa and Kuyava. These myths, however, introduce us to the general mode of life the Āryans lived — a life full of conflicts and clashes against their enemies, non-Āryans or Āryan, with Indra as their chief.

Atithigva

Among Indra's protégés Atithigva stands in the second position after Kutsa in respect of number of Ṛgvedic verses referring to him. Divodāsa was his name and *atithigva* an epithet qualifying his hospitable nature.[107] Atithigva's principal enemy was the *dā́sa* Śambara, the descendant of Kulitara (IV.30.14) and a master of innumerable ramparts. Indra fought against Śambara on behalf of Atithigva Divodāsa. Śambara was the master of ninety or ninety-nine or hundred(?) ramparts (*púr*). Indra killed Śambrá who considered himself immortal.[108] He devastated his ninety or ninety-nine castles (*púr*).[109] Indra, after destroying his ninety-nine castles entered into the hundredth.[110] For the sake of Divodāsa Indra devastated Śambara's hundred ramparts made of stone.[111] Indra also killed Karañja and Parṇaya for the sake of Atithigva (I.53.8). In the Dāśarājña-war, a fight between the Āryan chiefs, Turvaśa and Yadu stood against Atithigva. So, Indra is besought to subdue these two and to bring forth blessings to Atithigva (VII.19.8).

Indra, though a patron of Atithigva, did not hesitate to subjugate him along with Āyu and Kutsa in favour of Suśravas. This incident has been already referred to.

Ṛjiśvan

The next name in the list of Indra's protégés is Ṛjiśvan, the descendant of Vidathin (IV.16.13). His chief enemy was Pipru[112] against whom Indra protected him in the battle against the *dásyu*-s (*dasyuhátya* I.51.5cd). Ṛjiśvan, the descendant of Uśij, sang in praise of Indra, and his cows were released from the enclosure of Pipru (X.99.11). Pipru, like Śambara, was the master of many ramparts. Indra devastated those ramparts and showered wealth generously on Ṛjiśvan (VI.20.7). The other *dā́sa* enemies killed by Indra in favour of Ṛjiśvan were Mṛgaya[113] (IV.16.13) and Vaṅgṛda. Strengthened by Ṛjiśvan's assistance, Indra devastated a hundred cities of Vaṅgṛda (I.53.8). With Ṛjiśvan's assistance Indra also killed the women of the 'black' (or of Kṛṣṇa, the *dā́sa*):

> *prā́ mandíne pitumád arcatā váco*
> *yáḥ kṛṣṇágarbhā niráhan ṛjíśvanā* । (I.101.1ab)

> Utter words of praise accompanied with oblation to him who enjoys, and who with Ṛjiśvan's assistance killed women of the black breed.[114]

Dabhīti

Indra patronized Dabhīti against the *dásyu*-s, against Dhuni and Cumuri. He became glorious by killing the *dásyu*-s without the help of any cord[115] in order to favour Dabhīti (II.13.9). Indra surrounded the assailants and threw their weapons into fire and showered gifts of horses and cows on Dabhīti. Indra did all this in the exhilaration of Soma (II.15.4). He led them to slumber and then killed 30,000 of them (i.e., the *dásyu*-s) with his magical power (*māyā*);[116] this he did for the sake of Dabhīti. Dhuni and Cumuri were two specific enemies of Dabhīti. Indra put these two also to sleep and then killed them and protected Dabhīti (II.15.9; ***also see*** VI.18.8; VI.21.13; X.113.9).

It cannot escape one's notice that Indra applied magical power (*māyā*) to kill the *dásyu*-enemies of Dabhīti and his other two non-Āryan enemies, i.e., Dhuni and Cumuri. He put them to slumber by *māyā* and then killed them. Noticeably enough, he did not need to apply this power while killing other enemies in order to protect his protégés.

Babhru

Babhru, the seer of V.30, lost his cows; they were stolen by Namuci. Namuci commissioned some women whom he intended to use as weapons against Indra. Indra wondered what harm they could do him! He, however, kept two of them back and killed Namuci (V.30.8-11).[117] The verses of the *ṚV* state that Indra severed Namuci's head and it is mentioned only once that Indra did it with foam (VIII.14.13) — an event so frequently referred to in post-Ṛgvedic Vedic literature (***See*** *TaitBrā*, I.7.1.6; *VS*, X.14; *ŚatBrā*, V.4.1.9. *et al.*).

Purukutsa

Purukutsa, the son of Durgaha, was imprisoned by his enemies.[118]

Seven sages came to Purukutsānī, Purukutsa's wife, and (probably) suggested her to propitiate Indra and Varuṇa who favoured her with the gift of the son Trasadasyu — an *ardhadevá*, "a demi-god" — a very significant epithet of Trasadasyu with reference to Indra and Varuṇa. Indra devastated seven ramparts of Śarat, the *dā́sa* and showered prosperity and well-being on Purukutsa (I.63.7; 174.2; VI.20.10).

THE PROTÉGÉS SAFE-GUARDED AGAINST NON-DĀ́SA-/DÁSYU-ENEMIES

The Āryans fought not only against their non-Āryan enemies, but they also had to fight against each other. They were divided into several groups of tribes and clans. Indra was the chief of one such group, probably the storngest one of all. The *ṚV* verses glorify Indra, their chief, under whose leadership they conquered their Āryan enemies. The Āryan identity of these enemies of Indra-worshippers can be inferred from their names; they are never referred to as *dā́sa*-s or *dásyu*-s.

Suśravas

Indra conquered twenty local chieftains (*janarājñaḥ*) and their six thousand and ninety-nine people in order to safeguard Suśravas who was without an ally (I.53.9.10). Indra protected Suśravas, the overpowering (*tū́rvayāṇa*), and, for the sake of this great young king, subdued Kutsa, Atithigva and Āyu:

(a) *tvám āvitha suśrávasaṃ távotíbhiḥ*
(b) *táva trā́mabhir indra tū́rvayāṇam* ।
(c) *tvám asmai kútsam atithigvám āyúṁ*
(d) *mahé rā́jñe yúne arandhanāyaḥ* ।। (I.53.10)

'O Indra! you with your defence, with your aid protected the overpowering Suśravas. For that great young king you killed Kutsa, Atithigva and Āyu.' It is more logical to interpet the word *tū́rvayāṇa* occurring in (b) as adjective to Suśravas than as a king's name as has been done by Sāyaṇa (*etannāmānaṃ rājānam*), Geldner[119] and Griffith.[120] The singular number in the word *mahé* occurring in (d) refers to Suśravasam (a) and confirms our conjecture.·Āyu who had been favoured by Indra, however, is now subdued by him in favour of Suśravas. Indra declares: *ahám veśáṁ namrám āyáve 'karam* (X.49.5). Such narration of the *ṚV* hints at the mutual conflicts among the Āryans.

Turvaśa and Yadu

Indra portected Turvaśa and Yadu also Narya, Turvīti and Vayya (I.54.6). The righteous Turvaśa and Yadu were brought from afar by Indra (I.174.9 = VI.20.12).[121] Indra entangled Ahṇavāyya in war for the benefit of these two wards of him (VIII.45.27). Indra, however, was not a consistent patron of Turvaśa and Yadu; he subdued them in favour of Atithigva (VII.19.8).[122]

Cāyamāna Abhyavartin

Cāyamāna's descendant Abhyavartin was patronized by Indra against the Vṛcīvats, the descendants of Varaśikha (VI.27.4-6).[123] Indra with his thunderbolt killed them (on the bank of) the Hariyūpīyā.[124] He killed one hundred and thirty (or three thousand: *triṃśatśatam*?) armoured soldiers of Varaśikha (on the bank of) Yavyāvatī.[125]

Sudās

Divodāsa's son Sudās was the foremost of all the fortunate protégés of Indra. He was the hero of the great war (*dāśarājña*) against ten or more kings on the bank of Paruṣṇī. Those kings attacked Sudās together but as Indra was on Sudās' side, so victory came to him. Much has been already discussed on the *dāśarājña* war by scholars.[126]

The other prortégés of Indra who could be brought under this category are the Anus and the Druhyus. They like many others of Indra's protégés, have been depicted both as anti-Indra and his protégés.

Indra' protégés belonging to the third category, formed a

mixed group. While some were defended against their enemies, others were favoured with the regulation of waters, rivers, etc., and on still others was showered prosperity.

Piṭhīnas, Daśadyu and Śvaitreya

Indra killed sixty thousand (soldiers) in order to win the kingdom for Piṭhīnas (VI.26.6). He protected the strong Daśadyu and earned victory for Śvitrā's son Śvaitreya.[127]

Etaśa

Etaśa who challenged Sauvaśva Sūrya was protected by Indra (I.61.15). Indra with skill protected Etaśa, the mortal, his devotee (IV.17.14; 30.6). For him Indra controlled Sūrya's horses, the *haritaḥ* (***see*** V.29.5; 31.11). When the sun attacked Etaśa then Indra taking Arjunī's son on his chariot proceeded to fight against Sūrya (according to Sāyaṇa). A conflict between Indra and Sūrya is observed in the Etaśa episode. Hillebrandt finds in Etaśa the horse of Sūrya.[128] Etaśa appears to be a horse, but he also adds that it is difficult to decode this episode: ". . . sie ist vielfach dunkel."[129] The *TS* records that the Sūrya moves on Etaśa (*etaśena tvā sūrya devatāṃ gamayatu,* 1.6.4.3). In the *ṚV*, however, Etaśa is depicted as a mortal who had been safeguarded by Indra against Sūrya. Can Etaśa be connected in any way with the hero of the late Khila-hymns, *etaśa-pralāpa*, where he talks apparent nonsense but actually hints at the fertility cult?

Mudgala and Mudgalānī

Since very early days scholars of eminence have expressed their mutually contradictory opinions on the story of Mudgala and Mudgalānī. Here we simply record that these two who won the race (or fight?) riding on a chariot by only one horse, were Indra's protégés.[130]

Turvīti, Vayya and Manu

For Turvīti and Vayya Indra regulated the rivers so that they might easily go across them (II.13.12; IV.19.6). Indra released the waters, the rivers, for Manu. Geldner observes in this context, "Indra leitete die befreiten Flüsse in ihre Bahnen zurück und führte den Stammvater Manu durch in seine nachmalige Heimat. Eine historische Reminizenz an die Erinnerung der arischen stamme in östliche Pandschab".[131] 'Indra led the released waters in their courses again, and led Manu, the forefather of the Āryans through the rivers to their subsequent home. A historical reminiscence of the immigration of the Āryans towards east Punjab.' In this context we see in Indra a culture hero. Of many characteristics of a culture hero, one is that he, "regulates waters".[132]

King Vṛṣaśṛṅga's Five Sons

Ṛjrāśva, Ambarı́ṣa, Sahadeva, Surādhas and Bhayamāna are, according to the *Sarvānukaramaṇī*, the seers of the hymn I.100. Indra has won the sun for them (I.110.6). Indra riding on Ṛjrāśva's chariot, drawn by strong black and red mares, won riches for him (I.100.16); he killed their enemies the *dásyu*-s and the Śimyu-s[133] (I.100.18). The names of the brothers are mentioned in the seventeenth verse of the hymn.

Tuji, another of Indra's protégés, is known only from a single text which mentions that he earned prosperity through Indra's favour (VI.26.4).

PROTÉGÉS CURED OF PHYSICAL DISABILITIES

Through Indra's favour the lame stood erect and the blind got sight (II.13.12; 15.7; IV.30.19). This capacity of giving relief from ailment to the protégé is more associated with the Aśvins, the divine doctors, than with Indra. In II.13.12, an Indra hymn, one reads: *prā̆ndhám̐ śroṇám̐ śravā́yant sā̆sy ukthyaḥ.* In I.112.8, a hymn to the Aśvins, we read: *andhám̐ śroṇám̐ cákṣasa étave kṛtháḥ.* One observes not only the similarity of subject-matter but also the identical vocabulary of these two verses. Indra rescued socially condemned son (Parāvṛc) of the unmarried maiden;

he was covered by anthills, lost his eyesight and became crippled (II.13.12; IV.19.9; IV.30.16).[134] Vimada was showered with riches (I.51.3). The Aśvins, however, rescued Vimada's wife from the enemies (*Ṛ̣V*, I.112.19; 116.1 etc.). Atri who had been thrown into fire was rescued by Indra (I.51.3). The same kind of relief was given to Atri by the Aśvins (*Ṛ̣V*, I.112.7; 16; 116.8 *et al.*).[135]

CONCLUSION

From the stories of Indra's protégés we may infer that the Āryans had frequent clashes with their enemies, Āryans and non-Āryans. It is of no significance to us whether Kutsa or Atithigva or Ṛjiśvan were historical presons. And, with such scanty material, i.e., the Ṛgvedic text, it is next to impossible to identify them as historical figures.

The stories of Indra's protégés belonging to the first category confirm that the Āryans fought with the non-Āryans, the *dā́sa*-s and *dásyu*-s who, possessed fortified cities (*púraḥ*) and were settled in a better position. In the *Ṛ̣V* only the enemy-cities are mentioned and never those of the protégés; this also indicates that the Āryans had been immigrating in a new land and in course of their forward march they devastated some of the earlier settlements. It is also evident that the Āryans were militarily superior to thier non-Āryan counterparts because the Ṛgvedic poems are a series of songs of their victory. As it is quite natural for the average human being to be dissatisfied with their own station in life and to hanker something better something new which is very often illusory; the Āryans reacted in a similar manner and felt discontended with their lot. They often went against their leader and as a result we find that those who had once been Indra's protégés had occasionally to be suppressed and even killed by him in favour of some other protégés. Atithigva, Kutsa, Āyu were all Indra's wards, but in order to favour Suśravas they had to be destroyed by him. Life in a general way was not that divine, but quite a common place existence with its quota of love, jealousy or hatred against each other.

Indra's greatest achievement lies in his act of regulating the water courses and rivers.[136] This is narrated in the stories of Turvīti, Vayya and Manu. This highly beneficent feat of Indra led him to the highest position among the *ṚV* gods. Curing physical maladies was not the chief element of his character. This might be attributed to him in a manner of eulogy.

The *ṚV* is not a history book, but, indisputably, it is literature. In literature life is represented in an aesthetic manner which offers the reader a glimpse into contemporary history. In the Ṛgvedic text myth and history are so unidentifiably dove-tailed into each oher that it is very difficult to distinguish one from the other. Even then, in the stories of Kutsa, Atithigva, Suśravas, Cāyamāna Abhyavartin and others we get a glimpse of the historical background of life led by the predecessors of the *ṚV* singers. We say predecessors because the verbs in the texts are mostly used in past tense.

IV. Indra-Vṛtra

The Indra-Vṛtra combat forms the central theme of the mythology of the *Ṛgveda*; rather this myth is the central theme of the whole of the Saṃhitā mythology. Before entering the analysis of the opinions of scholars of East and West, on this theme an attempt to portray the different aspects of Vṛtra, (used both in masculine and neuter gender and also both in singular and plural number), as we find them in the *ṚV* texts, seems necessary.

DĀNU — VṚTRA'S MOTHER

Vṛtra is the strongest of Indra's enemies. We do not know, who in fact Vṛtra was. In the Saṃhitās and, specially, in the *ṚV* Vṛtra, in places, is very highly anthropomorphised — strong, irresistible earthly being who had arrested the waters, and in others symbolises resistance in a general way. The *ṚV,* I.32 narrates very poetically, bringing along some visual effect as it were, the story of Indra's killing Vṛtra. Indra killed not only Vṛtra but also his mother Dānu who lied low in order two shield her son against Indra's attacks. And lo! the mother's corpse was lying over her son's. The mother's efforts to protect her son failed; she tried to protect her son against Indra's attacks in the same manner as does the mother cow defends her calf:

> *nīcā́vayā abhavad vṛtráputréndro*
> *asyā áva vādhar jabhāra* ।
> *úttarā sū́r ádharaḥ putrá āsīd*
> *dā́nuḥ śaye sahávatsā ná dhenúḥ* ।। (I.32.9)

Nowhere in the *ṚV* is so distinctly mentioned that Vṛtra is Dānu's son except in this hymn.[137] Vṛtra is referred to in places as *dānava*, i.e., the son of Dānu. The following is one such verse:

> *nı́ māyíno dānavásya māyā́*
> *ápādayat papivā́n sutásya* ।। (II.11.10cd)

Exhilarated by Soma Indra crashed the strength of the mighty *dānava.*[138]

VṚTRA — HEADLESS AND FOOTLESS

But for the account that Vṛtra is headless and footless we have no·knowledge about Vṛtra's anthropomorphic features. I.32.7a states *apā́d ahastó apṛtanyad índram*, 'the headless and footless fought with Indra'. III.30.8cd may also be quoted in this connection *abhı́ vṛirā́ṃ várdhamānaṃ píyārum apā́dam indra tavásā jaghantha*, 'O Indra, you killed the terrific ever-increasing footless Vṛtra with your might'.

INDRA NEEDED EXTERNAL HELP TO KILL VṚTRA

Indra had to invigorate himself with the soma drink[139] in order to be strong enough to kill Vṛtra, his strongest enemy. After he drank profusely and was eulogised by the Maruts, he held the *vájra* in his arms, killed Vṛtra and released the waters (V.29.2). Viṣṇu assisted him in this feat (VI.20.2). The gods placed him in the position of the Vṛtra-killer (VIII.12.22ab). The assistance of Tvaṣṭṛ, Uśanas[140] and the Maruts was indispensable for him in killing Vṛtra. The Maruts, his associates, communicated to him the important message — which part of Vṛtra's body is to be hit at in order that he could be killed.[141] Thus, the cumulative assistance of all such divinities enabled Indra to accomplish the great task of killing Vṛtra what had been impossible so long.[142] The waters flew over Vṛtra's corpse gladdening men's mind; Ahi (= Vṛtra) was now lying under water, once eclipsed by him (***see*** I.32.8; 11 *et al*). Indra announces to the Maruts, his associates:

> *vádhīṃ vṛtrám maruta indriyéṇa* (I.165.8a)
>
> O Maruts, I killed Vṛtra with my own strength (***also see*** IV.17.3; 7; 8; 30.7).[143]

Heaven and the earth, the entire firmament shook in fear by the terrific sound made by Vṛtra before being killed by Indra (***see*** I.52.10; II.11.9-10).[144] Killing Vṛtra was to Indra as easy as it is for a horse to drive away the fly sitting on its body (I.32.12). Vṛtra's body was stuck between logs floating in water; Indra's enemy went into the eternal sleep (I.32.10).

Indra, undoubtedly, was the strongest hero to the Vedic seers, but equally strong was his enemy — Vṛtrāhi.[145] Indra was not fully confident of his capability to kill Vṛtra. Even after killing Vṛtra he had doubts in his mind whether he had really performed the great task. So arose the feeling of necessity in the poet's mind to remove Indra's doubts in a form of indirect praise:

> *áher yātā́raṃ kám apaśya indra*
> *hṛdí yát te jaghnúṣo bhī́r ágacchat* | (I.32.14ab)
>
> O Indra, whom else had you seen as the killer of Ahi, that you had fear (i.e., doubt) in your heart (whether you had really killed him)!

The same fear in Indra has been reflected in the *AitBrā,* III.15 and *TS,* II.5.3.6.[146] Human behaviour is very clearly observed in Indra here.

The word *vṛtrá* which has been formed from the Indo-European root **var* meaning to obstruct, is the symbol of resistance. This word was not a proper name originally but an abstract idea. As the invading nomadic Āryans settled down in the western part of India and gradually settled as an agricultural people, so along with the change of character of this people from nomadic to agricultural the significance of the word *vṛtra* also changed from resistance in general to 'cloud', obstructing rains and pervading the atmospheric region. And, the root *vṛ* started to be interpreted as 'to pervade' — the cloud pervades the atmospheric region. Yāska and the other authors of the *Nirukta*s composed their works after atleast one millennium from the age of the composition of the *Ṛgveda* hymns. By that time conditions of life had changed. Regular showers of rain was very much needed, and the service of a war hero was of not essential need in life as it had been previously. Accordingly, *vṛtra*, 'resistance in general' started to symbolise clouds obstructing rain. As *vṛtra* did not represent a person like most other *dāsa*-enemies of Indra so we find the use of *vṛtra* in masculine and neuter gender and as well as in singular and plural number. That *vṛtra* the earthly resistance has been transformed into atmospheric resistance (i.e., cloud) goes in favour of Mircea Eliade's statement. "A true myth describes an archetypal event".[147] The basic concept of *vṛtrá* — 'resistance' which lies in the earthly resistance put forward by the non-Āryans against the invading Āryans changed its significance along the change of conditions of life.

INDRA, THE RELEASOR OF WATERS

'That feat of Indra was glorious; he, for the first time, released the waters downwards, which (then) flowed down following the selfsame course providing food to the ocean'.[148] According to VI.72.3 Indra and Soma released the waters and they flowed into ocean (*prā́rṇāṃsy airayataṃ nadī́nām ā́ samudrā́ṇi paprathuḥ purū́ṇi*). Indra shouting in great anger cut Vṛtra into pieces part by part and the waters flowed into the ocean.[149]

The rivers released by Indra were navigable (*nāvyā*): 'O

Indra, your *vajrá* functioned variously (in order to release) ninety navigable rivers'.[150]

It has been mentioned several times that Indra released seven rivers, *sapta sindhavaḥ* — a phrase occurring frequently in the Vedic texts. We, however, do not know the story of this number — whether it has historical and geographical background or, whether this was a favourite number with the Vedic seers and was considered auspicious as it was in many early cultures and is also today to many Hindus (cf. *saptarṣi, saptapadī, sapta loka et al.*). Quite a good number of verses mention that Indra released seven rivers. A few such instances are: *ávāsṛjaḥ sártave saptá síndhūn* (I.32.12d) 'you released the seven rivers to flow'. *asyá śrávo nadyaḥ saptá vibhrati* (I.102.2a) 'the seven rivers possess his glory'. *yó hatvā́him áriṇāt saptá síndhūn* (II.12.3a) 'who after killing Ahi released the seven rivers'. *ahám saptá sraváto dhārayaṃ vṛ́ṣā dravitnvaḥ pṛthivyā́ṃ sīrā́ ā́dhi* (X.49.9ab) 'I the bestower, place the seven flowing rivers on the surface of the earth'.[151]

A few verses state in a general way that Indra released waters; nothing is mentioned about their source — whether they were river water, rain water or waters blocked because of some natural obstruction or calamity or waters enclosed in a dam for agricultural purposes. Synonym of waters occurring in these verses have been interpreted by Sāyaṇa variously. As for example, he interprets *apaḥ* as *vṛṣṭyudakam* in I.54.10; 56.5; 6; 103.2 etc. *sindhavaḥ* has been interpreted quite logically as *nadyaḥ* in I.61.11; IV.22.6 *et al.*) and *apaḥ* as *udakāni* in V.30.5; 31.6; VII.21.3; X.147.1. From the different interpretations of the same word in different places it becomes clear that the main point of the statement of the Vedic singers was to state that Indra released waters.

Of the many characteristics of a culture hero laid down by Smith Thompson one is: "Culture hero regulates waters".[152] Indra's greatest service towards his people was the release of the enclosed waters. This great feat of his raised him temporarily from the status of a culture hero to that of the highest god.

A few instances describing Indra as releaser of waters are quoted below from the *ṚV*:

I.56.6c: *tvám̥ sutásya máde ariṇā apáḥ*

'In the exhilaration of Soma you released the waters.'

I.103.2b : *vájreṇa hatvā́ nī́r apáḥ sasarja*

'After killing (Vṛtra) with *vájra* you released the waters'.

I.165.8cd : *ahám etā́ mánave viśvā́ś candrā́ḥ*
sugā́ apáś cakāra vájravāhuḥ ||

'Thunderbolt in arms, I let the waters flow smoothly for the sake of Manu'.

V.30.5d : *v'́vā apó ajayad dāsápatnīḥ* ||

'Indra conquered all waters, the wards of the *dāsas*.[153]

The word *apsujít*, 'conquerer of waters' is repeated in each and every verse, except in the last one, of VIII.36.

It becomes clear from the above discussion that Indra released the waters; Indra set them down into their original courses — the waters which were enclosed because of some reason. And this was the most important event in the life of the Ṛgvedic people irrespective of the nature of these waters.

PÁRVATA

The *ṚV* tells us many a time that Indra shattered the mountains (*parvata*) and released the waters. We are quoting below a few such verses:

tvám̥ tám indra párvatam̥ mahā́m urúm̥
vájreṇa vajrin parvaśáś cakartitha |
ávāsṛjaḥ nívṛtāḥ sartavá apáḥ
satrā́ víśvam̥ dadhiṣe kévalam̥ sáhaḥ || (I.57.6)

> *Várja*-holder Indra, you shattered part by part the great mountain, released the enclosed waters and they flowed down; you alone, in truth, possess that all-pervading strength.
>
> *bhinád valám áṅgirobhir gr̥ṇānó*
> *ví párvatasya dr̥ṃhitā́ny airat* ।
> *riṇag ródhāṃsi kr̥trímāṇy eṣāṃ*
> *sómasya tā́ máde índraś cakā́ra* ।। (II.15.8)
>
> Lauded by the Aṅgirases he killed Vala, blew out the strong mountain, destroyed the artificial barrier of waters — all this Indra did in the exhilaration of Soma.
>
> *ví yád várāṃsi párvatasya vr̥ṇvé*
> *páyobhir jinvé apā́ṃ jávāṃsi* । (IV.21.8ab)
>
> When he unclosed the doors of the mountain, the waters gained their speed.[154]

Párvata under I.57.6 has been interpreted by Sāyaṇa, Griffith and Geldner as cloud; under II.15.8 the word as has been interpreted by Sāyaṇa, Griffith and Geldner as mountain.

The majority of the *párvata*s occurring in the *R̥V-Saṃhitā* has been interpreted by Sāyaṇa as cloud and by Griffith and Geldner either as mountain or as cloud. If we read these verses with an open mind we do not find any occasion to interpret *párvata* as cloud, this word rather upholds the imagery of some rocky obstruction resisting the flow of the rivers. Why, how the waters were obstructed the *R̥V* does not give any adequate reasons in this regard. The obstruction was demolished by Indra and the rivers started flowing in their original courses. We do not find any logical justification to interpret *párvata* as cloud; Indra is hardly a rain god after the *R̥V-Saṃhitā*.

To Oldenberg the *parvata* as mentioned in the *R̥V* verses are real *párvata*s and the rivers simply rivers and not clouds and rain water. He says in this context, "Had it been the intention (of the Vedic singer) to speak about clouds and rains then it would not have been possible to repeat the metaphors in innumerable places instead of mentioning the subject by its real name in any place".[155] H. Lüders also thinks along the same lines and says that he considers it impossible that the *ṚV* singers always meant cloud and rain waters whenever they spoke about mountains and rivers or the seven rivers. Why should they, constantly use metaphoric language instead of expressing in clear language. He also adds that we would have understood the Veda more correctly, had we accepted them in their literal meaning.[156]

To us the *párvata*s were *párvata*s or similarly shaped rocky installations. We further believe that because of some reason, because of some natural calamity, or because of artificial installations raised to control the flow of the rivers for agricultural purposes, the river-courses were arrested. The *ṚV* Āryans, under Indra's leadership shattered those obstructions and let the rivers flow bringing forth the total fall of the economy of their non-Āryan enemies. We are also tempted to believe that as the rivers were enclosed by the Āryans' *dā́sa*-enemies so the coinage *dā́sa-patnī* (= rivers), i.e., that which is protected by the *dā́sa*s.

SCHOLARS ON THE INDRA-VṚTRA MYTH

From the late nineteenth century till today scholars have expressed different opinions on the Indra-Vṛtra myth. A few of these are analysed below.

Oldenberg does not rule out that the Indra-Vṛtra myth might be related to the primitive storm myth which existed in many mythologies. Germanic Donar-Thor myth is comparable in this regard.[157] To the later Vedic poets and their interpreters also Indra is explicitly a rain and storm god, but at the same time he confirms that to the poets of the *ṚV* Indra-Vṛtra myth narrates the breaking of the mountains (*Berge*) and the release of the earthly rivers.[158] Oldenberg has a very objective attitude towards his subject of discussion, but at the same time he is prone to some confusions also; he fails to correlates the pre-Āryan storm-rain myth with the Ṛgvedic Indra-Vṛtra myth in a logical way.

Our study of the *Ṛgveda* leads us to conclude that the Ṛgvedic Indra is not a storm-, rain-god. Parjanya is the real representative of the rain-storm-god in the *ṚV* and the Maruts also may be mentioned in this connection.

According to Hillebrandt the Vṛtra-myth is pre-Indian originated in Kashmir or further north-west. This perception was lost in India. In Vṛtra we meet with an example of melting of the snow of pre-Indian preception through the Indian sun.[159] Hillebrandt observes further that the Indian rivers are not the starting point of the Vṛtra myth. And this fight between the winter demon and the sun bears greater significance in the land situated in the north-west of India. The word *vṛtra* originated there and has immigrated carrying the same significance from the pre-Indidan age. But, when it came further east into India proper coming through a variety of circumstances it lost its original significance and the significance of the myth also faded.[160]

We are deeply indebted to Hillebrandt for his deep and far-fetched study on the Vṛtra myth. The *Ṛgveda* texts, however, do not tell us anything about the winter giant, the freezing of the rivers, etc. The *ṚV* repeatedly tells us that the waters were enclosed by Vṛtra (= Ahi) and Indra with his *vájra* destroyed the barriers, killed Vṛtra and let the rivers flow. Even now, in the absence of historical and archaeological evidence we have to depend mainly on the Vedic texts.

A group of scholars think that Vṛtra represented cloud. Their opinions may be recorded below.

Muir finds in Vṛtra a demon of drought, "hostile powers in the atmosphere who malevolently shut up the watery treasures in the clouds".[161] According to Perry, "Vṛtra is a cloud demon".[162] Hopkins observes, "For the oft-mentioned act cleaving the cave, where the dragon Vala or Vṛtra (the restrainer of enveloper) had coralled the kine (i.e., without metaphor, for the act of freeing the clouds and letting loose the rain)".[163] Griffith thinks that Vṛtra ". . . is the demon of darkness and drought supposed to take the possession of the clouds causing them to obstruct the clearness of the sky and keep back the waters."[164] Keith observes, ". . . winning of the light in the Vṛtra legend, which means, no doubt, the appearance of light after the thunderstorm."[165] Jalwant K. Shastri also is of the opinion that Vṛtra is cloud.[166]

In the *ṚV* we find very few verses which indicate that Vṛtra represents cloud. Two such instances:

> *vṛtrám̐ yád indra śávasāvadhīr áhim*
> *ā́d ít sū́ryam̐ divý ārohayar dṛśé* || (I.51.4cd)
>
> O Indra, no sooner had you with your strength killed Vṛtra the Ahi than you raised the sun in the sky for all to see.
>
> *ūrdhó hý asthād ádhi antárikṣe*
> *ádhā vṛtrā́ya prá vadhám̐ jabhāra* | (II.30.3ab)
>
> He stood high in the atmospheric region and killed Vṛtra.

The two verses quoted above give the idea that Vṛtra represented the cloud. With great endeavour we may find out one or two such verses bearing the same significance. But compared to the vast mass of literature these few examples are too meagre to establish that Vṛtra was really the cloud. If we are to base on the Vedic texts for drawing our conclusion, then Indra is by no means a rain god and Vṛtra also is not cloud.

According to Benveniste, Renou (*Vṛtra et vṛθrgna*, Paris, 1934) and M. Klostermeier Vṛtra is 'resistance'. Klostermeir says, "The basic clue may be taken from the work of Benveniste and Renou on Vṛtra and V r θragna. For them, the basic meaning of Vṛtra has been presented only in the Avestan Vṛtra (neuter) means 'resistance', from the root *var-*, to resist. It is not personified. . . It is an abstract power without a human or physical basis".[167] It is an accepted truth today that Vṛtra has been formed from **var* 'to resist'. In the *ṚV*, however, Vṛtra does not all along represent an abstract idea. In many places Vṛtra has been personified and consequently has been used in masculine also.

Griswold holds the view that Vṛtra means any kind of water obstraction, "vṛtra may be interpreted, then as anything which obstructs the waters, whether drought-demon in the case of heavenly waters, or mountain barriers or snow in the case of earthly waters".[168]

Hermann Güntert thinks that the Vedic Vṛtra-myth tells us about the release of waters which were obstructed in the source and in that connection he quotes I.32.11. 'The waters were arrested and stopped by force from flowing; to search more beyond this is fully unjustified and misguiding'.[169] He adds further, 'For the Vedic Vṛtra one is to think about enclosure, arrest of waters by all means'. Our search after the truth about Vṛtra follows the objective attitude of Griswold and Hermann Güntert.

With Lommel at their head quite a good number of scholars are of the opinion that the Indra-Vṛtra myth is a cosmic event and in it lies creation myth. After Lommel Norman Brown propounded this theory and then H. Lüders, Mircea Eliade and Kuiper. And, this is now more or less a widely accepted theory.

Lommel observes, 'The obstructors may have different names, Śuṣṇa, Viśvarūpa — and then also Vṛtra — but it is always the same: a cosmic event which is repeated till the end of the world, and it is presented in an imagery, as if it took place once only, but the same imagery is presented in different names, as if they were different events'.[170] Kuiper observes the 'myth of the eternal return' more or less in the same light when he says, "Therefore the myth was not merely a tale of things that had happened long ago, nor was it a rational explanation of how this had become what it is now. The origin of the world constituted the sacred prototype of how in an endlessly repeated process, life and this world renewed themselves again and again".[171] Analysis of any other myth would lead us to the same truth, that this myth is nothing but a repetition. If we do not take into consideration the concrete facts and look into the spirit which causes the conflict in life then we would visualise the function of *tejas* and *tamas* or the activities of the three *guṇas*, i.e., *sattva, rajas* and *tamas* which are guiding every event of life.[172] All the wars of the world that have ever been fought, represent the same theory, i.e., the establishment of the cosmos by the destruction of chaos. But, each conflict has its own distinct historical and social background. Our endeavour is to find out the backdrop of such events and to analyse the character of that particular event and in case of the Indra-Vṛtra myth mainly through the study of the Vedic literature.

Neglecting the whole mass of textual matter and taking into consideration only a few of them, it would be unjustified to entitle the Indra-Vṛtra myth a creation myth. We are grateful to the scholars for bringing into limelight what was underlying the Vedic texts, but at the same time we must admit the truth that in the *ṚV* Indra is basically a war hero, a war god, and not a creator. Mircea Eliade may be quoted in this regard. "But Indra is not a creator; he promotes life and diffuses it victoriously all over the universe but he does not make it".[173]

Kuiper says, ". . . Indra's combat with dragon Vṛtra . . . represents an Aryan myth of creation".[174] In this connection he says that Vṛtra represents inert resistance and resides in the primordial hill which floats on the surface of the cosmic waters. But, according to the *ṚV* texts, the hills described therein are very much earthly and they are never described primordial and the enclosed rivers which had been released by Indra are nothing but the real earthly rivers, which are navigable and which flow into the ocean. According to the Ṛgvedic description Vṛtra is not at all inert. At his shouts heaven and earth shook (I.52.10). All the gods with their diverse modes of assistance equipped Indra for the great task of destroying Vṛtra (VI.20.2). Why would so much of preparation be necessary for killing an inert enemy. Had Vṛtra been inert then why would Indra have to fear, if he had actually killed his enemy (I.32.14). Kuiper further adds, "Indra while slaying this Vṛtra, at the same time splits the hills, which is now riveted to the bottom of the waters, and Fire and Water (Agni-Sūrya and Āpaḥ-Soma) are forced to leave undifferentiated world of inertia and to join the ranks of the heavenly Gods (RV, X.124.2, 6)". Kuiper here supports himself on two verses (X.124.2; 6) which are not directly connected either with Indra or with Vṛtra and which are rather late verses belonging to the Book X in order to establish the theory of creation myth in the story of Indra-Vṛtra he neglects the whole mass of relevant Ṛgveda texts.

Expressing our deep appreciation for Brown's very thoughtful article on the creation myth of the *ṚV*[175] we would like to discuss here a few points related to his theory of ceation myth and our subject of present study. The creation myth has hardly been delineated in the *ṚV Saṃhitā* directly but it contains substantial material out of which a creation myth can be formulated, and has been formulated by Brown. The majority of the *Ṛgveda* poets were not theorists or philosophers. They sang in natural spontaneity mainly for the sacrificial purposes; the seed of philosophy was there but not in a systematic manner. We believe, each and every people of the world, in case of even very primitive people, have their own creation myth, so also had the Ṛgvedic people in a very indistinct manner, of course. Brown says, "The Danavas bind, restrain, hold in cheque, cover over, enclose. What they bind or cover over or enclose are the Cosmic Waters and the Sun, which is the embryo of waters". According to the *Ṛgveda* texts the waters enclosed by Vṛtra and released by Indra were, however, very much earthly. When the fight between Indra and Vṛtra, or in other words the releasing of enclosed waters — the most glorified feat of Indra, was deified through eulogy uttered by the beneficiaries in praise of and in gratification towards their master then along with Indra the waters were also described cosmic (X.124.9). Then again Brown observes. "The Dānavas are patrons of inertia and destruction; in the beginning they were opposed to creation."[176] We would like to comment here that the enemies are always mischeivous, evil-doers; they are the symbolised *tamas*. And, so were the enemies of the Indra-worshippers.

We would prefer to conclude that, the *ṚV* people did not start with a creation myth. They were marvelled by the contributions towards their well-being of their leader Indra who fought with enemies and rescued his protégés.[177] The immigrant Āryans had to fight very frequently against their non-Āryan early Indian enemies in order to settle down in the new land. But, the most important service of Indra towards his people was the release of enclosed waters. This brought back life to his followers as it were. Indra broke the barriers and let the rivers flow in their original course. Description of this event has been given profusely in the *Ṛgveda* verses. The history came first out of which the myth originated, basically through eulogy. Jung's and Kerényi's view has significant bearing in this regard, "The myth of a primitive society, i.e., in its original living form, is not a mere tale told but a reality lived".[178]

H. Lüders assigns Indra-Vṛtra myth as a creation myth before concluding his discussion on this topic. After a survey of all the materials in this regard it appears to him that to the Vedic poets Indra-Vṛtra myth was a kind of creation myth and in this regạrd one is not permitted to ask, what existed before. The archaic snake had eclipsed the world. Everything was in darkness. The waters enclosed in the mountain on which the dragon was lying down or which it had gulped, was arrested. Indra killed the snake, broke the stones (i.e., the barriers), the waters flowed down as the earthly rivers flow towards ocean.[179] Lüders further adds, 'it is possible, more I cannot confirm, that the Vṛtra-myth originally dealt with enclosure of water . . .'[180] While drawing conclusions Lüders takes into full consideration the textual material unlike some others scholars. He further confirms that Indra's achievement in bringing out the world order was considered as the last success in his fight with dragon. This also corresponds to the martial activities of this god on which is fashioned his whole character.[181] What we observe here is that, our thought that Indra's Vṛtra-killing made the path for his elevation to the status of the highest god, — creating the sun, enlarging the earth and heaven and the like has bearing with Lüders' conclusions.

Hans Schmeja's approach to the Indra-Vṛtra myth appears to be somewhat very pragmatic. He believes that at the base of the myth lies real history. The historical background of this myth lies in the heroic fight between Indra and the cobra. He thinks that a group of people led by a leader in the course of their sojourn arrived at a camping place around midday. Men and cattle were all thirsty and totally exhausted. They had been looking for water in a damp place and came in collision with a cobra. Their leader killed the cobra in a life and death fight and made out the path towards water-source free, bored it at the mountain slope and the waters flowed down for his men and cattle.[182] Schmeja concludes that Indra who was originally the leader of people, the king of all, later became the highest god (*oberster Gott*).[183] After interpreting *ṚV*, I.32 he observes that at the root of a myth lies history. The historical background of the Indra-Vṛtra myth lies in the dangerous fight between the brave hero Indra and the cobra. He killed the snake, released waters towards the well-being of his people. This myth, later, has been interpreted as a creation myth or a religious theme.[184] We appreciate Schmeja's realistic attitude towards interpretation of a myth, it appears to us that he takes a very easy path to solve a very intiricate problem.

CONCLUSION

From the use of the word *vṛtrá* in the masculine and neuter and both in singular and plural it appears that originally it was an abstract term symbolising that which resists, or covers. The Avestan term *v r θragna* leads towards the conclusion that it is not an Indian term but was used, probably, by those Indo-Europeans who migrated towards south and south-east from their original home. Vṛtra, though originally an abstract term, has been considerably anthropomorphised in some verses of the *ṚV*. In this connection I.32; I.52.10; I.56.5 *et al.* may be referred to. Ahi and Vṛtra are identical. What we feel is that, Vṛtra was the leader of that group of non-Āryans who were snake-worshippers. And, here the worshipped and the worshipper are identified. Such a phenomenon is not impossible. In many mythologies of the world we read about the conflict between snake-worshippers and their enemies. In Sumer there is the myth of Bel Marduk and Tiamat, in Egypt Ra and Apope, the Jews have the myth of Jehovah and the dragon Leviathan or Behemoth or Rahab, the Hittites have the myth of Innaras and Ilunkus; in the Greek mythology one reads the story of Apollo and Python; the Persians have the myth of Ferudin and Azi Dahak, etc.[185] We believe that Indra's non-Āryan enemies whose leader has been symbolized in Vṛtra were snake-worshippers and following a normal course Ahi and Vṛtra were identified.

To the scholars, specially, Norman Brown and Kuiper the rivers released by Indra were heavenly. Our findings, as we have already shown, lead us towards the conclusion that rivers described to be released by Indra were earthly; they were navigable and they flowed down into the ocean. The current of these rivers, because of some reason — not yet known to us, was arrested. A conclusion that the previous non-Āryan settlers blocked the river waters for agricultural purposes seems to be a cogent conclusion. This caused great inconvenience to Indra and his nomadic followers. The Āryan immigrants destroyed the barriers and nullified the agricultural system, rather the economy of their enemies. But, unfortunately, as no historical or archaeological evidence is available in support of our assumption, it is wiser not to draw any such conclusion.

Releasing river waters was the highest achievement of Indra. He started to be more respected than ever and loved by his followers. To them, he was no more a human being of flesh and blood. He was now set in the process of being deified and was gradually elevated to the status of the highest god in the Vedic pantheon. Along with the deification of their leader the waters released by him were also deified. But, we must admit the fact at the same time that only once in the whole of the *ṚV* the waters have been described as divine (X.124.9b *apāṃ divyā́nām*) and that also in a late hymn. Along with the elevation of Indra to the highest position as a divinity, his enemy Vṛtra was also demoted to a very low position; he became an inhabitant of a dark hell, hidden in darkness under water — a very apt residing place for a snake. Indra on the other hand, was glorified as one who settled heaven and earth which were paralysed by Vṛtrāhi.

Thus the creation myth of the *ṚV* seems to have originated from an earthly but very important event in the life of the Vedic Āryans. But, this was a temporary phase of Indra story which takes a different and less glorious turn in later Vedic literature, in the epics and also in the Buddhist literature.

V. The Epithets

Epithets of gods throw light on different aspects of their character and achievements; they are attributes and thus give a more accurate picture of the subject, i.e., the deity. With a view to getting such an all-round picture of Indra his epithets may be analysed furitfully.

About forty-five epithets of Indra are available. A thorough discussion on Indra's epithets would demand a separate independent work. Here only a short note on those adjectives will have to suffice, especially those epithets which are used more or less exclusively for Indra.

These epithets may be classified under separate heads like his martial qualities, his magnanimity, his royal, genealogical, anthropomorphic traits and those epithets which denote his friendship with other gods.

MARTIAL

Vájra the unique and unassailable weapon, but for the existence of which the history of the Indo-Āryans would have been otherwise than what we can assemble from the Saṃhitā texts, was chiefly the weapon Indra used against his non-Āryan enemies and above all against Vṛtra. The main and immediate cause of the defeat of the non-Āryans at the hands of the Āryans, the Indra-followers, was the *vájra*. The following are the cognates associated with Indra's *vájra*: *vajrin, vajrabhṛt, vajrahasta, suvajra, adriva*. All these attributive words give more or less the same idea, i.e., 'the possessor of *vájra*'. From these epithets it becomes evident that *vájra* played a very important role in the Indra-myth in particular and in the Vedic mythology in general. With the *vájra* in hand Indra won many battles against his enemies — the Āryans and the non-Āryans and consequently he was adorned with such epithets'.[186] *Adriva* though literally means one who is possessed of stones, or hills is used in the *Ṛ V* in the sense of one who possesses the *vájra*. *Adriva* has always been used in the vocative with reference to the narration of Indra's martial feats.[187]

Indra's most glorious achievement is his slaughter of Vṛtra. Vṛtra was the strongest of his enemies. Vṛtra blocked the rivers and thus caused great inconvenience to the followers of Indra. Indra killed Vṛtra and released the waters. Indra's epithets in this regard are: *vṛtrahan, vṛtraghna, vṛtrakhāda* and *vṛtra-hantama*. All these epithets indicate that Indra killed Vṛtra.

The chief enemies of Indra were *dā́sas/dásyus* — the aboriginal Indians. In contrast with the nomadic Āryans, they were city(?) dwellers. The invading Āryans under Indra's leadership destroyed their cities, ramparts and forts. Indra's epithets in this connection are *pūrphit, pūrbhittama, purohā* and *purandara* — all signifying — the destroyer of cities.

The epithets *satrāsāha* 'conquering', *abhimātihana* 'killer of enemies', *yudhma* 'fighter' *khajakṛt* and *khajaṅkara* 'fighter' indicate Indra's warrior character. *Śuṣmintama, vṛṣantama, vṛṣan* may also be mentioned in this connection. The word *śūra* occurs around a hundred and forty times in the *Ṛ V* and of these hundred and thirty times it describes Indra and the rest Agni or Mitrāvaruṇau.

Ākhaṇḍala 'killer of enemies' occurs only once (VIII.17.12) in the *Ṛ V* and that too in connection with Indra. Sāyaṇa interprets this word as *śatrūṇām ākhaṇḍayitaḥ*.

The Āryans as riders of horse-drawn chariots were in a more advantageous position than the non-Āryans who were probably not acquainted with this types of vehicles. The *Ṛ V* tells us about the non-Āryan cities, about the rivers blocked by them but never about their horses. The Āryans, on the other hand, rode chariots drawn by horses. Their leader Indra fought many battles riding on such chariots. Indra's twin horses were tawny and called Haris. The epithets *haryaśva, harivaḥ, harivat,* — all meaning possessor of horses, then *hariṣṭhā, hariśriya*, 'settled on horses' have relevance in this regard. Of these epithets *haryaśva* is of most frequent occurrence.

Indra, the greatest Āryan warrior needed the soma drink for exhilaration. The *Ṛ V* hymns were mostly composed for sacrificial purposes; the priests sang doxologies to the deities in the sacrifice. Very often the themes of these songs were based on the reminiscence of their past life; the majority of the hymns are composed in the past tense. Indra who for the accomplishment of his martial feets needed the exhilarating soma drink was now offered soma liabation in the sacrifices. Many gods were entitled to the soma libation but Indra was the foremost of them, the one who received it in all the three pressings. Indra's epithets in this regard are *somapā, somapāvan, somapātama*. These are almost exclusively used to describe Indra. With only one exception VIII.46.26 (— a *dānastuti*) in which Vāyu has been addressed as *somapā*. Indra is the best of all soma-drinkers; *sómapāḥ somapā́vnām*. He is also *somavṛddha* 'an experienced soma-drinker': *imā́ giráḥ sompāḥ somavṛddha juṣásva indra purutámāya kāróḥ* (III.39.7). *ṛjīṣin* also meaning 'a drinker of soma, except for three occasions,[188] has all along been used with reference to Indra only.

Of the forty-five epithets of Indra twenty-six signify Indra's martial character. This reveals the most significant aspect of his character.

SUPREMACY

Śakra, śacīvaḥ, śacīpati, śatakratu, purumāya and *maghavan* are intended to be brought under this division.

Śakra has been interpreted by Sāyaṇa as *śaktimat* (I.62.4) and *śaktiyukta* (I.54.2). This adjective describes Indra's manly power. Except for three occasions,[189] *śakra* has all along qualified Indra in the *ṚV*. *Śakra* > *Śakka* becomes Indra's most familiar name in the Buddhist literature. *Śacīvaḥ* also means 'possessor of strength or skill'. But for two occasions[190] it is an epithet for Indra. *Śacīpati* may also be referred to in this connection; Indra is never Śacī's husband in the *ṚV*. It seems to be a later back formation. *Śacī* in the *ṚV* indicates skill, strength. VIII.37 consists of seven verses. Three-fourths of each verse (b, c, d) containing *śacīpati* is a refrain in this hymn. The refrain goes as follows:

> *śacīpata índra viśvābhir ūtíbhiḥ* ।
> *mā́dhyandinasya sávanasya vṛtrahan*
> *anedya píbā sómasya vajrivaḥ* ॥

Once the Aśvins have been addressed as *śacīpatī*. *Śatakratu* speaks about multifarious function of Indra. Except for once (I.112.23) in which the Aśvins have been so addressed, it is a very oft-repeated epithet of Indra. *Purumāya* (Sāyaṇa: *bahuprajña*), indicates a tendency of Indra's elevation as magnanimous in a general way. This adjective occurs five times in the *ṚV*. Once it describes the Aśvins' (I.119.1) chariot; otherwise it is Indra's epithet.

Maghavan (according to Sāyaṇa *dhanavan*) is very often used with reference to Indra. *Maghavan* speaks about Indra's greatness in a general way. Around a hundred and thirty times this epithet occurs in the *ṚV* and each time it refers to Indra. There are only three exceptions (I.58.9; 127.11; VI.15.15) in which it describes Agni.

ROYAL

We can bring *viśpati* and *carṣaṇīdhṛta* under this division. *Viśpati* has been explicated by Sāyaṇa as *marutāṃ patiḥ*. But, why do we not expose it as the 'lord of the people'? Griffith translates this word 'lord of men'. *Viśpati* occurs several times. But we cannot say that it is exclusively Indra's epithet. It is also attributed to Agni, Soma and Yama. The majority of the occurrences of the term *viśpati* are, however, Indra's adjectives. *Carṣaṇīdhṛta* (Sāyaṇa; *sarvāsāṃ prajānāṃ dhāryāitā*) 'upholder of men' is a very apt epithet for Indra. It occurs nine times in the *ṚV*. Five times it refers to Indra in the others to Mitra, Agni, Varuṇa Viśvedevāḥ or *vájra*(?).

GENEALOGICAL

The word *kauśika* occurs only once (I.10.11) in the *ṚV* and that with reference to Indra. According to Sāyaṇa it means *kuśikasya putraḥ*, Griffith also translates, 'son of Kuśika'. It does not seem appropriate to comment on the term on such slender evidence. The verse is as follows:

> *ā́ tú na indra kauśika mandasānáḥ sutáṃ piba* ।
> *návyam ā́yuḥ prá sū́ tira kṛdhí sahasrasā́m ṛ́ṣim* ॥

ANTHROPOMORPHIC

Of all the Ṛgvedic gods Indra is the most fully anthropomorphic. The epithets in this connection are *śiprin*, *hariśipra, suśipra* which may be in a general way interpreted as 'fair-jawed'. These are exclusively Indra's epithets. *Suśipra*, however, has been used once in connection with Rudra (II.33.5).

EPITHETS DENOTING FRIENDSHIP WITH OTHER GODS

The Maruts were Indra's close associates. The epithets *marutta, marutsakha, marutvat, marutstotra* are very relevant in this regard.

A survey of Indra's epithets reveals the fact that the major aspect of his character is that of a mighty warrior and he is very anthropomorphic, to an extent few other gods are.

VI. Indra and Other Gods

SŪRYA

Of all gods the relation between Indra and Sūrya appears to be the most complicated. We shall first see how their relationship has been presented in the *ṚV* verses.

Indra Generated the Sun and the Dawn

Indra whose glorious and multifarious activities are never harmed and who supported the heaven and the earth, gave birth to the sun and the dawn:

> *índrasya kárma súkṛtā purū́ṇi*
> *vratā́ni devā́ ná minanti víśve* ।
> *dādhā́ra yáḥ pṛthivī́ṃ dyā́ṃ utémām*
> *jajā́na sū́ryam uṣásaṃ sudáṃsāḥ* ।। (III.32.8)

The whole hymn (III.32) eulogises Indra and so keeping in tune with the theme of the hymn this statement that Indra created the sun and the dawn might also be eulogy, III.49.4 also narrates: *kṣapā́ṃ vastā́ janitā́ sū́ryasya.* Indra is 'the illuminator of the night and a producer of the sun'. For the visibility of all, Indra places the sun in the high heavens:

> *índro dīrghā́ya cákṣase ā́ sū́ryaṃ rohayad diví*[191] ।
> (1.7.3)

Indra gladly let the dawn and the sun glitter (in the heaven):

> *haryán uṣásam arcayaḥ sū́ryaṃ haryā́n arocayaḥ*[192] ।
> (III.44.2ab)

Indra is Above Sūrya

Indra conquered the Sun: *saṃvárgaṃ yán maghávā sū́ryaṃ jáyat* (X.43.5b) and the sun does not disregard the limits of the daily courses set by the master of the Haris (i.e., Indra):

> *díśo sū́ryo ná mināti prádiṣṭā*
> *divédive háryaśvaprasūtāḥ* । (III.30.12ab)

It becomes evident that the sun admits Indra's excellence and functions at his command. Appointed by Indra Sūrya repels the nocturnal darkness:

> *sá ít támo' vayunáṃ tatanvát*
> *sū́ryeṇa vayúnavac cakāra* । (VI.21.3ab)

Rivalry

A rivalry between Indra and Sūrya is also observed. Indra stole one of Sūrya's (chariot-)wheels;

> *sū́raś cakráṃ prá bṛhaj jātá ójasā prapitvé*
> *vā́cam aruṇó muṣāyatīśānā́ ā́ muṣāyati* ।
> (I.130.9ab)
>
> Born mighty, he (Indra) steals the sun's wheel:
> the bright lord also steals speech.[193]

Indra and Sūrya Very Close to Each Other — Identified

One also notices friendly relations between these two deities; in the same verse they are invoked together. IV.31.5; 6 address them jointly and offer them oblation.[194] They are not only very close to each other; they are also identified. IV.31.5 is dedicated to Indra. The last verse addresses Indra as Sūrya.[195] VIII.93 is an Indra-hymn. The last foot of the first verse addresses Indra as Sūrya. In the second foot of the fourth verse of the same hymn also Indra is addressed as Sūrya and in the third foot as Indra himself. Sūrya is known to all as seven-rayed; II.12.12a, however, describes Indra as *saptaraśmī* (*yáh sáptaraśmir vṛṣabhás túviṣmān*). Indra, therefore, appears to be no other god but Sūrya himself when the poet sings: *jyótir vṛṇīta támaso vijānán* (III.39.7a) 'He embraces light distinguishing it from darkness'.

We find Indra in the process of being solarized, he is being elevated from the status of a war god to a solar god and being a solar god is a matter of dignity among the divinities. Many scholars are of the opinion that Indra is a solar deity and according to some he is none other than Sūrya. The pioneers of those who hold this view are Max Müller and J.J. Meyer.[196] Herman Lommel, however, observes in Indra's character three aspects; to him Indra appears as (i) a fighter, (ii) the sun, and (iii) the storm. And, he suggests that our duty is to find out how these different facets of his character have coalesced in one god, i.e, Indra.[197]

Because of his munificence Indra, basically a war hero, had been elevated higher and higher to such an extent that he reaches the status of the highest god. His becoming a solar deity is a step towards his rise to the highest position in the Vedic pantheon. A solar deity is basically a saviour who saves his people from the vital problems of life and so did Indra. In this regard we may refer to Kṛṣṇa, Viṣṇu, Zeus, Apollo, Marduk etc.[198] who were the saviours of their followers.

Indra has been fully identified with Sūrya in some *ṚV* verses. *TS* states *ādityaḥ indraḥ* (I.7.6.3). When Indra becomes Sūrya then the apparently inexplicable relation of Indra with Sūrya becomes very easy to interpret. Indra broke the chariot of Uṣas and threw it in the river Vipāt; poor Uṣas fled, or was it that Indra had actually killed her?[199] The base of such a metaphorical description is nature — as soon as the sun rises the dawn becomes non-existent. The relationship between Indra and Sūrya was not all along friendly and harmonious. The sun worked at the behest of Indra and Indra also had a feeling of rivalry against Sūrya, but it ended up in a cordial and harmonious mood. Indra was the saviour of the Vedic Āryans; he gave them shelter, water — all the primary necessities of life; he was their saviour; he earned the supreme position in the Vedic pantheon by dint of his benevolence towards the nomadic Āryans, all the groups of which were not his staunch followers. But his supremacy had to be admitted, a good relation with him had to be established. So, we find, that the Indra-worshippers and Sūrya-worshippers came in good terms with each other. Through the worshipper only the worshipped can be known.

We shall see, more or less same was the case with reference to Indra's relation with other important gods of the Vedic pantheon.

VARUṆA

In some *ṚV* verses the nature of the relation between Indra and Varuṇa is very clearly stated. The two deities are invoked together in sacrifice and supplicated for well-being, earthly prosperity, etc. They are invoked in the battlefield to fight against the enemy. They attacked Bheda in favour of Sudās (VII.83.4). They fought for the same Sudās against the ten kings (cf. *dāśarājña*).[200]

In a few verses of the four hymns dedicated to Indra and Varuṇa, of the seventh *maṇḍala* (82-85). It is very clearly stated about the specific sphere of function of these two deities. Indra is *svarāj* and, Varuṇa is, *samrāj*:

> *samrā́d anyáḥ svarā́j anyáḥ ucyate vām* ।
> *mahā́ntāv indrāváruṇā mahā́vasū* ।। (VII.82.2)

Samrāj holds a much higher position than *svarāj*. Indra's function is to fight the enemies in the battlefield and Varuṇa's to preserve the eternal law (*vratāni*):

> *vṛtrā́ṇy anyáḥ samithéṣu jíghnate* ।
> *vratā́ny anyó 'bhí rakṣate sádā* ।। (VII.83.9ab)

One protects the people including all their divisions and the other kills irresistible foes:

> *kṛṣtī́r anyó dhāráyati práviktā* ।
> *vṛtrā́ṇy anyó apratī́ni hanti* ।। (VII.85.3cd)

Varuṇa obviously holds a higher position than Indra. Varuṇa's responsibility is to maintain *ṛta*, i.e., the eternal cosmic law, whereas Indra's duty is to protect earthly people from enemies. But, what we find as presented by sage Vasiṣṭha the seer of the seventh *maṇḍala*, is that, these two gods function in their specified spheres and never interfere in each other's affairs. To quote R.N. Dandekar, "Indra the war god suponsored the Vedic Āryans' exploits of conquest and colonization, while Varuṇa, the moral governor, blessed their efforts in connection with law and order".[201]

Varuṇa's function is of much deeper significance than Indra's. But, in everyday life Indra's service is more needed. When the basic necessities of life are fulfilled, when there is peace and harmony in life only then can one think of higher things like cosmic law (*ṛta, vrata,* etc.). Consequently, Indra occupied a much more important place in the everyday life of the Ṛgvedic Āryans who believed that through sacrifice one could attain the ends of life. Varuṇa who is a passive god and maintains an Olympian attitude towards his devotees is given his due honour, but Indra is invoked much more frequently; he is a kṣatriya god, so naturally, very active — 'a god of second order' (according Dumezil), whereas Varuṇa is the highest god with the usual passive attitude of such a god towards his devotees.

VIṢṆU

In most of the verses dedicated to Indrāviṣṇū these two deities are very conventionally invoked, mainly, to the soma libation.

The principal feature in the relation between Indra and Viṣṇu is that, Indra invokes Viṣṇu's help in killing Vṛtra who had arrested the waters. "The mother told her strong son, 'those gods are leaving you, my son'. Then Indra, intent on killing Vṛtra says, 'friend Viṣṇu, step forward (i.e., extend your help)".[202] The gods accompanied by Viṣṇu, offered all their strength to Indra when he, the soma-drinker, was about to kill Ahi who enclosed the waters.

The feats which had been attributed to Indra are now being jointly attributed to Indra and Viṣṇu. In course of our discussion on the relation between Indra and Sūrya we referred to the fact that Indra generated Sūrya and Uṣas. Now we are told that Indra and Viṣṇu together generated Sūrya, Uṣas and also Agni:

urúṃ yajñā́ya cakrathur u lokáṃ
janáyantā sū́ryam uṣā́sam agním ||[203]

Indra is famous for destroying Śambara's ninety-nine castles; according to VII.99.5, however, Indra did not accomplish this feat single-handed but assisted by Viṣṇu:

índrāviṣṇū dṛṃhitā́ḥ śámbarasya
náva púro navatíṃ ca śnathiṣṭham |

VIII.12.27ab tells us that Viṣṇu belongs to Indra:

yadā́ te[204] *víṣṇur ójasā tríṇi padā́ vicakrame* |

In the Indrāviṣṇū legend is observed an attempt of establishing a rapport between Indra and the rising god Viṣṇu.

TVAṢṬṚ

Tvaṣṭṛ made the strong *vájra* with thousand edges and hundred joints for Indra:

ádha tváṣṭā te mahá ugra vájraṃ
sahásrabhṛṣṭiṃ vavṛtat śatā́śrim |
níkāmam arámaṇasaṃ yéna návantam
áhiṃ sáṃ piṇag ṛjīṣin || (VI.17.10)

Tvaṣṭṛ also sharpens the *vájra* for Indra.[205]

We further observe a kind of enmity between Tvaṣṭṛ and Indra. Indra severed the heads of Viśvarūpa — Tvaṣṭṛ's three headed son who deemed himself invincible.[206] This relates to the *TS*-story (II.4.12.1) of Tvaṣṭṛ's surrender to Indra's magnanimity. After the son's death Tvaṣṭṛ performed a sacrifice to which he did not invite Indra, the killer of his son. Indra, however, managed to drink the soma in that sacrifice.[207] Enraged Tvaṣṭṛ planned to kill Indra but failed completely in his endeavour and had to submit to Indra's greatness. This is the sum total of the story narrated in the *TS*.[208]

How do we analyse this phenomenon? Do we observe a conflict between the Indra worshippers and Tvaṣṭṛ worshippers which quite naturally ended in the victory of Indra worshippers?

SARASVATĪ AND THE AŚVINS

The demon Namuci stole soma from Indra along with his vitality. Aśvins, the divine physicians, and Sarasvatī requested by the gods, recovered soma and consequently Indra was again restored to his original form. Indra who without soma had been totally laid down was nourished by the Aśvins like parents, and nursed by Sarasvatī with all her skill. This is the story which we can gather about the relation of Indra with the Aśvins and Sarasvatī.[209]

The Sautrāmaṇī ritual is centered around this episode.

ADITI

Indra was born from his mother Aditi's womb not in the normal way but he was born at his own will from his mother's side putting the mother's life in jeopardy.[210] He appeared to be an unwelcome child to his mother who concealed him, the possessor of great might (*avadyámiva mányamānā gúhākar índraṃ mātā́ viryéṇa nṛ́yṣṭam,* IV.18.5ab). But later in the same hymn she shows her concern for her son when she found that all the gods had left him (11). She also proudly announced the glorious feats of her son who had killed Vṛtra and released the waters (7). The *ṚV* depicts a peculiar relation of love and hate between mother Aditi and her son Indra.

PŪṢAN

A friendly relation, of course, very sparse, is observed between Indra and Pūṣan. VI.57 has been jointly dedicated to Indra and Pūṣan and they are also invoked together conventionally in some stray verses.

Pūṣan was by Indra's side at the time of the slaughter of Vṛtra (VI.57.4).

Many a god invigorated Indra in order to make him competent for killing Vṛtra. At that time Pūṣan also cooked one hundred buffaloes for him.

Only one angle that is friendly all along is reflected in the relation between these two deities.

BṚHASPATI

Indra's relation with Bṛhaspati is in the main friendly and conventional, i.e., they are invoked together to the sacrifice. Bṛhaspati also helped Indra fight Kṛṣṇa the Asura who, advanced against Indra accompanied by his ten thousand people on the bank of the river Aṃśumatī. Indra with Bṛhaspati's help killed him:

> *ádha drapsó aṃśumátyā upásthe*
> *ádhārayat tanvaṃ titviṣāṇáḥ* ।
> *víśo ádevīr abhyā́ 3carantīr*
> *bṛhaspátina yujéndraḥ sasāhe* ।। (VIII.96.15)[211]

Bṛhaspati together with Indra is also prayed for *sumati* (good mind) and *dhīḥ* (intelligence) which is Indra seldom supplicated for:

> *bṛ́haspate indra várdhataṃ naḥ*
> *sácā sā́ vāṃ sumatír bhūtv asmé* ।
> *aviṣṭáṃ dhíyo jigṛtáṃ púrandhīḥ*
> *jajastám aryó vanúṣām árātīḥ* ।। (IV.50.11)

> O Bṛhaspati, O Indra, make us prosperous, possessors of good mind, protect our intelligence, arouse prayers in us your favourite, and fight our enemies.

It was a matter of dignity on the part of the Vedic gods to be associated with Indra who held the prime position in the Vedic pantheon. So we find that the relation of Indra with many gods is very conventional and with no specific motif. In this connection the relation between Indra and Agni and Indra and Vāyu may be referred to. There are a few hymns and a few stray verses jointly dedicated to Indra and Agni (I.21; V.86; VI.59; 60; VII.93; 94 *et al.*) and to Indra and Vāyu (I.135; IV.47 *et al.*). In these hymns these pairs of gods are jointly but very mechanically invoked to the soma libation. Invoking the gods to the sacrifice was the main purpose of these hymns.

The relation between Indra and the Maruts, however, is very close; they are his associates. We avoid discussion on this point as we have already delineated on this point in the chapter, 'The Maruts'.

VII. Indra, the Highest God — Through Gratification, Through Eulogy

The nomadic Vedic Āryans reached the land of Saptasindhu under Indra's leadership. Under Indra's guidance they overcame all troubles in their long journey, reached this new land and gained a home. To them he is no more a war hero but much more than that. Their hearts, full of gratitude towards their leader, prompted them to sing song in his praise. They endowed him with the dignity of a solar god and elevated him to the status of the highest god who settles the heaven and the earth, who is like their parents, whose capabilities are beyond the reach of any other's, whose glory can be observed in every object and every being. He is the king of all; he is above all.

Vedic society was chiefly sacrifice-oriented. And, who could be a better recipient of the sacrifice than Indra, the saviour. Indra is the most fortunate deity to be invoked in the sacrifice in the largest number of hymns.

In quite a good number of hymns Indra is eulogised as the highest god. Some of them are:

> O Indra, you have spread the surface of the earth and fixed the atmospheric region upon the heaven.[212]
>
> Indra, the performer of many glorious feats, like Bhaga, placed the heaven and earth (*ródasī*) in the venerable high region of sky.[213]

According to I.63.1ab the great Indra after being born supported both the heaven and earth which had been terrified, by his strength.[214] The Vedic singer marvelled at Indra's greatness looks upon him as their parents. 'For gracious Śatakratu, thou hast ever been a Mother and Sire to us'[215] (tr. Griffith) — what other attributes would be showered on him who saved their life from threats of enemies, who gave them water, shelter and security in life. The whole hymn X.120 glorifies Indra and endows upon him the highest attributes. 'The bright Indra, the Sóma-drinker, is beyond all measure; he is unrivalled among the gods and he by his magnanimity is beyond heaven, earth and the wide-spread atmospheric region'.[216] One observes Indra's greatness in all the heavenly, earthly, living, non-living existences. 'The seven rivers bear his glory far and wide; heaven and sky and earth display his comely form. The Sun and Moon in change alternate run their course, that we, O Indra, may behold and may have faith'[217] (tr. Griffith). Indra's greatness makes the black or brown cows yield white milk.[218]

Indra is also the king of men: *rā́jā kṛṣṭīnā́m* (IV.17.5b): *éko víśvasya bhúvanasya rā́jā* (III.46.2c); he is also a *svarāj*: *svarā́d índro dáma ā́ viśvágūrtaḥ* (I.61.9c)[219] and an *ekarāj* (VIII.37.3a) and a *samrāj*:

> *bhúvaḥ samrā́ḍ índraḥ satyáyoniḥ* (IV.19.2b)[220]

Even though Indra is the highest god who places permanently the sun, the moon, the earth, the atmospheric region, the mountains, i.e., all movable and immovable objects in their respective places but the contradiction lies in the statement of the *Ṛgveda* poets that Indra performed all these miraculous deeds in the repture of Soma. Such apparently contradictory statements hint at Indra's basic nature of a warrior. It is otherwise ridiculous to accept that the highest god needs exhilaration through soma drink for performing his most glorious feats.

VIII. Indra in the Yajurveda

In the texts of the *YV* we are introduced to a different Indra than the Indra whom we have known in the *ṚV*. The Ṛgvedic Indra is highly alive with his warlike feats and munificence towards his people. Where have the heroic feats gone now! His invincible weapon the *vájra*, the Haris — the pair of horses that drew his chariot, his killing the apparently invincible enemy Vṛtra and releasing the enclosed waters bringing back life to his people. These feats exist only in name and have lost all their original significance.

We may say that the tone of the *YV* is totally different from that of the *ṚV* and consequently the nature of Indra, the principal Ṛgvedic god also changes.

Indra in the *YV*, however, maintains his high status among the gods. He enjoys his usual share of soma libation in the sacrifice. His importance in the sacrifice may be inferred from the following passage uttered during the piling of the 'Fire-altar' ceremony; in this passage Indra is mentioned in each and every *yajus* along with some other deity. Indra remains the common deity whereas the other deity is replaced by another deity:[221]

> *agniśca me indraśca me somaśca me indraśca me savitā ca me indraśca me sarasvatī ca me indraś-ca me pūṣā ca me indraśca me bṛhaspatiśca me indraśca me mitraśca me indraśca me varuṇaśca me indraśca me tvaṣṭā ca me indraś ca me dhātā ca me indraśca me viṣṇuśca me indraśca me aśvi-nau ca me idraśca me marutaśca me indraśca me viśve ca me devā indraśca me pṛthivī ca me indraśca me antarikṣaṃ ca me indraśca me*

> *dyauśca me indraśca me diśaśca me indraśca me mūrdhā ca me indraśca me prajāpatiśca me indraśca me* || (IV.7.6)

Human elements are also very much manifest in Indra in the text of the *YV*. 'When Indra had been consecrated his power and strength fell away in ten places; the gods brought it together with Sautramaṇī'.[222] (tr. by Keith, *HOS* 18, p. 457). The Sautramaṇī sacrifice is performed in honour of Indra in order to bring back his strength and ability which he was totally shorn of because of over-drinking. The divine doctors Aśvins and Sarasvatī treated him with great care and cured him.[223] The soma which Indra drank for the exhilaration he needed in order to perform his martial feats now becomes a vice. Does the Sautramaṇī sacrifice not pale Indra's glamour? He behaves like a person addicted to drink.

TS, VI.4.6.2 records that the gods observe, Indra has now become what they are (*te devā amanyatendro vā idam abhūd yad vayaṃ sma iti*). Then again Indra is said to be the youngest of the gods (*indro vai devānām anujāvaraḥ*' — *TS*, VI.6.11.2). This hints at Indra's emergence as a god from a lower status (***also see*** *TS* VII.2.10.2). Of all the gods Vāyu comes closest to Indra. They are very often invoked together and offered soma.

The majority of the Indra stories narrated in the *YV* following the Yajurvedic style of narration attributes human behaviour to him; he behaves like an earthly being who has flaws, physical weakness, a sense of insecurity, and not as one possessed of the Olympian attitude. A few of such stories are retold briefly in order to get a correct picture of the Yajurvedic Indra.

All the texts of the *YV Saṃhitā* narrate the story of Indra's killing Viśvarūpa, the three-headed son of Tvaṣṭṛ and also of Vṛtra, Viśvarūpa's successor with some variations here and there. The gist of all the versions of this story is Indra's fear of being superceded by Viśvarūpa and Vṛtra which resulted in their slaughter by him. After killing Vṛtra with great endeavour and the help of all the gods Indra became void of strength. All the gods together cured him with great care.[224]

Indra had to adopt some tricky methods in order to kill his demon-friend Namuci who in fact was superior to him in strength. Indra who had destroyed innumerable *dā́sa-/dásyu-* enemies, the very strong Vṛtra with his *vájra* in hand in direct fight, adopted foul means to kill one single demon.[225]

Śuṣṇa possessed ambrosia (*amṛta*) when the gods and the demons were at war. Many gods, were lying dead while the demons were revived through *amṛta*. Indra following a device snatched the *amṛtra* away from Śuṣṇa. Indra transformed himself into a round honey-comb and lay, in Śuṣṇa's way. Śuṣṇa opened his mouth to have the ball and immediately Indra assumed the shape of an eagle and made off with the ambrosia.[226] There are more stories about Indra in the *YV*-texts. Here we have referred to just a few of them. These stories tell us that Indra is no more a war god now; of course he still holds an important position among the gods and solves their problems. But he solves them not in a straightforward manner by directly fighting against the enemies, but he seduces through trickery and by magic.[227]

IX. Indra in the Atharvaveda

In the *AV* Indra is a representative of both the traditions — the Great and the Little. The Ṛgvedic character of Indra, like that of a war god, a killer of Vṛtra, a lover of soma etc. has been maintained in an Atharvanic way in this Veda. The upholders of Little tradition who belonged to the so-called lower level of the society and to whom belonged the *AV* primarily, endowed Atharvanic elements on his character. And this Indra of the *AV* functions in a totally different manner than the Ṛgvedic Indra. The purpose of both these types of Indra is, however, common, i.e., service to the people, generosity.

Indra is still a war god in the *AV*, but his direct fight with the enemies are not much described. III.1.5 urges Indra to confound the enemies with the blast of fire, of wind and destroy them and the next verse asks Indra to confound the enemies who are desired to be killed by the Maruts and whose eyes are to be extracted by fire and thus the enemies go back defeated.[228]

Indra's Vṛtra-killing now becomes an established glorious fact of the past; it has earned the status of an example which is often quoted as a glorious instance. The seer of VI.134.1 states, 'Let the *vájra* sever the neck, crush up the headdress of his enemy as did Śacīpati of Vṛtra'. (*vṛtrasyeva sacīpatiḥ*). X.5 is a mixture of prose and verse. The same text, as quoted below, forms the subject-matter of the first part of the first six verses of this hymn:

> *indrasyouja sthendrasya sahas sthendrasya valaṃ sthendrasya nṛmṇaṃ stha*
>
> Indra's force are ye, Indra's power are ye; Indra's strength are ye; Indra's manliness are ye; . . . (tr. by Bloomfield, Vol. II; p. 579).

The text itself and the repetition of the same text in the six consecutive verses indicate Indra's established position in the status of a god of strength.

Indra's relation with the earth has become cordial. The earth is described as *indrarṣabhā* (XII.1.6) 'whose bull is Indra' (tr. by Whitney, Vol. II; p. 662). Indra protects her with care *mahāṃstvendro rakṣaty apramādam* (18). The earth has chosen Indra and not Vṛtra (37). Louis Renou observes in this connection. "Les rapport de la Terre avec Indra śexpliquent par la notion d'Indra-roi: ils sont conformes *à* la representation indienne bien connue".[229] The Atharvavedic Indra conquers his enemy by application of net (*jāla*).

> *bṛhat te jālaṃ bṛhata indra śūra*
> *sahasrārghasya śatavīryasya* |
> *tena śataṃ sahasram ayutaṃ nyarvudaṃ*

jaghāna śakro dasyūnām abhidhāya senayā ||
(VIII.8.7)

Great, O Indra, hero (śūra), is the net of thee that art great, that art worth a thousand, that hast hundred fold heroism; therewith encircling the army of the barbarians, the mighty one slew a hundred, a thousand, ten thousand, a hundred million. (tr. by Whitney, Vol. II; p. 504).

An earthly king, a kṣatriya, can prosper, can destroy his enemies and subjugate them only when Indra is by his side — this forms the theme of IV.22. This hymn consists of seven verses. The first five verses pray for Indra's favour on behalf of a kṣatriya king. Through Indra's favour only one becomes the sole master of his people (*viś*) and subdues the enemies. Indra's favour makes him the richest of the rich. In the three verses of VI.98 Indra is described as *rājā, adhirāja*, the overlord of all the directions and as the possessor of *kṣatra*. The second verse goes as follows:

tvam indrādhirājaḥ śravasyus
tvaṃ bhūr abhibhūtir janānām |
tvaṃ daivīr viśa imā vi rājā-
yuṣmat kṣatram ajaraṃ te astu ||

O Indra, the glorious, you are the supreme king (*adhirāja*), you are the subduer of the people, you are the king of the divine subjects (*viś*), O long-lived one, let the *kṣatra*, the immortality be yours.

According to the *ṚV* Aditi is Indra's mother. *AV,* III.10.12, however, states that Ekāṣṭakā[230] underwent penance and got Indra as her son through whom the gods killed their enemies and the Śacīpati became the killer of the *dásyus*. The next verse tells us that she who was Indra's mother, and also Soma's mother, was Prajāpati's daughter. According to VIII.10.12 Indra is the son (*vatsa*) of Virāj. The theme of this hymn is eulogy of Virāj.

Whoever Indra's mother might be — Aditi or Ekāṣṭakā, but she was very fortunate. VI.38 is a prayer for brilliance. The refrain in the whole hymn is: *indraṃ yā devī subhagā jajāna sā na etu varcasā saṃvidānā*, 'the fortunate goddess that gave birth to Indra — let her come to us, in union with splendour' (tr. by Whitney, Vol. I; p. 309).

So long the subject of our discussion was the Ṛgvedic characteristics of Indra as they have been maintained in the *AV*. We would now see how the Athavarnic Indra functions.

Indra's *vájra* is desired to kill the demons (*rakṣāṃsi*: II.3.6).[231] Indra is urged to suppress with his *vájra* the evil spirits — the Sadānvas who possessed the base of the house.[232] Indra's physical strength is not sufficient enough to kill the *asura*s and he had to wear some herbal medicine in an amulet on his arm and to consume the Pātā plant in order to be strong enough to fight against the enemies.[233] Indra has a big millstone with which he destroys the worms.[234]

The Ṛgvedic Indra who used to be exhilarated by the soma-drink in profuse quantity, with the thousand-edged and hundred-jointed *vájra* killed enemies in hundreds and thousands and devastated their ramparts now requires Pātā plant as a tonic and amulet to be worn in arms in order to enable him to fight his demoniac enemies — a god who belongs to the Little Tradition.

Urged by a devotee, Indra makes a man impotent and the process of making one impotent, as described in the *AV*, VI.138.2 is very vulgar and cruel indeed:

> *klīvaṃ kṛdhy opaśinam atho kuṛīriṇaṃ kṛdhi*
> *athāsyendro grāvābhyam ubhe bhinatv āṇḍyou* ||
>
> Do thou make him impotent *opaśa*-wearing, likewise make him *kurīra*-wearing; then let Indra with the two pressing stones split both his testicles.

Indra is also prayed to for a wife. The singer of a hymn wants to have a wife in the manner following which the Aśvins obtained Sūryā, the Sun's daughter.[235]

VI.30.1 describes Indra as a god of agriculture. The gods grew barley on the bank of the river Sarasvatī for Manu. Indra was the master of the furrow and the Maruts, his associates were the ploughmen.[236]

The merchant Indra is asked to lead his merchant devotees in order to drive away their enemies causing obstruction, and shower prosperity on them.[237] Safeguarding the merchants presents a new phase in the story of Indra. This is an indicator to the fact that new occupations are now coming up as the means of livelihood for a group of people.

The Atharvanic Indra is also a serpent-killer:

> *naṣṭāsavo naṣṭāviṣā hatā indreṇa vajriṇā* ı
> *jaghānendro jaghimnā vayam* ıı (X.4.12)
>
> Of lost lives, of lost poison (are they) slain by thunderbolt-bearing Indra, Indra hath slain, we have slain. (tr. by Whitney, Vol. II; p. 577).

In spite of the fact that Indra has maintained the principal Ṛgvedic traits of his character[238] still his Atharvanic character becomes more prominent in this Saṃhitā. He comes nearer people and solves their day-to-day problems. The method of solving the problem is also simple, like application of *jāla* (net), use of magical power to confound the enemies, use of millstone, etc. The great Vṛtra-killer here in the Saṃhitā is desired to kill snakes, make somebody impotant, give the devotee a desired wife, become a ploughmen, lead the clan of merchants and also to kill snakes. N.J. Shende rightly observes: "In the popular religion of the *AV*, it will be noticed that the Ṛgvedic Indra is transformed into a deity of popular appeal to redress the private and public appeal".[239]

From the *ṚV* to the *AV* new developments in the character of Indra are observed. The upholders of the Little Tradition earn comparatively prominent position in the society. Their way of life, beliefs, concepts are different from those of the sacrificing Vedic Āryans. If Indra is to be the god of this tradition then he is to change his nature according to their concepts and beliefs and he did so, and consequently he survived. The gods who change their character according to the change in the social situations of their worshippers, survive. This reminds us of the popular saying: 'Survival of the fittest'. Indra who evolved differently in the texts of the different Saṃhitās — a war god, a solar god, the highest god in the *ṚV*, a god full of trickery in the *YV* and Atharvanic in the *AV* survives throughout the Vedic period and also in the later literature following the same process. This phenomeon of change in the character of a god hints at his euhemeristic nature also. The gods of nature like Sūrya, Agni, Uṣas, Vāyu and others do not evolve in the like manner.

X. Opinions of Scholars on the Identity of Indra

Starting from Edward Perry (1882) and ending with Hans Schmeja (1987) scholars have expressed various opinions on the identity of Indra, the most popular, the most important and the most complicated god of the Vedic Āryans. Some find in his character pure elements of an atmospheric or a war or those of the highest god, others a mixture of different elements like those of a war and the highest, or of a war and atmospheric, or of fertility, war and the highest god; to some he is a solar so a saviour god, again to others a lunar, yet to some others despite all his greatness he cannot be assigned as the creator. Opinions of many of these scholars have already been discussed while we dealt with the Indra-Vṛtra problem — the central theme, specially, of the *ṚV* and the other Saṃhitās in general.

The principal upholders of the rain-, storm-god theory are Perry, Macdonell, Oldenberg, Schlegel and Keith. Perry says, "I consider that Indra belongs to not among the deities of the sky, but among, or rather at the head of those of the air — a distinction which we shall find a very important one when Indra mythology is concerned".[240] Then again, Perry concludes that he considers Roth's opinion which sees in Indra the head of the atmospheric god and also the national and the favourite god of Indo-Āryan tribes, a type of heroic power used for noble ends, as correct.[241] Two different characters, i.e., that of an atmospheric god and of a heroic god, i.e., the possessor of earthly qualities, have been attributed to Indra. But, Perry does not make an attempt to show how or what situations led the atmospheric god to possess elements of a heroic god also. Same may be said about Macdonell who also sees in Indra primarily a thunder god and then a god of battle of the Āryans.[242] Keith sees in Indra a storm god.[243] Oldenberg's opinion in this regard has already been discussed by us. It might be quite natural that these scholars have in their mind the primitive rain-god theory which was a common belief both to Semitic and Indo-European peoples.[244] But, the Ṛgvedic Āryans as we know them from the texts were not much concerned with rains of fertility, rather their main occupation was with fighting the enemies and settling in the new land under Indra's leadership. Later, along with the change in the situations of life they felt the need for a fertility god and so Indra emerged in the later literature as a rain/fertility god.

Bloomfield classifies the Vedic gods in three divisions — transparent, translucent and opaque. He includes Indra in the second group, i.e., according to him Indra is a translucent god who refuses to reveal his origin. He observes, "Indra's character is translucent, that is, we can no longer define his origin with certainly; but there is no doubt that he originated somewhere in the visible nature". He also considers Indra's origin as prehistoric.[245]

Schlegel thinks that Indra was originally a storm god who dislodged an earlier storm god.[246] This is a presumption of Schlegel. In the *Ṛgveda*, however, Parjanya and also the Maruts are the gods of rain and storm. Sudarshan Kumar Sharma sees in Indra the cloud and observes, Indra thus means, ". . . one having drops of water, i.e., *megha* . . . The etymology of Indra according to my interpretation could be *indavo rāyo yasya saḥ*, i.e., 'that which has its riches for the Soma drops or the drops of water which automatically gives 'Indra' — the variant sense of cloud".[247] On Indra's identity Veronica Ions says, "Indra is a storm god, wielder of thunderbolt, *vájra*, a weapon which he carries in his right hand".[248] Storm god is not the sole identity of Indra. We rather undermine Indra by introducing him as a storm god. Indra is much more than that.

According to A. Bergaigne, Adolf Kaegi, Louis Renou and Helmut Glasenapp Indra is a war hero, a protector of the fighting Āryans. Bergaigne "calls him a god of battle. . ."[249] To Kaegi also "Indra is thus a god of battle, the ideal of an everfighting, and never conquered hero, and, therefore the favourite of the race fighting for new homes and rich herds".[250] Louis Renou puts the highest importance on the warrior aspect of Indra's character when he says, "The Veda would have been entirely different in form if the battle-myths connected with Indra had not been introduced into it".[251] Glasenapp who sees in Indra a war god, observes, "In the *ṚV* Indra is the god of strength whose influence is manifest all over (i.e., in the Veda) where his mighty strength gets expression. He is therefore praised as a ideal hero by the fighting Āryans and is invoked as a protector against enemies in distress and danger, they glorify him as the protector against the enemies and as a liberal giver of cows and wealth".[252] It is true that Indra in the *ṚV*, was mainly a war god, a god of battle. But, the *ṚV* singers attribute to him with the qualities of the highest god also whose magnanimity is beyond the reach of anybody. In order to get the correct picture of a god we are to take into consideration all the phases of his character.

To Ragozin Indra's character was a puzzle. He says, "The personality of Indra though sufficiently transparent, still has enough of complexity in its duality (storm god and war god) to suggest evolution from simpler subject-matter to a more directly naturalistic conception".[253] To Ragozin Indra is more a "war god than a storm god". To Hermann Goetz Indra is mainly a storm god but he is aware of the warrior aspect of his nature also.[254]

Roth-Böhtlingk, Geldner, Barnett, Charpentier think that Indra was primarily a war god and then he had been raised to the status of the highest god for a period. *St. Petersburg Dictionary* introduces Indra as occupying the highest position among the gods of the atmospheric region but in conclusion it observes, "he originally was not the highest god, but the national and popular god of the Aryan Indians — a model of the executor of all the heroic feats needed in order to fulfill all kinds of noble purposes and gradually rising towards the highest position dislodging Varuṇa".[255] Geldner thinks, Indra's character has two aspects — a sky-god and world-creator on the one hand and a perfect enemy-killer on earth on the other. And, these two phases of character together give the true picture of this god. Barnett observes, "Very likely he was a chieftain on earth. The story of his great deeds so fascinated the imagination of men that they worshipped his memory and at last raised him to the rank of a cheif god".[256] Charpentier to whom Barnett's opinion is of deep significance, sees in Indra first a war hero whose heroic feats against the primitive Indians have been sung by the Vedic poets who later gave him the status of a war god who gradually dislodged the previous high gods like Mitra and Varuṇa and became the highest god in Vedic pantneon. The existence of two different phases of Indra's character that had been already observed by Roth-Böhtlingk and Geldner have been synchronized by Charpentier.[257] We have already discussed the opinion of the scholars who think that Indra is Sūrya or a solar deity.[258] We have nothing against saying that Indra is a solar deity. But this also is to be admitted at the same time that this is only a partial introduction of Indra. Indra has many other phases in his character. According to V.A. Gadgil, Indra is the representative of *tejas*, "Indra can be properly understood in view of the fact that the Sunlight (a form of *tejas* represented by Indra) possesses a remarkable degree of marvellous health giving properties and that plants, herbs, waters and the storms are contributory causes in this mysterious phenomenon of nature".[259] Indra in the *ṚV* is hardly a healing deity, neither is he a god who is much concerned about the moral or ethical aspects of his worshippers which in fact is Varuṇa's domain of function.

E.N. Ghosh, P.C. Sen Gupta, A.J. Karandikar identify Indra with the summer solstice.[260] By drawing such a conclusion we neglect the whole mass of Indra-literature of the *ṚV* and support ourselves on just a few of them which would fail to give a complete picture of the god.

Ernst Siecke recognises the lunar identity of Indra in its origin.[261] He thinks that the influence of the moon was stronger than that of the sun on the primitive people. Other phases of his character like those of a storm god, war god, a god who grants all manners of well-being developed later. Siecke also identified the Maruts, Indra's associates, with the stars.[262] He, like many scholars, sees many points of similarities between Indra and Herakles and is of the opinion that Herakles was originally a lunar deity who was later transformed into a solar god.[263] Siecke has logic in his thought but at the same time his argument is too hypothetical.

According to L. von Schroeder Indra is the Indian counterpart of Greek Hercules. They have many common points of similarity in their action. Some of them are: Hercules killed Hydra and Indra Ahi — both were the water snakes;[264] both Indra and Hercules were rain-bringers;[265] Hercules drank wine after killing Hydra and Indra drank soma;[266] Hercules killed three-bodied Geryones and Indra the three-headed Viśvarūpa[267] and so on. We would observe in this regard that both Indra and Hercules were culture heroes and so, quite naturally, they have some points of resemblance. Such similarities could be found among other mythologies of the world also. Such findings would not, however, help in obtaining an insight into the real nature of a particular god.[268] We have to see each god in his own perspective primarily, to get a true picture of him.

Many scholars belong to the historical school and describe Indra basically as a human hero, the chief of the Āryan invaders towards Saptasindhu. Names of R.N. Dandekar, Yajnik S. Natvarlal, Kalyan Ganguly, Sukumari Bhattacharji, B.H. Kapadia, Sudha Rastogi, Klaus Mylius, Hans Schmeja can be mentioned in this regard. Dandekar observes, "The Vedic God Indra must . . . have originally been a human hero, who possessing great virile power, led his Aryan followers from victory to victory in the numerous battles in which the latter must have been kept engaged by their many foes".[269] Yajnik S. Natvarlal believes that Indra was a human hero and the word *indra* must have been a title, ". . . Indra was a human hero. His various names, his friendship with various persons at various times, however, indicate that Indra was not one. Indra must have been a title . . ."[270] Sukumari Bhattacharji believes that Indra was a solar culture hero originally[271] and later was raised to the status of the highest god; she further believes that Indra was a title and refers to the *Rāmāyaṇa,* VII.30.35 and the *Brahma-vaivarta Purāṇa, Kṛṣṇa-janmakhaṇḍa,* XLVII; 50-161 with reference to this.[272] She observes about Indra's identity, "Indra's power lies in his being a culture hero of the Vedic Aryans. They needed a god in whom they could project their aspirations and experiences, a god who symbolized their national dreams. . . But simultaneously with his mundane career he symbolizes the cosmic creator. The resultant figure is 'a most complex personality. . . .' "[273] Kalyan Ganguly, a believer in the human origin of Indra observes, "Of all the gods of the *ṚV* Indra seems to have been endowed with the utmost of human qualities and his anthropomorphism does not appear to have proceeded from phenonmenal abstractions and through theriomorphism. . ."[274] B.H. Kapadia thinks that the Indra-Vṛtra fight represents no natural phenomenon but it was an actual fight. ". . . the entire hymn (I.32) which deals with the Vṛtra-fight has nothing in it which describes climatic phenomenon".[275] Sudha Rastogi also considers that Indra was not originally a divine being he had been gradually elevated to the status of the god-hood.[276] Klaus Mylius introduces Indra in the glossar which he attaches to his translation of a few Vedic hymns and passages, "Indra the divine king of the Vedic pantheon, divine personification of the fights of the Indo-Aryan against the pre-Aryan population . . ."[277] Hans Schmeja's opinion, broadly on the same line, has been discussed already under "Indra-Vṛtra". The scholars belonging to the historical school follow different courses in getting their common conclusion, i.e., the euhemeristic origin of Indra; the paths have been different but the destination is the same. Among these scholars Natavarlal S. Yajnik, B.H. Kapadia, Kalyan Ganguly overlook the solar aspect of Indra's character which forms a big gap and obstructs in reaching the real nature of Indra and also negligence would be shown towards those parts of Vedic texts which describe Indra as a solar god. Indra was not Sūrya but he was solarized.[278] A solar god is also fertility god.

Different aspects — fertility, solar, war, cosmogonic — of Indra's character have been revealed to Gonda during his life-long Vedic studies. He recognises in Indra a fertility god in pre-Vedic period which aspect again prevailed after the most glorious period of Indra myth was over. He says, "It may now be considered a matter of common knowledge that Indra who in the belief of the Vedic man represented force, energy and vitality in nature, was already at an early period regarded as being intimately connected with atmospheric phenomena and with various forms of fertility and vegetative life. In the religious undercurrents this trait of his character persisted after he had lost the high position accorded to him in former times".[279] Then again the warrior Indra was the most prominent in his mind when he says, "The Vedic Indra is a demon-slayer, a helper, a friend and deliverer of his worshippers. Hence he is the god of battle par excellence, and an irresistable warrior, whose mighty arm gains innumerable victories".[280] He recognises in Indra a god of second order (cf. Dumezil).[281] Gonda also refers to the present theory on the Indra mythology which is cosmic when he says in the introduction to his *The Indra hymns of the Ṛgveda*. Nowa-days, the prevalent views of Indra mythology are as follows, "The structure of the Indra myth is essentially cosmogonic, or rather demiurgic because there existed already a world before his birth". He, however, identifies the Indra myth as multivalent.[282] Gonda has studied the different facets of Indra's character but has not harmonized them.

Since very early days some scholars have seen Indra as the highest god. A. Barth notices the double aspects in Indra's character, ". . . the king of heaven and the national god of the Aryans; he gives victory to his people and is always ready to take in hand the cause of servants".[283] We would only like to add here that the 'national god' had been elevated to the status of 'the king of heaven' by the beneficiaries through eulogy expressed in deep gratification towards their benefactor. Václav Machek sees Indra as the highest and the strongest god in the Vedic mythology. He also adds that Indra has no exact counterpart among other branches of the Indo-European family.[284] He, however, concludes that there is nothing to prevent us from identifying Indra with Dīeus.[285] To identify Indra as the highest god of the Vedic Āryans and to unify him with Dīeus will be equal to evade the truth. Comparatively, only a very small number of *Ṛ V* hymns depict Indra as the highest god whereas the majority of them speak about his martial feats.

Kuiper, Lüders, Norman Brown see in the Indra-Vṛtra myth mainly the cosmogonic aspect of the character and consequently the first and foremost trait of Indra's nature to them is that of the highest god who regulates the world order. Of the many-sided Indra mythology this is only one phase and rather the last phase, and a temporary one. We restrain ourselves from discussion on the opinion of these scholars in order to avoid repetition.[286]

Conclusion

Indra the powerful leader of his nomadic Āryan followers was a culture hero. Like many other culture heroes, like Kṛṣṇa, Jesus Christ etc., his birth was abnormal. He was born from his mother's side and did not follow the usual path. The Āryans who were on their way towards the land of Saptasindhu had to face many hindrances on their way in search of a new land, a new home. Quite naturally, they had been resisted by the earlier inhabitants, namely, *dā́sa/dásyu*s. At Indra's leadership they fought many battles and conquered the people, the land. The warrior Indra used his invincible weapon *vájra* against the enemies, drank soma profusely became exhilarated and went to fight riding on his chariot drawn by the Haris — the two tawny horses. He was a devastator of cities (*purundara*), a killer of enemies (*vṛtrahan*). The *ṚV* contains many verses the theme of which is Indra's direct fight against the enemies. He killed Vṛtra, the strongest of his enemies and released the enclosed waters — releasing waters is the motif of a culture hero. This achievement of Indra, i.e., releasing waters was a turning point in the Indra mythology. To the beneficaries of this unique achievement he remained no more a leader — a chieftain. They were amazed at his supernatural capabilities and looked upon him as a god — a god of war. In the sacrifice-oriented society of the Vedic Āryans Indra had the right to soma libations in all the three pressings. He was a saviour to his people. A saviour god is normally a solar god. Indra was solarized and there lies dignity in being solarized. A solar deity is normally a god of fertility. To many scholars Indra is a fertility god. They who were his followers, became now his worshippers, his devotees. They through Vedic songs showered all kinds of heroic, noble, divine attributes on him. He is the most fortunate deity to be invoked in the maximum number of Ṛgvedic hymns. In course of the evolution of his character he emerged as the highest god, became cosmogonic — a sustainer of the world order. Every object of the universe bears his glory. He is above all. All the aspects of Indra's character like those of a culture hero, a war god, a solar deity, so consequently, a god of fecundity consummate him as the highest god in an evolutionary process. These different facets are complementary to each other and are not alineated and they together contribute to the formation of Indra's character in its entirety. Unfortunately, the most glorious phase of Indra mythology was a temporary one. Even in the *TS*, in the *AV* Indra is not so vibrant with his manliness, with his munificence and above all with his cosmic qualities. Indra in the post-Vedic age, in the epics and Buddhist literature is shorn of all his glamour, he is then a colourless titular head of the pantheon yielding place to some other deities — Viṣṇu or Śiva — whose service was felt more urgent by the people of the time, and whose prime occupation now turned to agriculture.

Notes and References

1. Herman Lommel *Die alten Arier*, Frankfurt am Main, 1935, p. 80: "Indra ist der meistgefeierte, der wichtigste Gott der Veda. Er ist der ausgeprägste Gestalt unter den altindischen Göttern. Sein Wesen ist am vielseitigsten und deshalb am schwersten zu verstehen. Wer es aber verstanden hätte der hätte den Veda zum grössten Teil verstanden".
2. Volker Moller is the author of the article "Die Mythologie der vedischen Religion und Hinduismus", in *Götter und Mythen des indischen Subkontinents*, ed. by Hans Wilhelm Haussig, Stuttgart, 1984.
3. *Nirukta*, X.8, ed. by Laksman Sarup, Part III, Motilal Banarsidass, (1st edn. 1926) reprint 1967, pp. 175-76.
4. *Ibid.*, part III, p. 176.
5. *Ibid.*, part II, p. 156.
6. *Ibid.*, part II, p. 176.
7. *Ibid.*, part II, p. 156.
8. *Bṛhaddevatā*, 11.6; ed. & tr. by A.A. Macdonell, *HOS*, Vol. V., p. 12.
9. *Ibid.*, II.35, p. 14.
10. *Ibid.*, V, 146-8, pp. 61-62.
11. *Ibid.*, II. 6, p. 12.
12. *St. Petersburg Dictionary*, Vol. I, p. 804.
13. *Le Monde Oriental*, Vol. V, XXV, 1-3, 1931, Leipzig, Otto Harrassowitz, pp. 1-2: "Dazu bemerkte Jacobi schon längst mit Recht, man könne von einer Wurzel *in-* nicht sprechen, da nur Präsenbildungen *i-na, i-nu,* und *i-nv-a* alle natürtich von einer Wurzel *i-* vorliegen".
14. Opinions of Benfey, Max Müller, Muir, Macdonell, Foy, Kirste, Grassmann, Bezzenberger and Jacobi have been collected from Charpentier's article mentioned above.
15. *Op. cit.*, p. 2.
16. *Op. cit.*, p. 2.
17. *Op. cit.*, p. 3.
18. *Op. cit.*, pp. 4-5.
19. Already referred to.
20. *Op. cit.*, p. 5.

21. ***See*** Hermann Güntert: *Der arische Weltkönig and Heiland,* Heale (Saale) 1923, pp. 13-14.
22. R.N. Dandekar: *Vedic Mythological Tracts*, Delhi, 1979, p. 186.
23. Alfred Hillebrandt: *Vedische Mythologie*, II, Breslau, 1902, p. 148.
24. For Benveiste's view A.B. Keith's "Indra and Vṛtra" (*Indian Culture*, Vol. I, 1934-35) has been consulted.
25. *Op. cit.*, p. 463.

    Benveiste's opinion suggests that the different peoples of the archaic world — the Hittites, the Mittannis, the Sumerians, the Indo-Europeans, etc. were not estranged from each other but, on the contrary, there was inter-trafficking between these peoples.

    One is, however, bound to be surprised and simultaneously tempted to be drawn towards the conclusion that the Hittite Innar and Indian Indra have linguistically a common base. But, one is definitely barred from drawing such a conclusion as so far no linguistic evidence has been found in its favour. We quote below Annalies Kammenhuber who while classifying different gods related to the Hittite innarauutar = Kalatar observes: "Der indische Gott Indra (*RHA*, 46.118) ist mit gutem Recht aus der Diskussion verbannt worden. *Münchener Studium zur Sprachwissenchaft*, Heft 3, 1953, 1958, p. 28. 'The Indian god Indra (*RHA*, 46.118) has been rightly excluded from this disscusion". ***Also see*** Edward Dietz Otto: *Reallexikon der Assyriologie und Vorderasiatischen Archäologie*, Vol. V., New York, Berlin, 1976-80, p. 96. From Jaan Puhvel's *Hittite Etymological Dictionary*, (Vol. I, Mouton Publishers, Berlin, New York, Amsterdam, 1984) is shown below the similarity of meaning and sound effect between Hittite *Innar* in its different derivatives and Indian Indra:

    Innarā — "explicitly, willfully, purposely, on one's own (account), of one's own accord. . .," p. 366.

    In(n)arah(h) — "make strong", "strengthen . . .", p. 367.

    Innarai- (?) or *innarwai* (?) "be strong . . .", p. 367.

    Innarauwah(h) "make strong, strengthen. . . .", p. 370.

    Innarwant seems to mean 'Sexually potent. . .", p. 372.
26. L.A. Waddel, *The Makers of Civilisation in Race and History,* S. Chand & Co., 1968, p. 79.
27. Mayrhofer, *Kurzgefasstes etymologisches Wörterbuch des Altindischen*, Band I, Heidelberg, 1956, p. 88. "Because 'indriya' and 'indra' signify 'the leader', 'the foremost' it is likely that Índraḥ is an old adjective meaning 'strong, powerful' and so its classification with Serbocroat, *jedar* full, powerful, strong (aksl, **jedri* *indro-s?) is recommended".
28. *Op. cit.*, p. 112.
29. Not only in the Vedic language, this is rather a common linguistic phenomenon, observed long before by Leonard Bloomfield in his work

Lnaguage (George Allen & Unwin Ltd., London, 1957 [1st edn., 1933]). He observes in the chapter entitled "Types of Phonetic Change" on p. 383: "In a good many languages we find an intermediate consonant arising in a cluster. A Primitive Indo-European (*sr*) appears as (*str*) in Germanic and in Slavic; thus Primitive Indo-European *(*srow-*) (compare Sanskrit [*sravati*] 'it flows') is reflected in Primitive Germanic *[*Strawmaz*] 'stream', old Norse (*strawmrl*), Old English (stream), and in old Bulgarian (*struja*) 'stream'. English, at more than one time has inserted a (*d*) in the groups of (*nr, nl*) and a (*b*) in the groups (*mr, ml*): Old English (*θunrian*) (*to*) *thunder*; Old English (*'alre*) (accusative case) *alder*".

30. ***See***, for example, the following:

OIA	*NIA*
vānara	*vāndara* (Hindi and many other Indian languages)
su-nara	*sundara* (Hindi and many other Indian languages)
tāmra	(**tāmbra*) *tāmbda* (Marathi)
āmla	(**āmbḍa*) *āmbaṭ* (Marathi)

31. ***See*** *St. Petersburg Dictionary:* "मन्त्र (von मन्)"; "तन्त्र (von तन्)"; "यन्त्र (von यन्)".

32. S.D. Laddu, (Bhandarkar Oriental Research Institute Pune), also has been thinking of for long, he tells me, along exactly the same lines.

33. I.53.2; 149.1; 164.21; II.20.2; VII.20.5; 36, 2; VIII.2.35; 33.5; X.3.1; 26.7; 44.4; 50.2; 115.2.

    I.149.1; 155.4; IX.77.4; X.23.6.

    III.49.2; X.120.6.

34. 'Whom the self-ruler, the best of men, riding Haris, nobody supersedes in the battlefield, the highest Lord accompanied by (his) fierce (people), traverses long distance and devastates the life of his enemy (*dásyu*)'.

35. Kṛṣṇa, we presume, was initially so-called because of his dark skin and later that became his name.

36. Most of the non-Āryan and also some of the Āryan enemies will be discussed in the section 'Indra's protégés'.

37. IV.20.6b:
    índraḥ sanā́d evá sáhase jātá ugráḥ ।

38. VII.20.5ab:
    vṛ́ṣā jajāna vṛ́ṣaṇaṃ ráṇāya
    táṃ u cin nā́rī náryaṃ sasūva ।

39. VIII.63.6ab:
    índre víśvāni vīryā̀ kṛtā́ni kártvāni ca ।

40. VIII.66.9ab:
    kád ū nú asyā́kṛtam
    índrasyāsti páuṃsyam ।

41. **See** *ṚV*: *vṛtrahátyena*, VIII.24.2; *vṛtrahátyāya*, V.29.7; VI.18.9; VIII.89.5; X.55.7; *vṛtrahátye*, I.52.4; 109.5; IV.19.1; 24.2; VI.23.2; 25.1; 8; 36.2; 47.2; VII.19.10; VIII.63.12; X.22.10; 48.8; *vṛtrahátyeṣu*, I.53.6; VII.1.10; 19.3; 32.15; X.65.2.

42. *Ibid.*, *ahihátyāya*, I.130.4; *ahihátye*, I.61.8; 165.6; III.32.12; 47.4.

43. *Ibid.*, *dasyuhátyāya*, I.51.6; 103.4; X.95.7, *dasyuhátye*, X.99.7; 105.11; *dasyuhátyeṣu*, I.51.5.

44. *Ibid.*, *śaṁbarahátye*, 1.112.14.

45. *Ibid.*, *śuṣṇahátyeṣu*, I.51.6.

46. Ludo Rocher, "*Vṛtrám Avadhīt Índraḥ*
Notes on the use of *vadh* in the *Ṛgveda*"

Wiener Zeitschrift für die Kunde Südasiens und Archiv für indische Philosophie, Vienna, 19, 1975, pp. 8-10.

47. *ṚV*, 1.51.5c:
tvám̐ píပpror nṛmaṇaḥ prā́rujaḥ púraḥ ।

48. *Ibid.*, I.53.8c:
tvám̐ śatā́ váṅgṛdasyābhinat púraḥ ।

49. *Ibid.*, I.63.7ab:
tvám̐ ha tyád indra saptá yúdhyan
púro vajrin purukútsāya dardaḥ ।

50. *Ibid.*, I.174.2:
dáno viśá indra mṛdhrávācaḥ
saptá yát púraḥ śárma śā́radīr dant ।
ṛṇór apó anavadyā́rṇā yū́ne
vṛtrám̐ purukútsāya randhīḥ ।।

Same is the theme of VI.20.10c.

The word *śā́radīḥ* occurs three times in the *ṚV* (I.131.4; I.174.2; VI.20.10). In I.131.4 it has been used as an adjective to *púraḥ*. And, on the other two occasions it refers to the seven ramparts which were destroyed by Indra in favour of his devotee, Purukutsa. Sāyaṇa interprets *śā́radīh* in I.174.2 as *pratyagrāḥ* । *yadvā́* । *etat saṃvatsaralakṣakaḥ* । *saṃvatsaraparyantaṃ dṛḍhīkṛtāḥ api* । He interprets *śā́radīḥ* under I.131.4 more or less in the same light. *śā́radīḥ* occurring in VI.20.10 has been exposed by Sāyaṇa as *etannāmako'suraḥ* ।

Griffith translates "autumn forts" and adds in n. 2. "Autmn forts: probably strongholds on high ground occupied in the rainy season". (*The Hymns of the Ṛgveda*, p. 120).

Wilhelm Rau after discussing the opinions of H. Zimmer who was supported by Macdonell adds: 'that which offers shelter in autumn (against overflowing rivers) and that of O. Böhtlingk and Roth, 'rich in year', 'old' and referring to Geldner who simply leaves to the choice to his readers, observes, '. . . I rather take *śā́radīḥ purā́ḥ* as *purā́ḥ* constructed in autumn against possible attacks, in other words as provisional defences to be repaired or rebuilt every autumn after the floods of rainy season'.

The Meaning of Púr in Vedic Literature, Munich, 1976, p. 37.

Rau's opinion tallies with Sāyaṇa's. His opinion is very rational. The autumn is the season even today, specially, in rural India, for any kind outdoor construction. But our question is, why the same was not said in connection with the other forts — those of Śambara, Pipru, Vaṅgṛda and others, who were also master of forts.

Our conjecture is, Śarat like Śambara, Pipru, Vaṅgṛda and Śuṣṇa is a proper name. The only difference is that it has been used in its adjective form — *śā́radī*.

51. *ṚV*, I.103.3ab:
sá jātū́bharmā śraddádhāna ójaḥ ।
púro bibhindán acarad ví dā́siḥ ।।

52. *Ibid.*, I.53.7ab:
yudhā́ yúdham úpa gha íd eṣi dhrṣṇuyā́ ।
purā́ púraṃ sámidáṃ haṃsi ójasā ।।

53. *Ibid.*, II.20.8cd:
práti yád asya vájraṃ bāhvóḥ dhúr ।
hatvī́ dásyūn púra ā́yasīr ní tārīt ।।

54. *áyas* has been accepted as copper by the majority of the present-day scholars.

Max Müller, however, takes *áyas* for iron: "Whatever the Old Aryan form may have been, it is clear that Skt. *ayas*, Lat. *ahes*, in *aheneus* and even the contracted from *aes, aeres* — Goth. *ais,* Old High German *er*, and English iron are names of cast in the same mould, and only slightly corroded even now by the rust of so many centuries". *Chips from a German Workshop*, Vol. II. "Comparative Mythology". London, 1856, p. 45.

55. *ṚV.*, I.121.12cd:
yáṃ te kāvyá uśánā mandínaṃ dād ।
vṛtrahánaṃ pā́ryaṃ tatakṣa vájram ।।

56. *Ibid.*, I.57.2d: *índrasya vájraḥ śnáthitā hiraṇyáyaḥ* ।
also see, VIII.68.3; X.23.3.

57. *Ibid.*, VIII, 96.3a. : *índrasya vájra āÿasó nímiślaḥ*
also see I.52.8c; 80.12; X.48.3. *et al.*

58. *Ibid.*, VIII.76.2:
ayám índro marútsakhā
ví vṛtrásyābhinat śíraḥ ।
vájreṇa śatáparvaṇā ।।
also see, VIII.89.3.

59. *ṚV*. II.11.4:
śubhrám nú te śúṣmam vardháyantaḥ ।
śubhrám vájram bāhvóḥ dádhānāḥ ।
śubhrás tvám indra vāvṛdhānó asmé
dā́sīr víśaḥ sū́ryeṇa sahyāḥ ॥

A play on the word *śubhra* is observed in this verse.

60. A few of these adjectives, however, have been used in the *ṚV* once or twice in connection with gods other than Indra also. For example, *vajrahastā* (I.109.8a) is addressed to Indrāgnī, *vajríṇaḥ* (VIII.7.32a) qualifies the Maruts. Such a phenomenon indicates that the significance of these terms is now moving from the particular towards the more general.

61. Wilhelm Rau: *Metalle und Metallgeräte im vedischen Indien*, Abhandlung der Geistes-und sozialwissenschaftlichen Klasse, Jahrgang, 1973, Nr. 8 Mainz, p. 37:

"Das Wort *vájra* m. früher durch 'Donnerkeil' (thunderbolt, foudre), heute gewöhnlich durch keule (die als Wurfgeschoss und als Schlagwaffe dienen kann, = mace, massue) übersetzt, bezeichnet in unserem Texten zwar meist das Kampfgerät eines Gottes, vor allem Indras, gelegentlich jedoch ebensowohl ein solches, das klärlich unter Menschen Verwendung fand. Wenigstens ein Teil des *vájra* war kupfern, denn seine Farbe wird als rötlichbraun beschrieben".

62. ***See*** *ibid.*, p. 45: "Müssen wir doch mit der Möglichket rechnen dass das Wort *vájra* seine Vorfahren im Laufe der zeit Badeutung wechselten, von der einen Wurfwaffe auf die andere übertragen wurden, vor allem wenn sich das Material änderte, aus dem man sie herstellte, und damit auch die From sich wandelte".

63. Tapan Kr. Das Gupta: *Der Vájra eine Vedische Waffe*, Hamburg, 1975, p. 66. "Obwohl in den meisten Fällen wenn in vedischen Texten vom *vájra* die Rede ist, damit die Waffe des Gottes Indra schlechtin gemeint ist, d.h. obwohl dieses Wort vor allem im Kontext des Mythos belegt ist, sind die Angaben über diesen *vájra* so genau so detalliert und in so hohem masse frel von Widersprüchen, dass kein ernsthafter Zweifel daran aufkommen kann, dass die vedischen Dichter dabei einen konkreten Gegenstand vor Augen hatten".

Interested readers may also consult B. Schlerath's "Vedisch *vájra* — die Keule des Indra *Orbis* 24(2), 1975, pp. 493-518., Schlerath's article is initially a rejoinder to Rau's thesis put forward in his work *Metalle und Metallgeräte im* vedischen *Indien.*

Wilhelm Rau rejects Schlerath's rejoinder in a small article, "Vedisch *vájra* die Keule des Indra" *Orbis* 25(2), 1976, pp. 376-78.

64. Today also the *vájra* to us is thunderbolt. Mention may be made of in this

connection of some other cognates of this word used in many Indian languages — *vajrapāt, vajrāghāt* (stroke of lightning), *vajranād* (a thunderous voice), *vajrāgni* (lightning), *vajranirghosh* (roar of thunder). A Tagore-song on rainy season comes to our mind: *bajramānik diye gānthā āshār tomār mālā*, 'O ashar (a rainy month), your garland is strung with the *varja* — jewels'.

Gitabitan, Vol. II, Vishvabharati Granthalaya, Calcutta, 1957, p. 450.

65. ***See*** *ṚV*, I.8.7ab:
yáḥ kukṣíḥ somapātamaḥ
samudrá iva pínvate
also see II.14.10ab; 11; IV.46.3cd, *et al.*

66. *Ibid.*, I.56.1ab:
eṣá prá pūrvī́r áva tásya camríṣaḥ
átyo ná yóṣām údayaṃsta bhurváṇiḥ ।

67. *Ibid.*, I.81.7ab:
mádemade hí no dadír
yūthā́ gávām ṛjukrátuḥ ।

68. *Ibid.*, IV.24.8:
yadā́ samaryáṃ vyáced ṛ́dhāvā
dīrgháṃ yád ājím abhy ákhyad aryáḥ ।
ácikradat vṛ́ṣaṇaṃ pátnī ácchā
duroṇá ā́ níśitaṃ somasúdbhiḥ ।।

69. Many are the verses which speak about the fact that Indra in the rapture of Soma performed best of his martial feats. A few such are: IV.32.10; VI.17.1; VII.98.3; VIII.33.7.

70. The question arises, had Indra been basically the highest god, the creator, then why should he need so much of impetus, so much of external impetus to rise to the occasion. He being the highest god he performs whatever he desires.

71. *ṚV*, III.48.2:
yáj jā́yathās tád áhar asya kā́me
'ṃśóḥ pīyū́ṣam apibo giriṣṭhā́m ।
táṃ te mātā́ pári yóṣā jánitrī
maháḥ pitúr dáme āsiñcad ágre ।।
also see, VII.98.3

72. ***Also see***, IV.18.3cd.

TS, II.4.12.1 states Tvaṣṭṛ whose son was killed by Indra brought soma for him.

73. I.130.3ab:
ávindad divó níhitaṃ gúhā nidhím
vér ná gárbhaṃ párivītam áśmani ananté antár áśmani ।

74. *áyas* has been interpreted as golden by Sāyaṇa and as iron by Griffith while interpreting this verse.

75. VIII.100.8:
mánojavā áyamāna āyasī́m atarat púram ।
dívaṃ suparṇó gatvā́ya sómaṃ vajríṇa ā́bharat ।।
also see, I.80.2; III.43.7; X.144.4-6.

This episode of the *śyena*'s bringing Soma from heaven resembles the similar episode in Greek mythology; the eagle (adler) brought ambrosia from heaven. Zues' excessive addiction to ambrosia which made him immortal is comparable to Indra's love for Soma.

Oldenberg observes Indo-European origin of this episode. ***See*** H. Oldenberg *op. cit.*, pp. 169-70.

76. *ṚV*, VIII.76.10:
uttíṣṭhan ójasā sahá pītvī́ śípre avepayaḥ ।
sómam indra camū́ sutám ।

77. *Ibid.*, VIII.77.4:
ékayā pratidhā́pibat sākáṃ sárāṃsi triṃśátam ।
índraḥ sómasya kāṇukā́ ।।

78. VII.98.1cd:
gourád védīyān avapā́nam índro
viśvā́hā íd yāti sutásomam icchán ।।

79. *Ibid.*, VIII.4.8cd:
mádhvā sáṃpṛktāḥ sāraghéṇa dhenávas
tū́yam éhi drávā píba ।।

80. For more detailed information about Soma the following book may be consulted:

Wasson, R.G., *Soma the Divine Mushroom*, New York, 1968.

81. This reminds us, of Kālidāsa. Duṣyanta before entering Kaṇva's hermitage asks his charioteer to wash the backs of the horses, i.e., to give them some relief *ārdrapṛṣṭhau kriyantāṃ vājinau, Abhijñanaśākuntala*, Act I, *Kālidāsa Granthāvalī*, ed. by Revaprasad Dwivedi, Varanasi, 1976, p. 433.

82. ***See*** *ṚV*, I.20.2; 111.1; 161.6; 7; III.60.2; IV.33.10 etc.

83. I.55.6ab:
sá hí śravasyúḥ sádanāni kṛtrímā
kṣmayā́ vṛdhāná ójasā vināśáyan ।

84. I.53.7ab :
yudhā́ yúdham úpa gha íd eṣi dhṛṣṇuyā́
purā́ púraṃ sám idáṃ haṃsi ójasā ।

85. I.102.4:
vayáṃ jayema tváyā yujā́ vṛ́tam
asmā́kam áṃśam údavā bhárebhare ।

asmábhyam indra várivaḥ sugáṃ kṛdhi
prá śátrūṇāṃ maghavan vṛ́ṣṇyā ruja ||

Again in I.100.2b we read : *bhárebhare vṛtrahā́ śúṣmo ásti* |

86. I.131.2c:
táṃ tvā nā́vaṃ ná parṣáṇiṃ
śūṣásya dhurí dhīmahi |
also see, VI.17.8.

87. I.174.7b : *kṣā́ṃ dāsā́ya upabárhaṇīm káḥ* |

88. II.30.4:
bṛ́haspate tápuṣā́śneva vidhya
vṛ́kadvaraso' surasya vīrā́n |
yáthā jaghántha dhṛṣatā́ purā́ cid
evā́ jahi śátrum asmā́kam indra ||

The above verse addresses Indra as Bṛhaspati. The interested reader may in this connection consult *Indra und Bṛhaspati* (Otto Harrassowitz, Wiesbaden, 1968) by Hans Peter Schmidt who observes in this work of him that the word Bṛhaspati was originally an adjective to Indra and later along with the development of sacrificial rituals and priestly perogative Bṛhaspati emerged as an independent god with priestly function.

89. III.34.6cd:
vṛjā́nena vṛjinā́n sáṃ pipeṣa
māyā́bhiḥ dásyūn abhíbhūtyójāḥ ||

90. VI.35.2.
kárhi svid tád indra yā́n nṛ́bhir nṛ́n
vīraír vīrā́n nīḷáyāse jáyā́jīn |
tridhā́tu gā́ ádhi jayāsi góṣu
índra dyumnáṃ svarvad dhehi asmé ||

91. VIII.24.5ab:
ná te savyáṃ ná dákṣiṇaṃ
hástaṃ varanta āmúraḥ |

92. X.99.3:
sá vā́jaṃ yā́tā́paduṣpadā
yán svarṣā́tā pári sadat saniṣyán
anarvā́ yát śatádurasya védo
ghnán śiśnádevān abhí várpasā bhū́t ||

śiśnadeva occurs twice in the *ṚV* (***see*** VIII.21.5d). The word has been translated by Griffith as the lustful demons and by Geldner as "Phallusanbeter" (X.99.3), "Phallusverehrer" (VII.21.5).

One can very well explain *śiśnadeva* as 'phallus-worshipper'. This rite of ling-*pūjā* — worshipping the male organ emerged later among the Hindus in the Tantras and is also prominently present among the contemporary Hindus. Does the origin of this rite lie among the *Śiśnadevas* who were, probably, pre-Āryan and definitely non-Āryan?

In worshipping the male organ nothing but prayer for the growth of facundity is reflected.

93. Griffith translates *anā́sa* as noseless and Geldner as "die mundlosen Dasyu's". Sāyaṇa, however, interprets: *āsyarahitān* ǀ *āsya-śabdena śabdo lakṣyate aśabdān mūkān.* We feel, Sāyaṇa by it meant that they did not speak the Āryan language. Sāyaṇa seems to us quite logical.

94. The Aṅgirases whose cows were recaptured by Indra from Vala's enclosure have not been, however, included within the scope of this discussion.

95. Many a time Kutsa has been described as *ārjuneya*. Sāyaṇa interprets once as: *arjuna iti indrasya nāma* ǀ *tathā ca vājasaneyakam etad vā indrasya guhyaṃ nāma yad arjunaḥ* (I.112.23). Arjuna is the name of Indra. According to the Vājasaneyin, 'Arjuna is the secret name of Indra. Otherwise he always exposes *Ārjuneya* as the son of Arjunī'. Griffith always translates *Ārjuneya* as the son of Ārjunī. (***see*** Griffith, *The Hymns of the Ṛgveda*, pp. 113, 428). Geldner accepts this translation when he says ". . . oder dem sohn der Arjunī (Sāyaṇa)". *HOS* 33, p. 198, n. 2d.

96. E.D. Perry, "Indra in the Ṛgveda", in *JAOS,* XI., p. 204.

97. Jan Gonda, *Vedic Literature*, Otto Harrassowitz, Wiesbaden, 1975, p. 247.

98. K.F. Geldner, *Der Rigveda*, in *HOS,* 33, p. 130, n. 2c, "*aśuṣam* dunkles Beiwort des Śuṣṇa, jedenfalls ein Wortspiel".

99. *Op. cit.*, p. 204.

100. ***See*** A. Hillerbrandt, *Vedische Mythologie*, Vol. II (2nd revised edn.), Breslau, 1929, pp. 258-61.

101. A.B. Keith, *The Religion and Philosophy of the Veda and Upaniṣads*, in *HOS* 31, p. 130.

102. *Op. cit.*, p. 125.

103. R.T.H. Griffith, *op. cit.*, p. 135, n. "Kuyava: perhaps a name given by the Aryans to one of non-Aryan cheiftains". ***Also see*** Geldner, *op. cit.*, *HOS* 33, pp. 134-35. Geldner thinks Kuyava may either be an adjective to Śuṣṇa or the name of a demon, Śuṣṇa's assistant; *op. cit.*, p. 134, n. 8a.

104. H. Oldenberg, *Die Religion des Veda,* pp. 159-61.

105. ***See*** *ṚV*, IV.16.10cd:
své yónau ní ṣadataṃ sárūpā
ví vāṃ cikitsad ṛtacíd dha nā́rī ǀǀ

'You two (i.e., Indra and Kutsa) who resemble each other in appearance (*sárūpā*) be seated in your own abode; the righteous woman (i.e., Indra's wife), however, had doubts (as to who of you are Indra).'

106. In the fn. of the *ṚV*, I.53.10 Griffith observes: "Kutsa has been mentioned (I.33.14) as a favourite of Indra, but is here represented together with

Atithigva and Āyu, as chastised by him". *Op. cit.*, Vol. I, p. 75. Velankar thinks that, there were altogether three Kutsas. (***see*** Velankar, H.D., "Divodāsa Atithigva and other Atithigvas" in *ABORI*, 23, (pp. 666-68). We, however, think that, such insufficient material, i.e., *Ṛgveda* texts, does not justify any definite conclusion based on history.

107. Sāyaṇa exposes *atithigva* under I.51.6: *atithibhiḥ gantavyāya*. *St. Petersburg Dictionary*, Vol. I; p. 95: ein zuname Divodāsas welchem die Götter den Śambara zu überwinden halfen". ***Also see*** Grassmann, H., *Wörterbuch zum Ṛgveda*, Leipzig, Otto Harrassowitz, 1936, p. 30.

108. ***See*** *ṚV*, I.51.6; 54.4; 103.8; VI.18.8 etc.

109. *Ibid.*, I.54.6; 130.7.

110. *Ibid.*, IV.26.3.

111. *Ibid.*, IV.30.20:
śatáṃ aśmanmáyīnāṃ purā́m índro vý āsyat ।
dívodāsāya dāśúṣe ।।

Ragozin says about Śambara and his forts: "Their (Tṛtsus') first great king, Divodāsa was engaged in continuous warfare with some fierce mountain tribes of the north ruled by a cheiftain named Śambara, who appears to have constructed a quantity of forts in defence of many passes which led from the highlands into the steeper and wilder Himalayan fastness. These forts, of course, were built of wood, so that the usual mode of attack and destruction in petty campaigns was fire." (*Vedic India*, London, 1915. (1st edn. 1895), p. 323). If the forts were built of wood, then how do we interpret *aśmanmáyīnāṁ purā́m*?

According to N.G. Chapekar, "The ninety-nine towns or forts of Śambara may be so many nights which are a normal phenomenon within the arctic nights". ***See*** his "Sudās", *Oriental Thought*, III. No. 1, 1957, p. 15. To a rational mind Chapekar's opinion is, however, not acceptable. Why would Śambara's *púr*s signify the arctic nights whereas the other *púr*s occurring in the *ṚV* symbolise 'cities', 'ramparts' etc.? Such an interpretation of the word *púr* is totally out of context also.

Wilhelm Rau summarises his opinion on *púr* in the following words: A *púr*-consisted of one or several concentric ramparts on a round or oval ground-plan (147-816-2.51): was built of mud (12.623) or stone (7.82124): was fortified with combustible defences, certainly gates and probably palisades (***see also*** *ṚV*, I.59.6 = 34.6; 1.130.4; 3.34 (268)3) wattle or prickly shrubs 625-30 34): was furnished with wooden sheds as quarters for human occupants (14.15)." — *The meaning of Pūr in Vedic Literature* Munich,1976, p. 41.

112. Perry thinks that the word *pipru* has been derived from *par* meaning overcomer. "He appears mostly in the company of Śuṣṇa and Śambara, "and like them is possessed of castles and strongholds, by which clouds are

meant". *Op. cit.*, p. 202. How do we explain the other descriptions of the word *púr* in other contexts if we accept that *púr* means cloud as has been thought by Perry?

113. Mṛgaya is sometimes interpreted as adjective to Pipru. (***See*** Geldner, *HOS* 33, p. 435, n. 13a).

114. This verse has been interpreted differently since the days of Sāyaṇa who, however, interprets it as follows: *kṛṣṇagrarbhāḥ kṛṣṇo nāma kaścid asuraḥ tena niṣiktagarbhās tadīyā bhāryāḥ . . . kṛṣṇam asuraṁ hatvā putrāṇām anupapatty' arthaṁ garbhiṇīs tasya bhāryā api avadhīt ity arthaḥ* । Griffith translates *kṛṣṇagarbhāḥ* as 'dusky brood'. According to Geldner, this verse speaks about the abortion of the child in mother's womb and he refers to Oldenberg who thinks the cities inside which the black people lived have been compared with pregnant women. (***See*** *HOS* 33 in the note of the translation of I.101.1).

    The word *kṛṣṇagarbhāḥ* is in the second case-ending plural number. It is the object of the verb *niráhan*. So Sāyaṇa's interpretation is logical even though it gives a cruel picture of Indra's behaviour towards his non-Āryan enemies' women.

    Renate Söhnen believes that Indra always maintained an ethical value in regard to his relation towards women. But so far as Indra's behaviour towards these *dā́sa* women (I.101.1ab) is concerned it can by no means be considered ethical. (***See*** Renate Söhnen, "Indra and Women", in *BSOAS*, LIV, 1991, pp. 68-74.

115. *ṚV*, II.13.9c: *arjjáu dásyūn sámunab dabhī́taye* । Sāyaṇa interprets *arjjaú* as *rajjurahite bandhanāgāre.* Griffith comments, "Not with chords; in a prison without chords — the grave". (*op. cit.*, p. 276, n. 9). Geldner translates, "der keinen Stricken bedarf" (*HOS*, 33, p. 273).

116. *Māyā* does not bear any specific meaning but the irresistible power inexplicable to human intelligence — a word which plays such an important role in the *Upaniṣads* and the *Vedānta* Philosophy, probably has its base in such verses of the *ṚV.*

117. *ṚV*, V.30.9:
    stríyo hí dāsá ā́yudhāni cakré
    kíṁ mā karann abalā́ asya sénāḥ ।
    antár hý akhyad ubhé asya dhéne
    áthópa práid yudháye dásyum índraḥ ॥

    In the fn. of the translation of this verse Griffith says, "His two different voices; the meaning may be that Indra heard the voices of women as well as the voice of Namuci, and so knew that he had not an army of demon warriors to fight against. Prof. Wilson following Sāyaṇa, translates: 'the two of his best beloveds (Indra) confined in the inner apartments'. *op. cit.*, p. 490. To us, however, Wilson appears more logical in this regard.

118. IV.42.8:

asmā́kam átra pitáras tá āsant
saptá ṛ́ṣayo daurgahé badhyámāne ।
tá ā́yajanta trasádasyum asyā
índraṃ ná vṛtratúram ardhadevám ।।

The word *daurgaha* occurring in the verse is interpreted in two ways: first as an adjective to Purukutsa, the son of Durgaha, and secondly as the sacrificial horse released by Purukutsa. Geldner, following *Nighaṇṭu*, I.14 suggests *daurgaha* might be a short form of *daurgahāśva*: comparable in this connection is *paidva auccaiḥśravas*. (***See*** *HOS* 33, p. 475n). We consider *daurgaha* in the above verse is an adjective to Purukutsa and in later texts it might mean the horse *Daurgahāśva*.

119. *Op. cit.*, Vol. 33, p. 69.

120. *Op. cit.*, Vol. I, p. 74.

121. Bringing one's own people across the ocean is an archaic motif. The same phenomenon is observed in the story of Moses in the old *Testament* in the Book of Exodus VI.6-8. Oldenberg comments on the story of Turvaśa and Yadu: "Indra hat Turvaśa und Yadu aus der Ferne hergeführt . . . Der Herr aller Kämpfe ist eben auch der Patrone der Wanderungen die sich damals durch das strömmliche Land bewegten". (*op. cit.*, pp. 163-64) 'Indra had led Turvaśa and Yadu from afar and made the rivers passable for them. The master of wars is also the patron of immgrations in course of which they had to cross lands full of rivers'.

122. In contrast to Indra's punishing Atithigva in favour of Suśravas, here he favours him. Such phenomena were the grounds which led Velankar to conclude that there were four Athithigvas. ***See*** his "Divodāsa Atithigva and other Atithigvas", in *ABORI* 23, pp. 657-58).

123. According to Sāyaṇa Varaśikha is an *ásura* but the texts do not say anything in support of it.

124. Griffith comments on Hariyūpīyā: "Hariyūpīyā (having golden posts), the name of a town, or according to others of a river", *op. cit.*, p. 302, n. 5. Sir Mortimer Wheeler observes that the modern name Harappa has its origin in the Ṛgvedic Hariyūpīyā: "The possibility has often been remarked that in the modern place the name Harappa may be reconsidered in the Hariyūpīya which is mentioned in the *ṚV*". *Civilization of Indus Valley and Beyond*, London, 1966, p. 78). This conjecture of Wheeler, however, has not yet been proved.

125. Sāyaṇa thinks, Hariyūpīyā and Yavyāvatī are identical rivers.

126. For Sudās and *dāśarājña*, ***see*** N.G. Chapekar, *Oriental Thought* 3, Umesh Chandra Sharma, *The Dāśarājña War*, Aligarh, 1982.

127. *ṚV*, I.33.14;
ā́vaḥ kútsam indra yásmin cākán

prā́vo yúdhyantaṃ vr̥ṣabháṁ dáśadyum ।
śaphácyuto reṇúr nakṣata dyā́m
úc chvaitreyó nr̥ṣáhyāya tasthau ।।

'O Indra, desiring (sacrifice), you protected Kutsa, protected the fighting, manly Daśadyu; the dusts raised from hoofs covered the sky, Śvaitreya stood up for victory (in the battle)'.

According to Geldner, Daśadyu is a bull (***See*** *HOS* 33, p. 40), but to us Daśadyu is a man. The R̥gvedic singers have very often used the term *vr̥ṣabha* as an adjective to indicate the manly power of a god. When the poet has been talking about Kutsa, a human being, why should the bull's story come in? Following Griffith, I would prefer to interpret Śvaitreya, occurring in the verse, not as a bull but as the son of a woman Śvitrā by name. (***See*** *op. cit.*, Vol. I, p. 47).

128. Alfred Hillebrandt, *Vedische Mythologie*, Kleine Ausagabe, Breslau, 1910, p. 98.

129. *Op. cit.*, *HOS* 33, p. 239, n. 8cd.

130. ***See*** M. Bloomfield, *ZDMG* 48; P. von Bradke, *ZDMG*, 46; P.S. Shastri, *Indian Historical Quarterly*, XXXIII, 3.

131. *Op. cit.*, *HOS* 33, p. 239, n. 8cd.

132. Stith Thompson, *Motif Index of Folk Literature*, Copenhagen, 1955, p. 116.

133. Sāyaṇa thinks, *Śimyu-s* were *rākṣasa-s*. Griffith, however, keeps the word as it is in translation (*op. cit.*, p. 130).

134. How Indra, the war god, was endowed with the attributes of a doctor? Does it indicate that the Āryan war god had been gradually emerging as the highest god who has the capacity to execute all kinds of feats? Or that in course of time the subject-matter of the hymns became of secondary importance because of sacrifice becoming more and more important in life than prayer?

135. On this aspect of the Aśvins' character has been directly discussed under the chapter, "The Aśvins".

136. History lies, though inscrutably concealed, in the geopgraphy and the topography of the North-Western India in the river names like Añjasī, Kuliśī, Paruṣṇī, Hariyūpīyā (?) etc. which point to actually existing water courses.

137. The *R̥V* verses mentioning *dānu* in the different declensional forms or with *taddhita* — suffixes are I.32.9; 51.4; II.11.18; 12.11; IV.30.7; V.68.5; X.120.6, *et al.*

138. The *R̥V* verses mentioning *dānava* are: II.11.10; V.29.4; 32.1; 4; 7; VIII.32.12 *et al.*

139. On this point we have discussed in the section entitled Soma.

140. We discussed this point in the section entitled *Vájra*.

141. In this connection we remember our Purāṇic stories of killing Droṇa (*aśvatthāmā hata iti gajaḥ*), the slaying of Karṇa by Arjuna through creating an artificial sunset, the last club-fight (*gadāyuddha*) between Duryodhana and Bhīma and others.

142. It reminds us of the goddess Durgā who, aided by all deities killed the demon Mahiṣa.

143. The question arises, had Indra been the highest god, had be been cosmogonic then why should he need so much external aid to kill Vṛtra. The highest god knows that he has to do and he accomplishes it through his sheer will, remaining fully passive. E.O. James characterises the High God as follows: "The High God is too lofty, unapproachable and functionless, and so he becomes otiose and shadowy. Although he stands head and shoulders above the rest of the pantheon as the climax of religious thought and experience, his very loftiness as the dweller in the sky makes him inaccessible." (*The Worship of the Sky-God*, University of London, 1963, p. 8). Thought about Varuṇa, Dyaus Pitar comes to our mind as we read E.O. James but by no means the very active, heroic Indra. The highest god knows what he is to do, he need not be assigned with duty, but Indra was commissioned by the gods with the duty of killing Vṛtra.

Agreeing with A.K. Lahiri, one may argue that the gods are created after men, so all manly qualities were attributed to Indra by his worshippers. Lahiri says: "We do not deny the fact that the human characteristics of Indra are dwelt upon more than those of any other god by the Vedic poets. But to deduce from this that Indra was originally a human hero is to miss the fundamental spirit of Indian religion. The ancient Indians portrayed their favourite gods as if they were very near and dear to them, and imposed human characteristic upon them". (*Vedic Vṛtra*, Motilal Banarsidass, Delhi, 1984, p. 209). From the Indra-hymns of the *ṚV* one presumes the background that the Āryans had passed through. They had real fights, real clashes with the aboriginal inhabitants and at Indra's leadership they fought all the battles against their enemies. The descriptions, though very precise, are so vivid, so true to life, and, the statements are so detailed and concrete that it is difficult to conclude that the god Indra had been endowed with all human virtues out of love and respect by his devotees; we would rather prefer to think the other way round.

144. Geldner comments in this regard, "Eine bestimmte Szene aus dem Mythos oder aus dem grossen Aufruhr in der Natur fortgesetzt ist" (*HOS* 33, p. 268, n. 8) 'a specific scene from myth or a great natural tumult has been depicted.'

145. That Ahi paralysed heaven (II.11.5) indicates his supremacy. Many other gods, according to the Vedic texts paralysed heaven. Some of them are Varuṇa (VII.86.1; VIII.42.1), Soma (IX.101.15), Indra (VIII.89.5; X.89.4;

X.113.4). What becomes clear to us is, that the capacity to paralyse heaven was a criterion to a Vedic god to reach a very high status. Vṛtra (= Ahi) also had the same capability but he was stopped from reaching so high a position because he belonged to the enemy block.

146. *AitBrā*, III.15, *indro vai vṛtraṃ hatvā nāstṛṣīti manyamanaḥ parāḥ paravāto' gacchat* "Indra having killed Vṛtra thought, 'I have not killed and went far away'."

TS, II.5.3.6, *indro vṛtraṃ hatvā parāṃ parāvatam-agacchat aparādhamiti manyamānaḥ* 'Indra after having killed Vṛtra thought, he had committed a crime and went far, far away'

147. Mircea Eliade: *Patterns in Comparative Religion*, London and New York, 1958, p. 413.

148. *ṚV*, II.13.2:
sadhrī́mā yanti pári bíbhratīḥ páyo
viśvápsnyāya prá bharanta bhójanam ।
samānó ádhvā pravátām anuṣyáde
yás tā́' kṛṇoḥ prathamáṃ sā́sy ukthyaḥ ।।
also see II.15.3; VI.17.12; X.111.9.

149. *Ibid.*, VIII.6.13:
yád asya manyúr ádhvanīd ví vṛtráṃ parvaśó ruján ।
apáḥ samudrám áirayat ।।
also see VIII.6.16; VIII.76.3.

150. *Ibid*, I.80.8ab: *ví te vájrāso asthiran navatī́ṃ nāvyā ánu* ।
also see, I.33.11.

151. X.104.8, however, tells us that Indra released ninety-nine rivers for the benefit of men. I.80.8 also speaks about ninety navigable rivers. I.62.6, on the other hand, speaks about four rivers.

152. Stith Thompson: *The Motif Index of Folk Literature*, Copenhagen, 1955, p. 116.

153. ***Also see***, I.54.10; 56.5;174.2; III.31.16; IV. 19.2; V.31.6; VII.21.3 *et al.*

154. ***Also see***, I.51.4; 54.10; II.11.7; V.32.1; 2; VI.30.5 *et al.*

155. H. Oldenberg *Die Religion des Veda*, Stuttgart, Berlin, 1923, (Ist edn. 1916), p. 137.

"Hätte man von Wolken Und Regen sprechen wollen könnte nicht an den zahllosen Stellen die Metaphor von Bergen und Flüssen gleichbleibend wiederkehren, ohne dass irgendwo die Sache beim rechtem Namen genannt wäre".

156. Cf. H. Lüders *Varuṇa*, Band I. Göttingen, 1951, p. 175, Ich hätte es in der Tat für unmöglich, dass die vedischen Dichter, wenn die von Bergen reden, damit immer die Wolken gemeint oder dass die Regengüsse als die Flüsse oder sieben Flüsse bezeichnet haben sollten. Warum sollten sie sich dann

stets der Metaphor und niemals der direkten und, unzweideutigen Ausdrücke bedient haben? Wir werden, glaube ich, nicht nur heir, sondern auch in zahlreichen anderen Fällen den Veda richtiger verstechen, wenn wir ihn buchstäblicher nehmen".

157. *Op. cit.*, ***see***, p. 138.

158. Cf. *op. cit.*, p. 141, Das Nachdenken der späteren Zeit hat ubrigens keine Schweirigkeit gefunden, den atmosphärischen Charakter von Indras Drachenkampf wieder aufzudecken; für die Veda-erklärer wie für die Dichter ist jetzt Indra der gewitternde und Regenspendende Gott. Das ändert aber nichts daran, dass er für die Sänger des Ṛgveda der Zerspalter irdischer Berge, der Berferier irdischer Flüsse gewesen ist".

159. ***See*** A. Hillebrandt: *Vedische Mythologie*, Vol. III, p. 191. "Die Sage von Vṛtrakampf nahmen die Inder aus Kashmir oder aus dem Nordwesten — ich will genz dahin gestellt bleiben lassen, wo sie ursprünglich erstanden ist . . . Diese Anschauung ging später in Indien. In Vṛtra begegnen wir einem weiteren Beispeil von der Umschmelzung vorindischer Anschauungen durch die indische Sonne".

160. ***See*** *ibid.*, p. 199.

"Die Flüsse Indiens sind nicht der Ausgangspunkt der Vṛtrasage. In den Indus westlich und nördlich gelegenen Ländern hat der kampf zwischen dem dämon des Winters und der Sonne noch grössere Bedeutung. Das Wort Vṛtra stammt dorther und mit dem Begriff aus der vorindischen Zeit herubergekommen. Aber Weiter im Osten, im eigentlichen Indien verblasst unter anderen Verhältnissen Ausgangspunkt und Bedeutung der Sage".

161. J. Muir, *Original Sanskrit Texts*, Vol. V, London, 1870, p. 95.

162. E.D. Perry, *JAOS,* XI, "Indra in the Ṛgveda", p. 20.

163. E.W. Hopkins, *Religions of India*, Boston, 1895, p. 20.

164. R.T.H. Griffith, *The Rāmāyaṇa of Vālmiki*, p. 387, n. 1.

165. A.B. Keith, *The Religion and Philosophy of the Veda and Upanishads*, Part I, p. 129.

166. ***See*** Jalwant Kumar Shastri, *Vedavāṇī* 32(7), 1980, p. 10. "*Vṛtra kon hei*" *vṛtra meghkā vāchak hei* । *kisi asurvishesh kā nam nehi hei* ।

167. M. Klostermeier, *Theistic Tradition of India*, "Mythologies and Philosophies of Salvation", Wilfred Lankrit University Press, 1984, p. 15.

168. H.D. Griswold, *The Religion of the Rigveda*, Oxford University Press, 1923, p. 182.

169. Hermann Güntert, *Der arische Weltkönig und Heiland*, Haale (Saale), 1923, p. 21.

"Die Wasser Werden gefangen, gewaltsam zurückgehalten; mehr dahinter zu suchen ist unberechtigt und führt in die Irre. . .

Für den vedischen Vṛtra ist jedenfalls zunächst an die Einschliessung und Gefangenhaltung der Wasser zu denken".

170. Herman Lommel, *Der Arische Kriegsgott*, Frankfurt/Main, 1939, p. 57.

"Die Verwehr mag verschiedene Namen haben, Śuṣṇa, Viśvarūpa — und dann auch Vṛtra —, er ist doch immer wieder derselbe; ein kosmi-sches Geschehen das sich wiederholt, solange die Welt steht, wird in ein Bild einmaliges Ereignis wäre und dieses wird mit wechselnden Namen abgewandelt, als ob es verschiedene Geschehnisse waren".

171. F.B.J. Kuiper, *Ancient Indian Cosmogony*, Vikas Publishing House, 1983, Sahibabad, p. 9.

172. The *Durgāpūjā* is celebrated alsmot all over India. In the annual worship of goddess Durgā people celebrate the victory of the goddess over the buffalo demon (Mahiṣāsura) who represents chaos. Durgā, the symbol of cosmic energy establishes cosmic order by annihilating chaos. The same may be said about the *Mahābhārata* war in which Duryodhana symbolises chaotic power and the war between Rāma and Rāvaṇa as narrated in the *Rāmāyaṇa*. In the *Dussera* festival people burn the effigy of Rāvaṇa who represents chaos. In the story of the ten incarnations of Viṣṇu also the same story of conqeust of cosmos over chaos is repeated.

173. Mircea Eliade *Patterns in Comparative Mythology*, London, 1958, p. 85.

174. F.B.J. Kuiper, *Indo Iranian Journal*, 4, 1960, "The Ancient Indian Verbal Contest", pp. 218-19.

175. Norman Brown, *JAOS*, 62, 1942, pp. 85-98. "The Creation Myth of the Rigveda".

176. *Ibid.*, p. 88.

177. ***See*** the section "Indra's Protégés" in this book.

178. C.G. Jung & Karl Kerényi, *Introduction to a Science of Mythology*, Routledge & Kegan Paul Ltd., 1951, p. 7.

179. Cf. *op. cit.*, p. 194.

"Überblicken wir das gesamte Material, so sheint es mir zu sein, dass für die Vedischen Dichter — und nur darum kann es sich zunächst handeln — der Vṛtrakampf eine Art von Schöpfungs mythus ist, bei dem man nicht fragen darf, was vorher war. Die Urschlange hat die ganze Welt umschlungen. Alles ist in Dunkel gehüllt. Die Wasser sind in dem Felsen, auf dem das Ungeheuer liegt, oder den es verschluckt hat, eingenschlossen. Indra erschlägt die Schlange und spaltet den Felsen. Die Wasser stürzen heraus und ergiessen sich als die irdischen Ströme in das Meer. Damit beginnt für die Menschheit das Leben auf der Erde".

180. *Ibid.*, p. 195, "Es ist möglich — mehr möchte ich nicht behaupten — dass der Vṛtramythus ursprünglich nur von der Einschliessung der Wasser handelete. . .".

181. Cf. *Ibid.*, pp. 193-94.

"... ich bin überzeugt, dass Indras Weltordnung immer als das letzte Ergebnis eines Dämonenkampfes angesehen wurden. Das entspricht dem Charakter des Gottes, der ganz auf kriegerische Taten eingenstellt ist; ...".

182. ***See*** Hans Schmeja, *Interpretations aus dem Rigveda*, Innsbrunck, 1987, p. 23:

"Stellen wir uns vor: Wandernde Scharen kommen unter Fühurung des Helden etwa um die Mittagszeit an einen Lagerplatz; Mensch und Veih sind dürstig und erschöpft; in einer feuchten Au suchen sie nach Wasser und stossen dabei auf die Kobra. Der Anführer erschlägt sie in gefährlichem Kampf und macht so den Zugang zur Qnelle frei, er bohrt die Quelle am Berghang auf, und nun fliesse das Wasser für Mensch und Tier (I.32, 1-2; 11.-12).

183. *Ibid.*, p. 26, Indra — zunächst als Führer der einwandernden Scharen, später als ihr Oberster Gott-gebietet dem Zug auf der Wanderschaft und beim Ausspannen; er ist Herr über Hornvieh und Jungvieh. Als könig herrscht er über die Länder und hält sie zusammen".

184. ***See*** *ibid.*, pp. 20-21. "Dass diese sangenhaften Erzälungen shon in der späteren rigvedischen Zeit als Weltschöpfungsmythen verstanden und religiös interpretiert wurden, sei nicht bezweifelt, doch möchte ich vermuten, dass ursprünglich nichts anders dahinter als Kämpfe und Abenteuer die eindringenden Arier bei der Inbesitznahme des Landes zu bestehen hatte, ..."

185. The following article of R. Ojha may be referred to in this regard: *The Journal of the Bihar and Orissa Research Society*, Vol. XXVIII, 1942, pp. 56-64. "Indra Vṛtra War and the Serpent People".

186. We have discussed on *vájra* in details elsewhere in this book.

187. Jan Gonda's *Epithets in the Ṛgveda*, Mouton & Co., 1959 may be consulted for more information about Indra's epithets.

188. Once in connection with Soma (VIII.86.4) and twice to describe the Maruts (I.87.1; II.34.1).

189. I.166.1 addresses the Maruts as *śakrāḥ*, II.39.3 the Aśvins and V.41.15 uses the word in a general way in connection with the gods.

190. III.21.4 describes Agni and X.74.5 the *yajamāna* as *sacīva*.

191. ***Also see*** I.52.8d: *ádhārayo diví ā́ sū́ryaṃ dṛśé* ।
VIII.89.7b: *ā́ sū́ryaṃ rohayo diví* ।

192. ***Also see*** VI.17.3; VIII.98.2.

193. ***Also see***, II.19.3.

194. IV.31.5; 6:
5. *pravátā hí krátūnām ā́ hā padéva gácchasi* ।

ábhakṣi sū́rye sácā ।।

6. *sáṁ yátta indra manyávaḥ sáṃ cakrā́ṇi dadhanvire* ।
ádha tvé ádha sū́rye ।।

195. IV.81.15:
asmā́kam uttamáṃ kṛdhi śrávo devéṣu sūrya ।
várṣiṣṭhaṃ dyā́m ivopári ।।

196. ***See*** Max Müller *Chips from a German Workshop*, Vol. II, 1856, p. 92, ***also see*** Alfred Hillebrandt *Vedische Mythologie, Kleine Ausgabe*, Breslau, 1910, p. 88; 98 ff. J.J. Meyer, *Trilogie Altindischer Mächte und Feste der* Vegetation, Vol. III, p. 134.

197. Herman Lommel *Der arische Kriegsgott* Frankfurt/Main, 1939, pp. 72-73.

"Nur weil in unserer Gedankenwelt die Sonne nicht ein Kämpfer und Krieger, Sonne und Gewitter zwei vollig getrennte Vorstellungen sind, neigen wir dazu, diese Wirkungsbereiche des Gottes als ursprünglich selbständig zu betrachten und fragen, wie diese sich verient hätten und welches von inhen der Kristallisationskern gewesen sein dürfte, an den die anderen Motive in einer Entwicklung angeschlossen wären".

198. The following article may be referred to in this connection: Sukumari Bhattacharji "The Sun-god and Soteriology" *Anvikṣā*, Vol. V. 1972, pp. 25-43.

199. ***See*** *ṚV*, IV.30.8-11.

200. ***See*** *ṚV*, VII.83.6-8.

201. R.N. Dandekar, *Vedic Mythological Tracts*, 1970, p. 348. Dandekar has dealt at length on *Indrāvaruṇau* with reference to Vasiṣṭha, the Vedic seer, keeping an eye to the historical background of the nomadic Āryans on their way towards India under the leadership of Indra under the section "Vedic seer Vasiṣṭha" of this book.

202. *ṚV*, IV.18.11:
utá mātā́ mahiṣám ánvavenat
amī́ tvā jahati putra devā́ḥ ।
áthābravīd vṛtrám índro haniṣyán
sákhe viṣṇo vitaráṃ ví kramasva ।।

203. VII.99. 4ab — a hymn to Indrāviṣṇū.

204. Sāyaṇa interprets *te* occurring in *a* as *tavānujaḥ* — 'Your younger brother'. This has been interpreted by Dandekar as, Viṣṇu derives his power of taking three steps from Indra, i.e., Viṣṇu is here described as subordinate ally of Indra. (***See*** *ibid.*, p. 71).

205. I.52.7cd:
tváṣṭā cit te yújyaṃ vāvṛdhe śávas
tatákṣa vájram abhíbhūtyojasam ।।
also see, X.48.3.

206. ***See***, X.8.9cd:
tvāṣṭrásya cid viśvárūpasya gónām
ācakrāṇáḥ tríṇi sīrṣā́ párā várk ||

207. *ṚV,* III.48.4cd refers to this incident and states that the powerful Indra drank soma from Tvaṣṭṛ's laddle following unfair means (according to Sāyaṇa by stealing *corayitvā*):

tváṣṭāram índro janúṣā abhibhū́ya
āmúṣya sómam apibac camū́ṣu
also see, X.8.7-9, this *tṛc* deals with Indra's killing Viśvarūpa.

208. ***Also see,*** *JaiBrā,* II.152-157; *MS* II.4, 1; *KS* XII.10; *ŚatBrā,* I.6.3.1-22; V.5.4, 2-13; XII.7.1.1-14.

209. *ṚV,* X.131.4; 5:
yuváṁ surā́mam aśvinā námucāv āsuré sácā |
vipipānā́ śubhasaptī índram kármasv āvatam ||
putrámiva pitárāv aśvínobhéndrāváthuḥ kā́vyair daṃsánābhiḥ |
yát surā́maṃ vyápibaḥ śácībhiḥ sáraswatī tvā maghavann abhiṣṇak ||
also see, *VS,* XIX.34; XX.59; 67; 68; *ŚatBrā,* XII.7.1.1-14.

210. ***See*** *ṚV,* IV.18.1-2.

Norman Brown, however, considers Indra's birth a normal one. ***See*** *India and Indology*, ed. by Rosane Rocher, Delhi, 1978, pp. 37-39; "Indra's infancy according to Ṛgveda".

211. ***Also see*** VIII.96.13; 14.

212. I.62.5cd:
ví bhū́myā aprathaya indra sā́nu |
divó rája úparam astabhāyaḥ ||

213. I.62.7cd:
bhágo ná méne paramé vyóman |
ádhāryad ródasī sudáṃsāḥ ||

214. ***See***, I.63.1ab:
tvám mahā́n indra yó ha śúsmair
dyā́vā jajñānáḥ pṛthivī́ áme dhāḥ |

215. *ṚV,* VIII.98.11:
tvám hí naḥ pitā́ vaso
tvám mātā́ śatakrato babhū́vitha |
ádhā te sumnám īmahe ||

216. III.46.3:
prá mā́trābhī ririce rócamānaḥ
prá devébhir viśváto ápratītaḥ |
prá majmánā divá índraḥ pṛthīvyā́ḥ
prórór mahó antárikṣād ṛjīṣī́ ||

217. I.102.2:
asyá śrávo nadyaḥ saptá bibhrati
dyāvākṣā́mā pṛthivī́ darśatáṃ vápuḥ ।
asmé sū́ryācandramásābhicákṣe
śraddhé kám indra carato vitarturám ।।
also see, II.12.2.

218. ***See*** VIII.93.13; ***also see*** III.30.14.

219. ***Also see*** III.45.5a, 46.la; VIII.61.2a.

220. ***Also***, IV.21.10a; VIII.16.1; VIII.46.20c.

221. A.B. Keith, *Veda of the Black Yajurveda*, *HOS*, Vol. 18, p. 381.

'May Agni for me and Indra, may Soma and Indra, may Savitṛ and Indra, may Sarasvatī and Indra, may Pūṣan and Indra, may Bṛhaspati and Indra, may Mitra and Indra, may Varuṇa and Indra, may Tvaṣṭṛ and Indra, may Dhātṛ and Indra, may Viṣṇu and Indra, may the aśvins and Indra, may the Maruts and Indra, may the All-gods and Indra, may earth and Indra, may the atmosphere and Indra, may sky and Indra, may the quarters and Indra, may the head and Indra, may Prajāpati and Indra (be auspicious for me through the sacrifice)'.

222. *TS*, V.6.3.4:
indrasya suṣuvāṇaṣya daśadhendriyaṃ vīryaṃ
parāpatat tad devāḥ sautramaṇyā samabharan

223. Each and every text of the *YV* deals with the Sautrāmaṇī, but we find that the *VS* deals with it more elaborately.

224. There are different versions regarding how Indra was cured of complete debility. The *JaiBrā* says that all the gods cured him with different kinds of treatments whereas the *KS*, the *MS*, the *ŚatBrā* state that by the performance of Sautramaṇī Indra was brought back to his original shape when he was totally indisposed after killing Vṛtra.

225. ***See*** *MS* IV.3.4 and ***also*** *TaitBrā,* 1.7.1.6-8; *ŚatBrā*, XII.7.3.1-16.

226. ***See*** *KS*, 37.14.

227. In getting the Indra-stories of the *YV* Wilhelm Rau's article "Twenty Indra Legends" in *German Scholars on India*, Varanasi, 1973, pp. 119-23 was drawn upon.

228. III.1.5; 6:
indra senāṃ mohayāmitrāṇām ।
agner vātasya dhrājyā tān viṣūco vi nāśaya ।।
indraḥ senāṃ mohayatu maruto ghantv ojasā ।
cakṣuṃsy agnir ā dattāṃ punar etu parājitā ।।

229. Louis Renou; "Indra dans L'Atharvaveda" *New Indians Antiquary*, 1946, July-december; p. 128.

'The rapport of the earth with Indra is explained by the notion of Indra-king; they conform to well-known Indian conception'.

Tr. by James Laine, Department of Religious Studies Macalester College, St. Paul MN 55105 USA. I am deeply grateful to Mr. Laine who took the trouble of translating the whole article of Renou for me.

230. Whitney thinks, Aṣṭakā is the name and *eka* is an adjective meaning 'sole'. So Ekāṣṭakā is translated by him as "the sole Aṣṭakā". (***See*** *HOS* 18, p. 102).

231. II.3.6: *indrasya vajro apa hantu rakṣasaḥ* ।

232. II.14.4:
bhūtapatir nirajatv indraś cetaḥ sadānvāḥ ।
gṛhasya budhna āsinās tā indro vajreṇādhi tiṣṭhatu ।

233. II.27.3; 4:
indro ha cakre tvā vāhāv
asurebhyas tarītave ।
prāśaṃ pratipāśo jahya-
rasān kṛṇv oṣadhe ।।

pātāṃ indro vyāśnād
assurebhyas tarītave
prāśaṃ pratiprāśo jahy
arasān kṛṇv oṣadhe ।।

234. II.31.1ab:
indrasya yā mahī dṛṣat
krimer viśvasya tarhaṇī ।

235. VI.82.2:

This, of course, is a point of controversy whether the Aśvins or Soma got Sūryā as wife.

See "The heavenly twins and a maiden" under the *Aśvins* in this book.

236. *devā imaṃ madhunā saṃyutaṃ yavaṃ*
sarasvatyām adhi maṇāv acarkṛṣuḥ
indra āsīt sīrapatiḥ śatakratuḥ
kīnāśā āsan marutaḥ sudānavaḥ

237. ***See*** *AV*, III.15.1:
indram ahaṃ vaṇijaṃ codayāmi
sa na etu pura etā no astu ।
nudann arātiṃ paripanthinaṃ mṛgaṃ
sa īśāno dhanadā astu mahyam ।।

238. Lakṣmīkānta Sharma hints at the same truth that in the *AV* Indra's earlier traits of character have not been totally extinct when he says: *yadyapi vede'smin indrasaṃbandhīni sūktāny alpatarāṇy eva santi tathāpi tair asya devasya mahimnaḥ samyag unmīlitaṃ jātam* । *satyametat yadatra nimnakoṭikābhicāre saṃyojitas tathāpi tasya prākkālikaṃ gauravaṃ sarvathā nirmṛṣṭaṃ na bhūtam.*

Medhā "Atharvavedasaṃhitāyām indrasya svarūpavimarśaḥ", Vol. 10, p. 4, 1973-74.

239. N.J. Shende, "Indra in the Atharvaveda", *Proceedings, All India Oriental Conference*, XXIII, 1946, p. 60.

240. E.D. Perry, "Indra in the Rigveda", in *JAOS,* XI, p. 120.

241. *Ibid.*, p. 123.

242. A.A. Macdonell, *The Vedic Mythology* (rept.) Indologiocal Book House, Delhi, 1971, p. 54, Ist edn. 1897.

243. *Mythology of All Racess*, Vol. VI, Boston, p. 32.

244. ***See*** E.O. James, *Worship of the sky-god*, London, 1963, p. 139: "Both in Semitic and Indo-European modes of expression the belief in a celestial Supreme Being who created the earth and fertilized by sending rain upon it has been almost universal".

245. Maurice Bloomfield, *The Religon of the Veda*, New York, London, 1908, p. 176.

246. Leopold von Schlegel, *Reden und Aufsätze vornämlich über Indiens Literatur und Kultur*, Leipzig, 1913, p. 377.

247. Sudarshan Kumar Sharma, "Indra is a synonym of cloud", in *Journal of the Ganganath Jha Research Institute*, 1979, (July-December), p. 98.

248. Veronica Ions (1983, 2nd edn.) *Indian Mythology*, Standard Indian Literature Co., (P) Ltd., India, p. 17.

249. Quoted from Perry's article on the Ṛgvedic Indra, *JAOS*, XI, p. 119.

250. Adolf Kaegi, *The Rig Veda*, tr. by Arrowsmith, R (1886), Ist Indian edition, New Delhi, 1972, p. 43, (Ist German edn. 1880).

251. Louis Renou, *Religions of Ancient India*, new Delhi, 1972, p. 21 (Ist. edn. 1953).

252. Helmut von Glasenapp, *Die Religonen Indiens*, Stuttgart, 1955, p. 65, "Indra ist im Veda der Gott der Stärke, dessen Wirken überall dort in die Erscheinung tritt, wo eine machtvolle Kraft sich äussert. Er Wird deshalb von kriegerischen Ariern als das Muster eines Recken gepriesen als Schirmherr in Not und Gefahr angerufen. Ihm jubeln Menschen zu als dem Beschutzer gegen die Feinde, ihn priesen sie als freigebiegen Spender von Kuhen und Schätzen".

253. A.Z. Ragozin, *Vedic India*, London, 1915, p. 5.

254. ***See*** Hermann Goetz, *Epochen der Indischen Kultur*, Leipzig, 1929, p. 37. ". . . Indra der Gott des Gewitters. Er dessen Blitze in die am Rande des Himalayas zu schweren Bänken stauenden Wolken fallen, ist zum Schätzer der Arier im Kampfe gegen die aus ihren Trutzburgen im Himalaya verbrechenden Überwohner geworden. Und als solcher verkörpert er auch die ganze reckenhafte Kraft und Barbarai dieser alten Krieger".

255. *St. Petersburg Dictionary*, Vol. I, p. 802.

"Er ist im Urspung nicht der oberste, aber der nationale gott und Liebling der arisch-indischen Stämme, ein Vorbild der zu edlen Zwecken thätigen Heldenkraft und tritt mit der allmähligen Verdunkelung Varuṇa's mehr an die Spitze . . ."

256. Barnett's opinion has been quoted from Charpentier's article; Charpentier quoted the same from Barnett's *Hindu Gods and Heroes*.

257. J. Charpentier "Ein Versuch der Aufklärung", in *Le Monde Orientale*, Vol. XXV, 1-3, 1931, Leipzig, p. 25.

" . . . während der unaufhörlichen Kämpfe mit den Ureinwohnern, deren Widerhall wir so oft im *Rigveda* vernehmen, wurde Indra zum siegrischen Führer, zum Kriegsgott erhoben, drängte allmählich die hoheren Götter Mitra und Varuṇa deren Götterkreise zurück und führte dann — wahrscheinlich während einer relativen kurzen Periode — als höchster konig des indischen Pantheon".

258. ***See*** in the section "Indra and other gods — Sūrya."

259. V.A. Gadgil, "Indra the representative of the highest physical aspect of Nature", in *ABORI*, 1942, p. 139.

260. E.N. Ghosh, "Studies in the Rigvedic deities — astronomical and meteorological", in *Journal of the Asiatic Society of Bengal*, New Series, Vol. VIII, 1932, p. 40.

"He (Indra) is intimately connected with the ecliptic. Again the passages in which he is stated to have produced the brightness of the sun, to have made the sun ascend in sky, to have produced dawn and again to have destroyed her through the sun, all makes us believe that he is connected with that part of the ecliptic which corresponds to the summer solstice".

We have given our interpretation of Indra's producing Uṣas or destroying her while discussing the relation between Indra and Sūrya.

P.C. Sen Gupta, "When Indra became Maghavan" in *Journal of the Royal Asiatic Society of Bengal*, Vol. IV, 1938, p. 447.

"The story of the great deeds of Indra suggests to us that this great god was none other than the gods of summer solstice".

A.J. Karnadikar, "The Riddle of Indra and Soma", in *Poona Orientalist*, Vol. 22, p. 18.

"In the *ṚV* Indra is the deity of the solstice. This hypothesis is accepted by almost all the astronomers and ridiculed by the philologists." Karandiar's words are self-explanatory.

261. Ernst Siecke, *Indras Drachenkampf*, Berlin 1905, p. 3, "Indras Gestalt ist vom Monde ausgegangen".

262. *Ibid.*, p. 17, "Ich glaube jetzt, dass die Marut ursprüglich die sterne bezeichnen".

263. *Ibid.*, p. 18, "Herakles hat unverkennabare Ähnllchkelt mit Indra: ursprüglich ein alter Mondgott, der in gewisser Zeit Züge eines Sonnengottes angegangen hat, zum Helden-ideal angestaltet".
264. **See** L. von Schroader, *Herakles und Indra*, Wien, 191, p. 34.
265. **See**, *Ibid.*, p. 38.
266. **See**, *Ibid.*, p. 34.
267. **See**, *Ibid.*, p. 62.
268. Cf. Herman Lommel, *Die Alten Arier*, Frankturt/M, 1935, p. 16.

    "Wir wollen die altindischen Götter in ihren eigenen Wesen, das ihren zu gekommt, sehen, und sie nicht an griechischem Mass herabsetzen . . .".
269. R.N. Dandekar, "*Vṛtrahā Indra*", in *ABORI*, Vol. XXXI, I-IV, p. 44, 1950.
270. N.S. Yajnik, "Indra, son of Brāhmaṇa", in *R.B. Trivedi Commemoration Volume*, 1958, p. 106.
271. Sukumari Bhattacharji, *The Indian Theogony*, Calcutta, 1978, p. 273 (Ist edn. 1970).
272. *Ibid.*, p. 282.
273. *Ibid.*, p. 281.
274. Kalyan Ganguly, "Indra a tribal hero who became a god", in *Indian Historical Congress*, 24th Session, (Summary), Calcutta, p. 1963, p. 68.
275. B.H. Kapadia, "Vṛtra-fight in the Ṛgveda", in *Vishveshvarananda Indological Journal*, 14(2) 1976, p. 191.
276. Sudha Rastogi, *Ṛgved me indra*, Varanasi, 1981, p. 182, *indra prārambh me devatā nahī thā, kramaśaḥ sopāno kā ārohaṇ karte huye vaḥ devatva pad par āsīn huā.*
277. Klaus Mylius, *Älteste Indische Dichtung und Prosa*, 1981, Leipzig, p. 254.

    "Indra der Götterkonig des vedischen Pantheons göttliche Personifikation des Kampfes der Indoarier gegen die vorarische Bevölkerung . . .".
278. The solar aspect of Indra's character has been treated with while Indra's relation with Sūrya has been discussed.
279. Jan Gonda, *Aspects of Viṣṇuism*, Motilal Banarsidass, 1969, p. 284 (1st edn. 1954).
280. Jan Gonda, *Ancient Indian Kingship from the Religious Point of View*, Leiden, 1969, p. 28.
281. Jan Gonda, *Die Religionen Indiens*, Kohlhammer, 1979, p. 54, (Ist edn. 1960).

    ("Er ist der Vertreter der zweiten Funktion (in Sinne Dumezils), der Kraft und weltlichen und Kriegrischen Macht".
282. Jan Gonda, *The Indra-hymns of the Ṛgveda*, Leiden, New York, Kopenhagen, Köln, 1989, p. 4.

283. A. Barth, *The Religons of India*, 5th edn. 1921, London, p. 12.

284. Václav Machek, "Name und Herkunft des Gottes Indra" in *The Archiv Orientalni*, Vol. 12, 1941, p. 143.

"Die höchste und mächtigste Gottheit der vedischen Mythologie, Indra, hat merkwurdigerweise bei den Indo-europäern keine genaue Entsprechung".

285. *ibid.*, p. 154 ". . . es gibt keine wesentliche Hindernisse gegen die Identifizierung Indras mit dem alten Diēus".

Machek's opinion has bearing to Wendy Doniger O'Flaherty's words, "For although the *Ṛ̣V* knows a sky father called Dyaus — Pitṛ, who is literally cognate of Zeus-pater and Jupiter, it is Indra who truly fills the shoes of Indo-European celestial sovereign".

Enclyclopaedia of Religion, Macmillan, 1987, Vol. VII, p. 214.

286. We have discussed on the opinion in this regard of these scholars in the section "Indra-Vṛtra".

Bibliography

Source Material

Aitareya Brāhmaṇa, Anandashram Press, Poona.

Āpastamba Dharmasūtra, Bombay Sanskrit Series.

Āpastamba Gṛhyasūtra, Chowkhamba Sanskrit Series.

Āpastamba Śrautasūtra, Baroda Oriental Institute.

Atharvaveda, ed. by Satavalekar, Sripad Damodar, Satara.

———, HOS, VII & VIII.

Bṛhadāraṇyaka Upaniṣad, Calcutta.

Bṛhadddevatā, HOS, V & VI.

Gopatha Brāhmaṇa, E.J. Brill, 1936.

Jaiminīya Brāmaṇa, ed. by Prof. Raghuvīra, and Dr. Lokesh Chandra, Nagpur, 1954.

Kāṭhaka Saṃhitā, Svādhyāya Maṇḍala, Bombay.

Mahābhārata, critical edn., Poona.

Maitrāyaṇī Saṃhitā, ed. by S.D. Satavalekar, Satara.

Nighaṇṭu and Nirukta, ed. & tr. by Lakshman Sarup, Motilal Banarsidass, Benaras, 1938.

Pāraskara Gṛhyasūtra, Benaras, 1938.

Ṛgveda, Vaidika Samshodhana Mandala, Poona, 1936.

Śatapatha Brāhmaṇa, Bombay, 1940.

Śāṅkhāyana-Brāhmaṇa, Calcutta, 1970.

Śāṅkhāyana Gṛhyasūtra, ed. by S.R. Sehgel, New Delhi, 1960.

Śrautakośa, Vaidika Samshodhana Mandala, Poona.

Sāmaveda, Svādhyāya Maṇḍala, Bombay.

Taittirīya Āraṇyaka, Anandashram Press, Poona.

Taittirīya Brāhmaṇa, ed. by Mahadev Shastri, (reprint), 1987, Delhi.

Taittirīya-Saṃhitā, S.D. Satavalekar, Satara.

Veda of the Black Yajurveda, HOS, Vols. 18 & 19.

Vājasaneyisaṃhitā, Svādhyāya Maṇḍala, Bombay.

Reference Books

Abhijñānaśākuntala in Kālidāsa Granthāvalī, 1976: ed. by Revaprasad Dwivedi, Varanasi.

Allchin, B & R, 1968: *The Birth of Indian CIvilization*, Penguin.

———, 1968: *The Rise of Civilization in India and Pakistan*, Cambridge University Press.

Arbman, Ernst, 1932: *Rudra*, Uppsala.

Arora, U.P., 1983: *Motifs in Indian Mythology*, New Delhi.

Barnett, L.D., 1977: *Hindu Gods and Heroes*, New Delhi.

Barry, W.T., 1958: *Sources of Indian Tradition*, Columbia University Press.

Barth, A., 1932: *Religions of India*, tr. by J. Wood, London.

Basham, A.L., 1963: *The Wondar that was India*, Bombay.

Basu, Jogiraj, 1969: *India of the Age of the Brāhmaṇas*, Calcutta.

Bender, H.H., 1922: *The Home of the Indo-Europeans*, Princeton University.

Bhattacharji, Sukumari, 1971: *The Indian Theogony*, Cambridge.

Bhargava, P.L., 1971: *India in the Vedic Age*, Lucknow.

Blair, C.J., 1961: *Heat in the Rigveda and Atharvaveda*, Connecticut.

Bloomfield, L., 1957: *Language*, London.

Bloomfield, M., 1908: *Religion of the Veda*, New York and London.

Brandon, S.G.F., 1963 (ed.): *The Saviour God,* Manchester University Press.

Brunhofer, G.H., 1910: *Arische Urzeit*, Berne.

Campbell, J., 1962: *The Masks of God*, Warbung, London.

Chakladar, H., 1920: *Social Life in Ancient India*, Calcutta.

Charpentier, J., 1911: *Kleine Beiträge zur Indo-Iranischen Mythologie*, Uppsala.

Childe, V.G., 1926: *A Study of the Indo-European Origin*, London.

Choudhury, Usha, 1981: *Indra and Varuṇa in Indian Mythology*, Delhi.

Clemen, C., 1962: *Religions of the World*, Allen & Unwin.

Conze, E., 1963: *The Saviour God,* Manchester.

Dandekar, R.N., 1979: *Vedic Mythological Tracts*, Delhi.

Das Gupta, Tapan Kumar, 1975: *Der Vájra eine vedische Waffe*, hamburg.

Deshmukh, P.S., 1933: *The Origin and Development of Religion in the Vedic Literature*, Oxford University Press.

Dumezil, Georges, 1970: *The Destiny of the Warrior*, University of Chicago Press, (trans. into English by Alf Hiltebaitel).

———, 1973: *From Myth to Fiction*, Chicago, London.

Eliade, Mircea, 1958: *Patterns in Comparative Literature*, London, New York.

———, 1964: *Myth and Reality*, London, New York.

———, 1967: *From Primitive to Zen*, London.

Farquhar, J.N., 1920: *An Outline of Religious Literature of India*, Oxford University Press.

Frazer, Sir James George, 1933: *The Golden Bow,* Macmillan & Co.

Geldner, K.F., 1928: *Vedismus und Brahmanismus*, Tübingen.

———, *Der Rigveda, HOS*, 33-35.

Ghurye, G.S., 1979: *Vedic India*, Bombay.

Gladstone, M.S., 1928: *Viṣṇu in Ṛgveda*, Cambridge University Press.

Glasenapp, Helmut von, 1953: *Die Religionen Indiens*, Stuttgart.

Gonda, Jan, 1969: *Aspects of Viṣṇuism*, Motilal Banarsidass, (1st edn. 1954).

———, 1959: *The Epithets of The Ṛgveda*, Mouton & Co.

———, 1978: *Die Religionen Indiens*, Kolhammer (Ist edn. 1960).

———, 1969: *Ancient Indian Kingship from the Religious Point of View,* Leiden.

———, 1974: *The Dual Deities of the Ṛgveda*, Amsterdam.

———, 1975: *Vedic Literature*, Wiesbaden.

———, 1989: *Indra Hymns of the Ṛgveda*, Leiden.

Goetz, Hermann, 1929: *Epochen der indischen Kultur,* Leipzig.

Gowen, H.H., 1931: *History of Indian Literature*, New York, London.

Griffith, R.T.H., 1971 (reprint): *The Hymns of the Ṛgveda*, Chowkhamba Amaravati Prakashan.

———, 1871: *The Rāmāyaṇa of Valmīki*, London.

Griswold, H.D., 1971 (Ist Indian edn.): *The Religion of the Ṛgveda*, Delhi.

Gupta, Uma, 1987: *Materialism in the Vedas*, New Delhi.

Güntert, Hermann, 1923: *Der arische Weltkönig und Heiland*, Halle, (Saale).

Hardy, Edmund, 1893: *Vedisch-Brahmanische Periode der Religion des alten Indien,* Munster.

Hariappa, H.L., 1953: *Ṛgvedic Legends Through Ages*, Poona.

Harris, J. Rendel, 1906: *Cult of the Divine Twins*, Cambridge.

Haussig, Wilhelm, 1984 (ed.): *Götter und Männer des indischen Subkntinents*, Stuttgart.

Hays, H.R., 1963: *In the Beginning: Early Man and His God*, New York.

Hillebrandt, Alfred, 1927, 1929: *Vedische Mythologie*, I, II & III, Breslau.

———, 1910: *Vedische Mythologie — Kleine,* Ausgabe, Breslau.

Hook, S.H., 1958: *Myth, Ritual and Kingship*, Oxford.

Hopkins, E.W., 1970 (reprint): *The Religions of India*, New Delhi.

Ions, Veronica, 1983 (2nd edn.): *Indian Mythology*, Standard Literature Co. (P) Ltd., India.

James, E.O., 1963: *The Worship of the Sky God*, University of London.

Jayne, W.A., 1962: *The Healing Gods of Ancient Civilization*, New York.

Jhala, G.C., 1978: *The Aśvins in the Ṛgveda and other Indological essays*, Munshiram Manoharlal Publishers.

Joshi, J.R., 1970: *Some Minor Divinities in Vedic Mythology and Ritual*, University of Poona.

Jung, C.G., 1933: *The Archetypes and the Collective Unconscious*, Kegan Paul.

Jung, C.G. & Kereny, Karl, 1951: *Introduction to a Science of Mythology*, Routledge & Kegan Paul.

Kaegi, Adolf, 1972: *The Ṛgveda*, (tr. by Arrowsmith), New Delhi.

Keith, A.B., 1917: *Mythology of all Races*, Vol. IV, “Indian Mythology”, Boston Marshall.

———, *Religion and Philosophy of The Veda and Upaniṣads*, *HOS*, 31, 32.

———, *Veda of the Black Yajurveda*, *HOS* 18.

Kosambi, D.D., 1962: *Myth and Reality*, Bombay.

———, 1965: *The Culture and Civilization of Ancient India in Historical Outline,* London.

———, 1975: *An Introduction to the Study of Indian History*, Bombay.

Kramer, S.N., 1961: *Mythologies of the Ancient World*, New York.

Kuiper, F.B.J., 1983: *Ancient Indian Cosmogony*, Sahidabad.

Lahiri, A.K., 1984: *Vedic Vṛtra*, Delhi.

Larson, Gerald, J., 1974 (ed.): *Myth in the Indo-European Antiquity*, University of California Press.

Lommel, Herman, 1935: *Die Alten Arier*, Frankfurt/Main.

———, 1939: *Der arische Kriegsgott*, Frankfurt/Main.

Lüders, H., 1951: *Varuṇa*, Göttingen.

Macdonnell, A.A., 1971 (reprint): *The Vedic Mythology*, Delhi.

———, 1925: *Lecutres on Comparative Religion*, London.

Malinowski, B., 1955: *Magic, Science and Religion,* New York.

Marshall, J.H., 1931: *Mohenjodaro and Indus Civilization*, London.

Meyer, J.J., 1937: *Trilogic altindischer Mächte und Feste der Vegetation*, Zürich.

Mitra, Majumdar Dakshinaranjan, (21st edn.): *Thakurmar Jhuli*, Calcutta.

Muir, J., 1870: *Original Sanskrit Texts,* Vol. V, London.

Müller, Max, 1856: *Comprative Mythology*, London.

———, 1856: *Chips from a German Workshop*, Vol. II, London.

Mylius, Klaus, 1978: *Älteste indische Dichtung und Prosa*, Leipzig.

Myriantheus, L., 1876: *Die Aśvins*, Munich.

Nève, Félix, 1847: *An Essay on the Myth of the Ṛbhus*, Paris, tr. by G.V. Davane, Asian Publications, Delhi, 1985.

Oldenberg, H., 1923: *Die Literature des alten Indien*, Berlin.

Oldenberg, H., 1894: *Die Religion des Veda*, Berlin.

———, *Pāraskara Gṛhyasūtra*, (tr.) *SBE* 29.

Ovid, *Metamorphoses*.

———, 1975: (tr. James, Mary, M.), Penguin.

Petazzani, R., 1955: *The All-knowing God*, London.

Piggot, S., 1950: *Pre-historic India*, Pelican.

Pischel, R., Gedner, K.F., 1889, 1897, 1901: *Vedische Studien*, Stuttgart.

Potdar, K.R., 1953: *Sacrifice in the Ṛgveda*, Bombay.

Puhvel, J., 1970 (ed.): *Myth and Law among the Indo-Europeans*.

———, *Studies in the Indo-European Mythology*, Berkeley and Los Angeles.

Raglan, Lord, 1949: *The Hero*, London.

———, 1949: *The Origins of Religion*, London.

Rahurkar, V.G., 1964: *The Seers of the Ṛgveda*, Poona.

Ragozin, A.Z., 1895: *Vedic India*, London.

Rao, S.R., 1973: *Lothal and Indian Civilization*, Asia Publishing House.

Rastogi, Sudha, 1981: *Ṛgved me Indra*, Varanasi.

Rau, Wilhelm, 1973: *Metalle und Metallgeräte im Vedischen Indien*, Mainz.

———, 1976: *The Meaning of Púr in Vedic Literature*, Munich, 1976.

———, 1957: *Staat und Gesellschaft in alten Indien*, Otto Harrassowitz, Wiesbaden.

Redfield, R., 1960: *The Little Tradition*, Chicago University Press.

Rele, Vasant G., 1931: *The Vedic gods as Figures of Eulogy*, Bombay.

Rendall, G.H., 1989: *The Cradle of the Aryans*, London.

Renou, Louis, 1957: *Vedic India*, (tr. by Phillip Spratt), Calcutta.

———, 1972: *Religions of Ancient India*, New Delhi.

———, 1963: *The Destiny of the Veda in India*, Delhi.

Ruben, Walter, 1956: *Beginn der Philosphie in Indien*, Berlin.

Sankhalia, H.D., 1950: *Pre-history and Protohistory in India and Pakistan*, University of Bombay.

Schwab, G., 1950: *Gods and Heroes*, Routledge.

Sharma, Umesh Chandra, 1982: *The Dāśarājña War*, Aligarh.

Schlegel, Leopold von, 1913: *Reden und Aufsätze vornämlich über Indiens Literatur*, Leipzig.

Schmidt, Hans Peter, 1968: *Indra und Bṛhaspati*, Otto Harrassowitz.

Schroeder, L. von, 1908: *Mysterium und Mimus im Ṛgveda*, Leipzig.

Siecke, Ernst, 1905: *Indras Drachenkampf*, Berlin.

Swanson, G.E., 1960: *The Birth of the Gods*, University of Michigan.

Tagore, Rabindranath, *Gitabitan*, Vol. II, Calcutta.

Thieme, Paul, 1957: *Mitra and Aryaman*, Yale University Press.

Thompson, Smith, 1955 (ed.): *Motif Index of Folk Literature*, Copenhagen.

Tilak, B.G., 1925: *The Archtic Home in the Vedas*, Poona.

Konow, S. and Tuxen Paul, 1949: *Religions of India*, Copenhagen.

Von Schroeder, L., 1914: *Herakles und Indra*, Wien.

Wace, C.S., 1888: *Serpent-worship and other Essays*, London.

Waddel, L.A., 1968: *The Makers of Civilization in Race and History*, S. Chand and Co.

Ward, Donald, 1968: *The Divine Twins,* Berkeley and Los Angeles.

Wasson, R.C., 1968: *Soma the divine Mushroom*, New York.

Watts, A.W., 1963 (ed.): *Pattern of Myth*, New York.

Weber, Albrecht, 1873: *Indische Beiträge*.

Weber, M., 1958: *The Religion of India*, Illinois.

Wheeler, Sir Mortimer, 1959: *Early India and Pakistan*, Bombay.

———, 1966: *Civilization of Indus Valley and beyond*, London.

Whitney, W.D., (ed. & tr.): *Atharvaveda-Saṃhitā*, *HOS*, VII & VIII.

Wikander, Stig, 1938: *Der arische Männerbund,* Lund.

Winternitz, M., 1962: *A History of Indian Literature*, tr. by Ketkar, S., Calcutta University, First German edition, 1907.

Zimmer, Heinrich, 1897: *Altindisches Leben*, Berlin.

Articles in Journals

Agrawala, V.S., "Cyavana and Aśvinau", in *Sarda Commemoration Volume*, Ajmer, 1937.

Apte, V.M., "The Name Indra — an Etymological Investigation", in *J. Bom. U.* 19(2) 1952.

Bajpai, K.D., "Indra in Early Indian Literature", in *Ṛtam*, July, 1969.

Barnett, L.D., "A study of Indo-European Psychology", in *JRAS*, IV, 1929.

Baunack, Th., "Nachträgliches zu Bhujyu", in *KZ*, XXXVI, 254.

———, "Über einige Wunderthaten der Aśvin", in *ZDMG*, L. 263.

Bhargava, P.L., "The Comparative Antiquity of Indra and Varuṇa", in *Ludwick Strenbach Felicitation Volume*, Lucknow, 1979.

Bhat, G.K., "Minor Ṛgvedic Enemies of Indra: Śambara", in *J.Bom.U.*, 38, 1969.

Bhattacharji, Sukumari, "The Sun-god and Soteriology", in *Anvīkṣā*, V., Calcutta, 1972.

———, "Rudra, the Rudras and the Maruts", in *Anvīkṣā*", III(I), Calcutta, 1968.

Bloomfield, M., "Contributions to the Interpretation of the Veda", in *ZDMG*, 48, 1894.

Bradke, P. von, "Ein lustiges Wagenrennen in Altindien", in *ZDMG*, 46, 1892.

Brown, Norman, "King Trasadasyu as a Divine Incarnation", in *Kunhan Raja Presentation Volume*, Madras, 1946.

———, "The Creation Myth of the Ṛgveda", in *JAOS,* 62, 1942.

———, "Prelude to the Indra-Vṛtra Battle (*ṚV*, X.124)", in *Journal of the Indo-European Studies*, 2, 1974.

———, "Indra's Infancy according to Ṛgveda", in *India and Indology*, Delhi, 1978.

Chandravarkar, G.L., "Asvins as Historical Figures", in *J.Bom.U.*, Vol. III, May, 1934.

Chapekar, N.G., "Nastya", in *ABORI*, Vol. 45, 1964.

———, "The Ṛbhus", in *JBBRAS* 29 (ii).

———, "Sudās", in *Oriental Thought,* Vol. III, 1957.

Charpentier, J., "Indra — ein Versuch der Aufklärung", in *Le Monde Oriental*, Vol. 1-3, 1931.

Chatterjee, Sachindranath, "Indra Fights the Demons: a Vedic Myth", in *Calcutta Review* 120(2), August, 1951, Calcutta.

Chattopadhyaya, Kshetresh Chandra, "Indra in the Ṛgveda", in *Proceedings, 4th All India Oriental Conference*, 1928.

———, "The Cradle of the Indra-Vṛtra Myth", in *Proceedings VI, AIOC*, 1930.

Chaube, B.B., "Myth and Reality in the Ṛgveda with Special reference to Indra-Vṛtra Myth", in *Vishveshvarnanda Indological Journal*, 17(1-2), 1979.

Dandekar, R.N., "Vṛtrahā Indra", in *ABORI*, XXXI, I-IV, 1950.

Dange, Sadashiv, A., "Survivals in the Ṛgvedic Indra-myth", in *Nagpur University Journal*, 15(2), April, 1965.

Devasthali, G.V., "Indra and His Devotees", in *R. Dravid Felicitation Volume*, 1971.

———, "Epithets of the Ṛbhus in the Ṛgveda", in *Indian Antiquary*, (3rd series), Vol. 2, No. 2, 1967.

Gadgil, V.A., "Indra the Representative of the Higher Physical Aspect of Nature", in *ABORI*, 1942.

Ganguly, Kalyan, "Indra a Tribal Hero who Became a God", in *Indian Historical Congress,* 24th Session, Summary, Calcutta, 1963.

Ghosh, B.K., "Varuṇa", in *JGIS*, 1941.

———, "Birth of the Gods", in *Indian Culture*, 1940.

Gnoli, G., "The Tyche of the Dioscuri in Ancient Sculptures from the Valley of Swat", in *East and West* 14(1-2), 1963.

Godbole, G.H., "Indra in the Śatapatha Brāhmaṇa", in *J.Bom.U.* 25(2), September 1956.

Hazra, R.C., "The Historical Background of the Maruts' (or Rudras') Association with Indra and Rudra and of the Puranic Story of their Origin", in *Purāṇam* 23(3), 1981.

Hillebrandt, A., "Indra and Vrtra", in *ZDMG*, L. 665.

Hopkins, E.W., "Indra as God of Fertility", in *JAOS*, XXXVI, 1917.

———, "Indra and Other Gods of War and Fertility", in *JAOS*, XXXVII.

Jog, K.P., "The Aśvins in the Ṛgveda and Their Traces in Later Literature", in *J. Bom. U.*, Vols. 33(2) Sept. 64, 34(2) Sept. 65.

Joshi, S.B., "Is Indra the Vṛtrahan Supreme God in the Ṛgveda", in *P.B. Desai Felicitation Volume,* 1971.

Kammenhuber, Annalies, *Münchener Studium zur Sprachwissenschaft,* Heft 3 (R.H.A., 46.118).

Kapadia, B.H., "Characteristic Activities of Indra", in *Sri Venkateshvara University Oriental Journal*, Tirupati, 14(1), June, 1971.

———, "Vṛtra-fight in the Ṛgveda", in *Vishveshvarananda Indological Journal*, 14(2), 1976.

Karandikar, A.J., "The Riddle of Indra and Soma", in *Poona Orientalist*, 22, 1957.

Keith, A.B., "Indra and Vṛtra", in *Indian Culture* I, 1934-35.

———, "The Home of Indo-Europeans", in *Indian Historical Quarterly*, XIII, No. 1, 1937.

Klostermeier, M., "Mythologies and Philosophies of Salvation", in *Theistic tradition of India*, Wilfred Lankrit University Press, 1984.

Konow, Sten, "Note on the Vajrapāṇi Indra", in *AO*, 8, Leiden/ Copenhagen.

Kramrisch, Stella, "The Ṛgvedic Myths of the Kraftsman the Ṛbhus", in *Artibus Asiae Acona*, 22(1-2), 1960.

———, "The Banner of Indra", in *Coomaraswamy Felicitation Volume*, 1947.

Kuiper, F.B.J., "The Ancient Indian Verbal Contest", in *Indo-Iranian Journal*, 4, 1960.

Lahiri, A.K., "The Marduk-Tiamat", in *Vishvabharati Quarterly*, Saṇtiniketan, 13-14, 1973-74.

Lommel, H., "Blitz und Donner im Ṛgveda", in *Oriens*, 8, 1955.

Machek, Václav, "Origin of the Aśvins", in *Archiv Orientalni*, Vol. XV.

———, "Name und Herkunft des Indra", in *Archiv Orientalni*, Vol. XII.

Müller, Reinhold, F.G., "Die beiden indischen Götterärzte", in *Archiv Orientalni*, Vol. XXVIII, 1960.

Oberlies, Thomas, "Die Aśvins: Götter der Zwischenbereich", in *Studien zur Indologie und Iranistick*, 18, 1993.

Obettinger, N., "Ein mythologischer Versuch zum Dualismus Zarathustras", in *Studien Indogermanica et Salvicia (Festgabe für Werner Thomas)*, Munich, 1988.

Ojha, R., "Indra-Vṛtra war and Serpent People", in *Journal of the Bihar and Orissa Research Society*, Vol. XXVIII, 1942.

Perry, E.D., "Indra in the Ṛgveda", in *JAOS*, XI.

Potdar, K.R., "The Ṛbhus in the Ṛgveda", in *J. Bom. U.*, 21(2), 1952.

Pradhan, Sitanath, "Apotheosis in the Ṛgveda", in *ABORI*, XII, 1930-31.

Rajvade, V.V., "Indra's Enemies", in *JAS Bom.* III.28.

Rau, Wilhelm, "Vedish Vajra die keule des Indra", in *Orbis,* 25(2), 1976.

———, "Twenty Indra Legends", in *German Scholars on India*, Varanasi, 1973.

Renou, Louis, "Indra dans L'Atharva-veda", in *New Indian Antiquary*, July-December, 1946.

Rocher, Ludo, "*Vṛtram avadhīt indraḥ*, on the use of *vadh* in the *Ṛgveda*", in *Wiener Zeitschrift für die Kunde Südasiens und Archiv für indische Philosophie*, Vienna, 19, 1975.

Ryder, A.W., "Die Ṛbhus im Ṛgveda", in *KZ*, 1901.

Satavalekar, S., "*Vedamantreṣu vīrapuruṣāṇāṃ varṇanam*", in *Gurukul Patrikā*" 18 (1-2), 1965.

Schlerath, R., "Vedisch Vajra — die Keule des Indra", in *Orbis* 24(2) 1975.

Schmeja, Hans, "Interpretations aus dem Rigveda", in *Innsbrucker Beiträge zur Kulturwissenschaft*, Sonderheft 61, Innsbruck, 1987.

Sen Gupta, P.C., "When Indra Became Maghavan", in *JAS Ben* IV, 1938.

Shamashastry, R., "The Ṛbhus and the Four Soma-cups", in *Poona Orientalist*, VII, 3 & 4, 1942-43.

———, "Indra's war with Śambara", in *F.W. Thomas Commemoration Volume*, 1939.

Sharma, B.R., "The Vedic Ṛbhus: Whom do They Represent", in *Sri Venkateshwar University Oriental Journal,* Tirupati, Vol. V (1-2), 1962.

Sharma, Lakshmikanta, "Atharvavedasaṃhitāyaṃ Indrasya svarūpa-vimarsaḥ", in *Medhā* 10(1-2), Raipur, 1973-74.

Sharma, Nigam, "*Marudgaṇaḥ*", in *Gurukul Patrikā* 20(1-2), 1967.

Sharma, Sudarshan Kumar, "Indra is a Synonym of Cloud", in *JGJRI*, 1979, (July-December).

Shastri, Biharilal, in "*Vṛtradyasura*", in *Vedavāṇī* 17(1), November, 1964.

Shastri, Jalwant Kumar, "*Vṛtra kon hei*", in *Vedavāṇī* 32(7), 1980.

Shastri, P.S., "Ṛgvedic Ballads of Association and Love", in *IHQ*, XXXIII, 3, 1957.

Shende, N.J., "Indra in the *Atharvaveda*", in *Proceedings of All India Oriental Conference*, XIII, 1946.

Shustery, M.A., "Rustam the Indra of Iran", in *III AIOC (Summary)*, Madras, 1924.

Sing, Fatah, "The Interpretation of Indra Myth", in *JBHU*, 5, 1940.

Söhnen, Renata, "Indra and Women", in *BSOAS,* LIV, 1, 1991.

Srinivasan, Doris, "The myth of the Paṇis in the Ṛgveda", in *JAOS* (1), 1973.

Srivastava, V.C., "The Aśvins in the *Ṛgveda*", in *JAHRS* XXX (1-4), 1964-65.

———, "A New Approach to the Personality of the Ṛgvedic Indra", in *JAHRS* XXXI, 1965-66.

———, "Indra and Ahalyā", in *ABORI*, 23, 1942.

Vader, V.H., "Twin Gods Aśvins", in *Indian Historical Quarterly*, 1932.

Velankar, H.D., "Divodāsa Atithigva and other Atithigvas", in *ABORI* 23, 1942.

Venkatasubbaiah, A., "On Indra's winning of cows and waters", in *ZDMG* 115, 1965.

Ward Donald, "Separate Functions of the Indo-European Divine twins", in *Myth and Law among the Indo-Europeans*, ed. by Jaan Puhvel, Berkeley and Los Angeles, 1970.

Wijeshekar, O.H. de A., "Ṛgvedic Bharata, A survival from Aryan Prehistory", in *University of Ceylon Review*, VII.3, 1949.

Yajnik, N.S., "Indra, son of Brāhmaṇa", in *R.B. Trivedi Commemoration Volume*, 1958.

Encyclopaedias and Dictionaries

Altiranisches Wörterbuch, (C. Bartholomae, Strassburg, 1905).

The enclyclopaedia of myths and legends of all nations, (H.S. Robinson and K. Wilson, London, 1962).

The encyclopaedia of Religions, (Macmillan Publishing Company, 1987).

Hastings' encyclopaedia of religion and ethics, 1958.

Larousse encyclopaedia of Mythology, London, 1954.

The new Schaff-Herzog encyclopaedia of religious knowledge, Michigan, 1958.

Wörterbuch zum Ṛgveda (H. Grassmann, Leipzig, 1936).

Kurzgefasstes etymologisches Wörterbuch des Altindischen, (M. Mayrhofer, Heidelberg).

Motif Index of folk literature, (S. Thompson, Copenhagen).

Practical Sanskrit-English Dictionary, (V.S. Apte, Poona).

Sanskrit Wörtebuch, (St. Petersburg).

A Sanskrit-English Dictionary, (M. Monier-Williams).

Śabdakalpadruma, (Calcutta).

Vācaspatyābhidhāna, (Varanasi).

Glossary

ádri	:	thunderbolt (also a stone, a rock, a mountain, cloud).
adriva	:	possessor of *vájra*.
ágohya	:	not to be concealed or covered, bright.
ahihátya	:	killing of Ahi.
ahutāda	:	not allowed to partake of a sacrifice; eaters of *bali*-offering.
amr̥ta	:	ambrosia, the nectar.
áṃsatra	:	shoulder-band, an armour to protect the shoulder.
anā́sa	:	flat-nosed (lit. nose-less), used contemptuously against the non-Āryan enemies.
anindrá	:	non-worshipper of Indra, Indra-haters.
áśvamagha	:	enriched with the treasure of horse.
áyaḥśipra	:	strong-jawed.
ā́khaṇḍala	:	killer of enemies.
āmīkṣā	:	clotted curd, offered as oblation.
Bhahiṣpavamāna	:	name of a *stotra* or *stoma*.
bhīmásaṃdr̥śaḥ (in pl. no.)	:	terrible in appearance.

bhrājadr̥ṣṭayaḥ	:	of bright appearance.
camasá	:	a vessel used at sacrifice for drinking the Soma, kind of flat dish or cup or ladle.
caru	:	an oblation of rice, barley and pulse boiled with butter and milk for presentation to the gods and manes.
citrábhānavaḥ (in pl. no.)	:	shining with light.
dásrā (in dual no.)	:	attractive in appearance, accomplishing wonderful deeds (chiefly said of the Aśvins).
dasyuhátya	:	killing of the *dásyu*s, a fight with the *dásyu*s.
devaviśaḥ	:	the subjects of gods (used in connection with the Maruts).
dhī́ḥ	:	intelligence, prayer.
dhr̥ṣṇú	:	bold, courageous, fierce.
gadāyuddha	:	club-fight.
gaṇá	:	group.
ghorávarpasaḥ (in pl. no.)	:	of frightful appearance (the Maruts).
Hári	:	generally used in the *ṚV* in dual number. The names of two horses of Indra's chariot.
hariṣṭhá	:	borne along by Haris Indra's horses (adj. to Indra).
hárivat/ hárivaḥ/ háryaśva	:	master of Haris, the two horses. (an adj. to Indra).
híraṇyaśipra	:	golden-jawed, having a golden helmet.
híraṇyavartanī	:	having a golden path.
hutāda	:	oblation-eater.

índrajyeṣṭha	:	one whose chief is Indra, led by Indra. (generally an adj. to the Maruts, used in pl. no.).
indrarṣabhā	:	(lit.) whose bull is Indra : the *Atharvaveda* poet uses it metaphorically with reference to the relation between Earth and Indra (*AV*, XII.1.6).
índravat	:	associated with or accompanied by Indra.
jāla	:	net.
Kāmyeṣṭi	:	a sacrifice performed for the fulfilment of some desire.
Karīrīṣṭi	:	sacrifice performed for rains.
krīḍin	:	playful (said of the Maruts, used in pl. no.).
kṣatrá	:	the royal power (strength).
madhupáu (in dual no.)	:	drinkers of *madhu* (said of the Aśvins).
madhupā́tamā (in dual no.)	:	the best drinkers of honey (said of the Aśvins).
mádhuvarṇā (in dual no.)	:	honey-coloured (said of the Aśvins).
Madhuvidyā	:	'science of sweetness' name of a particular mystical doctrine. It is also called *Pravargyavidyā*.
mághavan	:	bountiful, munificent.
marúdvṛdha	:	rejoicing in the Maruts (said of Indra).
marútstotra	:	a prayer to the Maruts.
marúttat / *marútva*	:	associate of the Maruts (i.e. Indra).
Marutvatīya graha	:	a vessel used to offer oblations to the Maruts in the midday libation along with Indra.
Marutvatīya pragātha	:	Name of a prayer to the Maruts.

máryāḥ	:	a band of young men (said with reference to the Maruts).
mayū́raroman	:	peacock-haired (said of Indra's horses).
mā́dhvī (in dual no.)	:	honeyed (said of the Aśvins).
nā́satyā (in dual no.)	:	truthful (a name of the Aśvins, the dual deities).
nāvyā	:	navigable.
nīlapr̥ṣṭha	:	dark-backed (an adj. to the Maruts, the storm gods).
nr̥tú	:	dancing (said of the Aśvins, Indra and the Maruts).
purumāyá	:	strong.
Pravargyavidyā	:	**see** *Madhuvidyā.*
Prātaranuvāka	:	'morning recitation'. Agni, Uṣas and the Aśvins are lauded in this recitation before sun-rise. This is a part of the Soma-sacrifice.
prātaryā́vānā (in dual no.)	:	yoked early in the morning (i.e. the Aśvins).
Pŕ̥śni	:	the Maruts' mother; the Maruts are called *pŕ̥śnimātaraḥ.*
pŕ̥śnimātaraḥ	:	whose mother is Pŕ̥śni.
pŕ̥ṣadaśva	:	having spotted horses (said of the Maruts).
Pr̥ṣatī	:	the name of the Maruts' horses.
puroḍā́śa	:	sacrificial cake.
pūrbhít, pūrbhíttama, purohā́, purandará	:	destroyer of cities.
rákṣas	:	an evil being or demon.
r̥bhú	:	handy, dextertous.

rayí	:	property, wealth.
ṛjīṣín	:	drinker of soma.
Ródasī	:	the female associate of the Maruts.
rudrásya sūnúḥ / sūnávaḥ	:	Rudra's son/s.
rudrávartanī (in dual number)	:	having a golden path (said of the Aśvins).
rudráḥ	:	fearful (an adj. to the Maruts in the *ṚV*).
rukmávakṣasaḥ (in pl. no.)	:	having golden ornaments on the breasts (said of the Maruts).
śakrá, śácīvaḥ, śacīpáti, śatákratu	:	strong.
śambarahátya	:	killing of Śambara, a fight with Śambara.
śárdhas	:	a host, troop (esp. of the Maruts).
śávaso nápātaḥ	:	childern of strength (said of the Ṛbhus).
śíprin, suśiprá, háriśipra	:	fair-jawed.
śiśnadeva	:	phallus worshipper.
śoṇau (in dual no.)	:	red-coloured (said of the Haris, the two horses of Indra).
śubhrá	:	radiant, shining, beautiful.
śubhráyāvānau (in dual no.)	:	going in a radiant chariot (as the Aśvins).
śuṣṇahátya	:	killing of Śuṣṇa.
Ṣoḍaśin	:	name of *stotra* or *stoma* consisting of sixteen parts.
Sadānvas	:	evil spirits (*AV*) which were supposed to possess the base of the house.
sámanyavaḥ (in pl. no.)	:	of equal mind (said of the Aśvins).
sánīḷāḥ (in pl. no.)	:	having the same nest, closely united and

		related, kindred, akin (said of the Maruts).
satrāsā́ha	:	conqueror of battles.
saúdhanvanāsaḥ	:	childern of Sudhanvan, the Ṛbhus.
Soma	:	juice, extract of the Soma plant (or mushroom? or Ephidra?) which was pressed between the stones by priests then sprinkled with water, and purified in a strainer; then it was mixed with clarified butter, flour, etc. and offered in libations to the gods (cf. Avesta : Haoma).
sómapati	:	lord of Soma (said of Indra).
somapá *somapā́vam*	:	Soma-drinker (entitled to drink *soma*).
sómapā́tama	:	the best drinker of Soma (said of Indra).
sómavṛddha	:	rich in Soma (said of Indra).
sudhánvan	:	having an excellent bow; believed to be the name of the fore-father of the three brothers: Ṛbhu, Vibhavan and Vāja.
suhásta	:	having beautiful hands, skilful with the hands.
sukṛ́t	:	doing good, benevolent, virtuous, pious.
sumatí	:	good mind.
suniṣká	:	decorated with beautiful ornaments.
sū́racakṣas	:	radiant as the sun.
svásvau (in dual no.)	:	possessors of excellent horses (said of the Aśvins).
sviṣúḥ	:	having good (swift) arrows.
tamas	:	(lit.) darkness, (philosophically) darkness of ignorance.
tejas	:	brilliance (spiritual or moral or magical power or influence).

tridhā́tu	:	best; used as an adjective to cow — yielder of best milk.
tveṣá	:	brilliant.
tveṣádyumna	:	having glittering brilliancy.
tveṣápratīka	:	of brilliant appearance.
udbhíd	:	bursting through, overflowing (used with reference to the Maruts).
ugrā́ḥ (in pl. no.)	:	violent (said of the Maruts).
vadhūyu	:	wooer, suitor.
vájra	:	a thunderbolt esp. that of Indra; sometimes also applied to similar weapons used by various gods or superhuman beings, or to any mythical weapon destructive of spells or charms.
vájradakṣiṇa	:	with *vajra* in the right hand.
vájrahasta / *vájravāhu*	:	with thunderbolt in hand.
vajrín, *vájriva*, *vájrabhṛt*, *suvájra*	:	possessor of *vájra*.
vatsá	:	a child, an offspring, a son, a calf.
vā́ja	:	strength, prosperity, wealth, speed, etc.
vā́jaratna	:	rich in goods or treasure (as the Ṛbhus).
víś	:	subjects, people.
viśpáti	:	chief of men, a king.
vrā́ta	:	group, host (said of the Maruts).
vṛtrahán, *vṛtraghná* *vṛtrakhādá*	:	killer of Vṛtra.
vṛtrahántama	:	the best killer of Vṛtra, i.e., the enemy.
vṛtrahátya	:	killing of Vṛtra or enemies in general.
yudhmá, *khajakṛ́t* *khajaṅkará*	:	fighter.

Index